W9-BXX-653

Presented to:

_____

From:

_____

JESUS ALWAYS

365 DEVOTIONS FOR KIDS

JESUS ALWAYS

ALWAYS

365 DEVOTIONS FOR KIDS

Sarah Young

Adapted by Tama Fortner

Edited by Kris Bearss

A Division of Thomas Nelson Publishers

© 2017 Sarah Young

All rights reserved. No portion of this book may be reproduced, stored in a retrieval system, or transmitted in any form or by any means—electronic, mechanical, photocopy, recording, scanning, or other—except for brief quotations in critical reviews or articles, without the prior written permission of the publisher.

Published in Nashville, Tennessee, by Tommy Nelson. Tommy Nelson is an imprint of Thomas Nelson. Thomas Nelson is a registered trademark of HarperCollins Christian Publishing, Inc.

Tommy Nelson titles may be purchased in bulk for educational, business, fund-raising, or sales promotional use. For information, please e-mail SpecialMarkets@ThomasNelson.com.

Unless otherwise noted, Scripture quotations are taken from the Holy Bible, New International Version˙, NIV˙. Copyright © 1973, 1978, 1984 by Biblica, Inc.˙ Used by permission of Zondervan. All rights reserved worldwide. www.zondervan.com. The "NIV" and "New International Version" are trademarks registered in the United States Patent and Trademark Office by Biblica, Inc.˙

Scripture quotations marked CEB are from the Common English Bible. Copyright © 2011 Common English Bible.

Scripture quotations marked CEV are from the Contemporary English Version. Copyright © 1991, 1992, 1995 by American Bible Society. Used by permission.

Scripture quotations marked ESV are from the ESV® Bible (The Holy Bible, English Standard Version®). Copyright © 2001 by Crossway, a publishing ministry of Good News Publishers. Used by permission. All rights reserved.

Scripture quotations marked GNT are from the Good News Translation in Today's English Version—Second Edition. Copyright 1992 by American Bible Society. Used by permission.

Scripture quotations marked HCSB are from the Holman Christian Standard Bible®. Copyright © 1999, 2000, 2002, 2003, 2009 by Holman Bible Publishers. Used by permission. HCSB® is a federally registered trademark of Holman Bible Publishers.

Scripture quotations marked ICB are from the International Children's Bible®. Copyright © 1986, 1988, 1999, 2015 by Thomas Nelson. Used by permission. All rights reserved.

Scripture quotations marked MSG are from The Message. Copyright © by Eugene H. Peterson 1993, 1994, 1995, 1996, 2000, 2001, 2002. Used by permission of NavPress. All rights reserved. Represented by Tyndale House Publishers, Inc.

Scripture quotations marked NASB are taken from the New American Standard Bible®. Copyright © 1960, 1962, 1963, 1968, 1971, 1972, 1973, 1975, 1977, 1995 by The Lockman Foundation. Used by permission. (www.Lockman.org)

Scripture quotations marked NCV are from the New Century Version®. © 2005 by Thomas Nelson. Used by permission. All rights reserved.

Scripture quotations marked NKJV are from the New King James Version®. © 1982 by Thomas Nelson. Used by permission. All rights reserved.

Scripture quotations marked NLT are from the Holy Bible, New Living Translation. © 1996, 2004, 2007, 2013, 2015 by Tyndale House Foundation. Used by permission of Tyndale House Publishers, Inc., Carol Stream, Illinois 60188. All rights reserved.

Scripture quotations marked NLV are from the New Life Version. © Christian Literature International.

Scripture quotations marked TLB are from The Living Bible. Copyright © 1971. Used by permission of Tyndale House Publishers, Inc., Carol Stream, Illinois 60188. All rights reserved.

ISBN 978-0-7180-9688-5

Library of Congress Cataloging-in-Publication Data on file

Printed in China
17 18 19 20 21   DSC   10 9 8 7 6 5 4 3 2 1

Mfr: DSC / Shenzhen, China / September 2017 / PO# 9448087

Introduction

*J*esus Always: 365 Devotions for Kids* is a book about Joy—how you can find Joy in Jesus no matter what is happening in your life. If you already belong to Jesus, you know that the story of your life has the happiest ending you could ever imagine: a home in heaven with Him forever! Just knowing this can fill your life here on earth with Joy—in good times *and* in hard times.

If you don't yet belong to Jesus, please know I'm praying that you'll ask Jesus to forgive all your sins and be your Savior. Also, that you'll try to follow Him and do what is pleasing to Him. Then you too will know the amazing Joy of having Jesus as your very best Friend—and having an awesome forever-after home in heaven.

I'm convinced that being thankful for all Jesus does is one of the most important ways to have a joyful heart. To help me start my day with a thankful attitude, I like to sing this little song soon after I wake up:

> *This is the day, this is the day that the Lord has made.*
> *We will rejoice, we will rejoice and be glad in it.*

These words help me remember that each day is a precious gift from God.

Another way I invite the Joy of Jesus into my life is by looking for the little treasures He sends to brighten my day: a cardinal flying by, a friend's hug, some "good luck" that I know is really God working in my life. When I find these blessings, I try to hold on to them and write them down in my "Thanks Book" later. On days when life is extra tough, it seems harder to find things to thank God for. But if I take time to look closely, I find plenty of good things. I hope you'll start your own "Thanks Book" so you can remember the little treasures in your life. They are always there, even on your hardest days.

I want you to remember that the Bible is our greatest treasure. It is the *only* inspired Word of God—it never changes, and there's not a single mistake in it. That's why I try my best to make what I write consistent with the teachings in the Bible. Each devotion in *Jesus Always: 365 Devotions for Kids* includes a Bible verse for you to read, along with others for you to look up on your own. I hope you will look up those verses and read them carefully. They are God's words of Life.

Jesus Always: 365 Devotions for Kids is written as if Jesus is talking right to you. So when you see the words "I," "Me," "My," or "Mine," they mean Jesus. And the words "you" and "your" mean . . . well . . . *you.*

I pray that you will grow closer to God as you read this book and your Bible—and that He will fill you with His Joy. Also, I hope you'll remember these things: Jesus is with you *always*. Jesus *always* hears your prayers. And Jesus *always* loves you!

With love, prayers, and blessings,

Sarah Young

JANUARY

Your word is a lamp to guide my feet
and a light for my path.

—Psalm 119:105 NLT

The Gift of Today

*This is the day that the L*ORD* has made; let us rejoice and be glad in it.*
—Psalm 118:24 ESV

Don't waste today worrying about things that happened yesterday. Today is a new day, and *I am doing new things* for you in it. As this new year begins, remember that I'm always with you and always working in your life. Don't let mistakes or failures take away your Joy—your mistakes do not decide who you are! This is the time to make a fresh start. I am an endlessly creative God—just look at this world I've made. Expect Me to do surprising and even amazing things in your life this year.

Today is My gift to you—because it is in today that I come to meet you, My child. Look for Me in *this day that I have made*. Search for all the wonderful details I've carefully prepared just for you. I want you to be filled with My Joy and to *be glad* today.

I have placed signs of My loving Presence all throughout your day—sometimes in surprising places. Do you see them? The smile of a friend, the gift of a small flower blooming in a sidewalk crack, a hug from someone who loves you. Thank Me for every gift you see. Your thankfulness will keep you close to Me and help you find Joy in each day.

READ ON YOUR OWN

Isaiah 43:18–19; Psalm 16:11

I Am Your Joy!

Be full of joy in the Lord always. I will say again, be full of joy.
—Philippians 4:4 ICB

I am your Joy! Let those four words light up your life. Because I am always with you, the Joy that comes from being in My Presence is always available to you. All you have to do is love Me and trust Me. Try saying these words out loud: "Jesus, *You are my Joy.*" As you learn to trust Me more and more, the Light of My Joy will shine down on you and inside you—it will light up your heart and soul. Think about all I have done for you and all I have given you. Remembering your blessings this way will help you through hard times.

When you decided to follow Me, I gave you My Spirit to live inside you. He is your Holy Helper, and He has unlimited Power. He can help you find Joy even on your worst day. I have promised that I am *preparing a place* in heaven just for you. And one day *I will come back and take you to be with Me* in heaven. Whenever your day is looking dark, fill it with light by thinking about Me. Take a deep breath and relax as you hear Me whisper, "I love you, and I am your Joy!"

READ ON YOUR OWN

Psalm 21:6; John 14:3

Be Still with Me

*"Be still and know that I am God. I will be praised in all
the nations. I will be praised throughout the earth."*
—Psalm 46:10 ICB

*B*e *still and know that I am God.* You may have heard those
words before, but do you understand them? They simply
mean that I want you to take time to sit—still and quiet—with
Me. I want you to think about Me. As you do, My Presence grows
in your life, while all your troubles shrink and seem less and
less important.

When you spend time with Me, My blessings flow into your
life like *streams of living water.* So take time, *make* time, to be
with Me. Your thoughts can get all tangled up like knots, but
when you spend time with Me, I untangle those knots and help
you see things as I see them. Remember, *My Word is a lamp to
guide your feet and a light for your path.* My words in the Bible
will show you the way to go.

It's so very important to know that *I am God,* and that *I made
you and you are Mine.* You are like a *sheep in My pasture.* Sheep
don't always understand what their shepherd is doing for them,
but they follow him anyway. In the same way, because you are
one of My "sheep," I want you to trust Me and follow wherever
I lead you.

READ ON YOUR OWN

John 7:38; Psalm 119:105 NLT; Psalm 100:3

The Joy of the Lord

Don't be sad. The joy of the Lord will make you strong.
—Nehemiah 8:10 ICB

Find Joy in Me, because I make you strong. You will need My Joy in your life, especially when you are faced with troubles. Whenever you are struggling through hard times, guard your thoughts and be extra careful of what you say. If you think too much about all the things that are going wrong, you'll only become more upset and discouraged—*and* you'll feel weaker. As soon as you realize that's happening, stop whatever you are doing. Turn to Me and ask Me to help you.

Take time to praise Me—yes, even when everything seems to be going wrong. Sing songs. Read Bible verses that tell you about My goodness and My Joy.

Remember that your problems are temporary—they will not last. *I* am eternal, and so is your relationship with Me. As you find Joy in Me and in My Love that never fails, you will get stronger. For *the Joy of the Lord will make you strong*—now and forever!

READ ON YOUR OWN

Psalm 66:1–3; Psalm 143:8

Pour Out Your Heart

*Trust in him at all times, O people; pour out
your hearts to him, for God is our refuge.*
—Psalm 62:8

When worry bubbles up inside you, let Me *comfort you.* Let Me *bring Joy to your soul.* Come and sit with Me. *Pour out your heart* to Me and tell Me all your troubles. Then sit quietly with Me while I comfort you. I will help you see things as I see them. I will remind you that you are Mine and that I have a wonderful plan for you. Remember that you are on your way to heaven. When you pour out your heart to Me, I will pour My Joy and Peace into your heart, mind, and soul.

Being joyful changes the way you see the world around you. Even though you'll still notice bad things happening, you will also see My goodness shining through—in the way My children love and help each other. The Joy of seeing My goodness will help you face the problems in your own life. And you'll even be able to help others face their problems. You'll be able to comfort them with the same kind of comfort that I give you. Your Joy will spread, "infecting" everyone around you with Joy in *their* souls!

READ ON YOUR OWN

Psalm 94:19; 2 Corinthians 1:3–4

Joy and Fear

Nothing can separate us from the love God has for us. Not death, not life, not angels, not ruling spirits . . . will ever be able to separate us from the love of God that is in Christ Jesus our Lord.
—Romans 8:38–39 ICB

Did you know that it's possible to be both afraid and joyful— at the same time? Think about this: When the women came to My tomb after I had been crucified and they saw the angel, they were *"afraid, but they were also very happy."* They were afraid because they didn't understand what was happening, but they were happy because the angel said I was alive!

Don't let fear keep you from feeling the Joy of My Presence. Joy isn't just for happy times or for when you don't have any troubles. My Joy is for *all* times because My Presence is with you today, tomorrow, and forever!

Don't let troubles or worries about what might happen in the future steal your Joy. Remember that *nothing*—no problem, no worry, no person—*will ever be able to separate you from My Love*.

Talk to Me about your fears. You can tell me anything, anything at all. Especially the things that make you angry, sad, or afraid. Trust Me with your troubles. Then ask Me to give you My Joy, which *no one can take from you*.

READ ON YOUR OWN

Matthew 28:8; John 16:22

Think About Me

*He will keep in perfect peace all those who trust in
him, whose thoughts turn often to the Lord!*
—Isaiah 26:3 TLB

The more often you think about Me, the more I will fill you
with My *perfect Peace*. Keeping your thoughts on Me is a
challenging goal, but it's also a wonderful gift. That's because
I—the Shepherd of your soul—am always with you.

Just as you must practice math or sports or ballet, you
must practice thinking about Me. Train yourself by trying these
things: When you see something beautiful, thank Me. When
someone makes you happy, thank Me for that person. Write
verses from My Word on your notebooks or post them on your
mirror or refrigerator. Push yourself to see how many of My
verses you can memorize.

By choosing to think about Me, you show Me that you trust
Me. Even when you're sad or having a bad day, your troubles
can remind you to talk to Me. Remembering that I am with
you helps to keep your thoughts from getting stuck on your
problems—you won't be going over and over them in your mind
without doing anything to fix them.

What new ways can you find to help you remember Me?
Think of as many ways as you can. Because the more you think
about Me, the more Peace and Joy you will have in your day.

READ ON YOUR OWN

1 Peter 2:25; Philippians 4:6–7

The Adventure

You have not seen Christ, but still you love him. You cannot see him now, but you believe in him. So you are filled with a joy that cannot be explained, a joy full of glory.
—1 Peter 1:8 NCV

In Me you will discover amazing Joy, *a Joy that cannot be explained.* You won't find this kind of Joy anywhere else—not in your best friend, not in winning the game, not in anything here on earth. You can only find it in your relationship with Me. So trust Me, My precious child. Yes, you'll still have troubles, and some of them may be big and hurtful and so very hard. But don't let them throw you off course or keep you away from Me. When you are with Me, you can have Joy *even* in the middle of sadness and trouble.

Your life with Me is an adventure, and there are always dangers in adventures! Ask Me to give you courage so that you can face your troubles bravely. Keep your thoughts on Me and on My promise of your heavenly reward. Your Joy will grow and grow—bigger than you could ever possibly imagine—when you reach your heavenly home. There you will see me *face to Face*, and your Joy will have no end!

READ ON YOUR OWN

2 Corinthians 6:10; 1 Corinthians 13:12

A Treasure of Joy

In him all the treasures of wisdom and knowledge are safely kept.
—Colossians 2:3 ICB

Do you ever feel frazzled or frustrated? Do you ever feel pulled in all different directions at once? Your parents want you to do this, but your friends want that, and the teacher expects this other thing. You find yourself rushing around all over the place and feeling . . . frazzled. It can make your mind race with thoughts about how to make everyone happy, worries about what might happen, and wondering how to fix your problems. When you feel so busy that you can't breathe, stop and remember that *all the treasures of wisdom and knowledge are safely kept in Me*. Whisper to yourself, "Jesus, You are my Treasure. You're all I really need."

When I am your greatest Treasure, I protect you from feeling frazzled. If your thoughts start spinning in a million different directions, just stop and think about *Me.* Living near Me, enjoying My Presence, helps you to *obey My commands*—to live the way I teach you. I'm telling you these things so *My Joy may be in you* and *your Joy may be complete*—the fullest Joy!

READ ON YOUR OWN

Colossians 2:2–3; Revelation 2:4; John 15:10–11

Thirsty for Me

God, you are my God. I search for you. I thirst for you like someone in a dry, empty land where there is no water.
—Psalm 63:1 NCV

Be careful of thinking too much about things that don't really matter. When your mind is wandering, it's easy to start making plans for the future before you even really need to do so. You try to take control of your life, and that's a waste of time. Often, you'll just end up changing your mind or forgetting what you hoped to do. Yes, there's a time to plan, but it's not all the time—and it's not even most of the time.

Live in this moment, the one you're in right now. That's where *I* am. I am right here beside you. Let My Love soak deep down into your heart and soul. Relax and stop thinking about your problems. Give your attention to Me so that you can be filled with My Love.

Even though you may not realize it, your soul is *thirsty for Me*—more than you would thirst for a drink of water on a hot summer day. Sit with Me. You don't even have to say a thing. Just *let Me lead you beside quiet waters*. I will *guide you* ever closer to Me, and I will satisfy the thirst in your soul.

READ ON YOUR OWN

Ephesians 3:17–19; Psalm 23:2–3

A Right Time

My times are in your hands.
—Psalm 31:15

There is a right time for everything. Everything on earth has its special season. When you try to live close to Me, I will guide you. I will show you the next step, but sometimes you have to wait until the right time to take it. Don't rush full speed ahead without checking with Me first. Wait for Me to show you *when* to take that next step. I understand how hard it is for you to wait, but trust that I know the perfect time for everything.

There is a season, a time and place, for everything that needs to happen. This means that even the very best times in life must end so that something new can begin. Some of My followers can't wait to get to the next new thing in life. But others don't want anything to change. I understand that change can be uncomfortable, and even scary, but trust Me—hold on to Me in your thoughts and prayers. Be ready to follow wherever I lead you and *whenever* I choose. *Your times are in My hands*, and I will take good care of you.

READ ON YOUR OWN

Ecclesiastes 3:1 ᴵᶜᴮ; Isaiah 43:19; 2 Corinthians 5:17

Have Courage!

Jesus quickly spoke to them. He said, "Have courage! It is I! Don't be afraid."
—Matthew 14:27 ICB

*D*on't be terrified or discouraged. I am with you wherever you go. It's easy to look at bad things happening in the world and feel afraid. Just thinking about the troubles you see and hear on the news can act like a poison, making you feel sick inside. The cure for this poison is Christian courage. And that comes from Me—from believing that I am always with you.

It's so important to remember that what you see of this world is *not* all there is. I am *here!* There was a time when the prophet Elijah was upset and discouraged because he felt like he was the only person in Israel who still loved God. But that wasn't true. There were thousands who still loved Me and hadn't bowed down to the false god Baal. But Elijah's feelings kept him from seeing that. Another time, the prophet Elisha's servant was terrified because he thought their enemies were about to kill them. But the servant couldn't see what Elisha saw: an army of angels with *horses and chariots of fire all around* who were protecting them.

I love you, My child. I am with you, and I have unlimited power to help you. Don't just look at the troubles of this world—look at *Me*. Hear Me saying, *"Have courage! Don't be afraid."*

READ ON YOUR OWN

Joshua 1:9; 1 Kings 19:14; 2 Kings 6:17

Faith—Another Way to See

Jesus looked at them and said, "With man it is impossible,
but not with God. For all things are possible with God."
—Mark 10:27 ESV

*A*ll things are possible with Me! Let these powerful words light up your mind and bring Joy to your heart. Don't be afraid because of how things might look at this moment. I'm training you to *live by faith, not by sight.* That means don't worry about the troubles you see; instead, trust Me to take care of you.

Your eyes are an amazing gift from Me. Use them with Joy, and thank Me for them. But don't be hypnotized by all that you see around you and then forget about Me.

Faith is another way of seeing—one that keeps you close to Me. It is choosing to see *Me* and not just the world your eyes show you. It's also daring to trust Me and My promises no matter what is happening.

I'm your Savior and your Friend, but remember: I am also God. When I lived on this planet, I did many miracles, and *My disciples put their faith in Me.* Even today, I continue to do miracles in your world. So trust Me. Do My will by doing the things I say in My Word, like being kind and putting the needs of others ahead of what you want. Try to see things through My eyes. Show your faith in Me by asking Me to do big things—and then watch to see what I will do.

READ ON YOUR OWN

2 Corinthians 5:7; John 2:11; Micah 7:7

Fully Known and Forever Loved

*The L*ORD *delights in those who fear him, who*
put their hope in his unfailing love.
—Psalm 147:11

You are fully known. I know absolutely everything about you, and I love you. My Love for you is perfect and complete, and it will never fail. So many people struggle to understand themselves and even to *like* themselves. But what they really want is for someone to understand them and to love them for who they are. I am that Someone. And I can help you discover who you really are.

Be real with Me—you don't have to pretend or try to impress Me. Just be yourself. Come to Me and whisper this prayer from My Word: *"Examine me and know my heart. Test me and know my thoughts. See if there is any bad thing in me."* I'll show you what you need to change. But don't worry—I'll help you too. Just stay with Me, talking to Me and resting in My Presence. Let My Love flow into you, filling up all those empty places inside. And be filled with My Joy—because you are *fully known* and forever loved by Me.

READ ON YOUR OWN

1 Corinthians 13:12; Psalm 139:23–24

I Never Let Go

Your hand shall lead me, and Your right hand shall hold me.
—Psalm 139:10 NKJV

Living a Christian life is all about trusting Me: in good times *and* in hard times. I am Lord over your whole life and over all that's happening in it. So I want you to include Me in every part of your life. You can reach out to Me at any time by simply whispering My Name.

When everything seems to be going wrong and you choose to trust Me anyway, My Light shines through you for others to see. Your faith actually makes the evil forces of this world weaker. And My Light shining through you blesses those around you and makes them stronger too.

Holding on to Me when things are going badly is a choice you have to make. It takes willpower! But when life is especially hard, remember that I am holding on to *you*. I won't ever let go of you! *Plus*, I have given My Spirit to all My children, and this Holy Helper has unlimited Power. When you feel like giving up, call out, "Help me, Holy Spirit!" and this quick prayer will give you strength to keep holding on to Me. Even when everything around you seems dark and difficult, My Light keeps on shining—and it can chase away the darkness!

READ ON YOUR OWN

1 John 1:7; John 1:5

I Am in Control

I trust in your love. My heart is happy because you saved me.
—Psalm 13:5 ICB

When things aren't going your way, refuse to get upset. Instead, stop whatever you're doing and take a deep breath. Then take another one. Look up to Me—and spend a few moments just remembering and enjoying the fact that I'm with you. Then, tell me what's upsetting you. I'll help you see things more clearly, and I'll help you sort out what's important and what isn't. Trust Me and keep talking to Me, and I will show the right thing to do.

I know that you want to be in charge of your life and take care of things yourself. And when you can't, it frustrates you. You plan out your day, but then other people mess up your plans! When that happens, you have a choice to make: Get upset or trust Me.

Remember that *I* am God and I am in control. *My ways are higher than your ways—just as the heavens are higher than the earth.* This means you can't expect to understand all that I do. It also means that when your day doesn't go the way you'd planned, you don't have to get upset. Use it as a reminder to talk to Me. I am your Savior God, and you are My beloved child. Trust that I'm in control, and that I love you with *a Love that will never fail.*

READ ON YOUR OWN

Psalm 27:8; Isaiah 55:9; Psalm 43:5

A Robe of Righteousness

*He led me to a place of safety; he rescued
me because he delights in me.*
—Psalm 18:19 NLT

I have led you to a place of safety. I rescued you because I delight in you.

You are in the safe place of salvation—you have been saved from being a slave to your sins. Your salvation is the greatest, most wonderful gift you could ever receive. Never stop thanking Me for this priceless gift!

When you wake up in the morning, thank Me for adopting you into My royal family. Before you go to sleep at night, praise Me for My amazing grace that takes away your sins. Live each day in a way that helps others see Me.

I delight in you, not because of anything you've done. I *choose* to delight in you and to rain down My Love on you. Because there was nothing you could do to make yourself good enough for heaven, I gave you My perfect righteousness. I gave it to you to wear like a beautiful robe that covers all your sins and mistakes. Wear this *robe of righteousness* gratefully—with Joy. Remember you are a child of the King. You are royalty in My kingdom, where My Light shines forever and ever. *Live as a child of Light*, safely robed in My shining righteousness and perfection.

READ ON YOUR OWN

John 8:34; Isaiah 61:10; Ephesians 5:8

I Guide You

I am always with you; you hold me by my right hand. You guide me with your counsel, and afterward you will take me into glory.
—Psalm 73:23–24

I am always doing something new in your life. So when something unexpected happens—something you haven't seen before or even imagined—look for Me.

Don't turn away from new things before you take time to see if they might be from Me. Think about a trapeze artist: She must swing out and let go of the trapeze bar she is holding on to so she can move toward the next one. When she lets go, she is flying through the air for a short time—until she grabs hold of the next trapeze bar.

At times *you* may feel as if you're "flying through the air" when something new and uncomfortable comes your way. It's tempting to avoid the change and stick with what you know. Instead, come and talk to Me in prayer. Tell me what you're worried about, and ask Me to help you see what's happening the way I see it. Remember, *I am always with you. I hold you by My right hand. I guide you*, showing you the best way to go.

READ ON YOUR OWN

Matthew 9:17; Proverbs 18:10; Matthew 11:28

I Know You

"My sheep listen to my voice; I know them, and they follow me."
—John 10:27

I call you by name and lead you. *I know you*—I know every single thing about you. I know things your friends don't know and things your parents don't know. You are never just a number or just another person to Me. So you can *follow Me* with Joy in your heart.

When I rose up out of the grave, Mary Magdalene thought I was the gardener. But I only had to speak one word: "Mary." When she heard Me say her name, she instantly knew Me and *cried out in Aramaic, "Rabboni!" (which means Teacher).*

My child, I also call *your* name. When you read your Bible, try putting your name into the verses, like this: *I have loved _____ with an everlasting love.* Remember, *I called you out of darkness into My marvelous Light.* I chose to give you My Love. Take time to "hear" Me speaking to you personally through the words of the Bible. Listen as I tell you how much I love you. And let your knowledge of My Love give you strength and courage to follow Me joyfully, praising Me all through your life.

READ ON YOUR OWN

John 10:3; John 20:16; 1 Peter 2:9; Jeremiah 31:3

This World Lies

*The fruit of the Spirit is love, joy, peace, patience,
kindness, goodness, faithfulness, gentleness and
self-control. Against such things there is no law.*
—Galatians 5:22–23

The fruit of the Spirit includes Joy. Even on your very worst days, My Spirit can give you the amazing gift of Joy. The Holy Spirit lives deep inside you, so His work is very helpful. It's just what you need. You can ask the Spirit to fill you with Joy—every day, every couple of hours, even every minute! Then cooperate with the Spirit by reading your Bible and asking Him to show you what My words mean.

One way the Holy Spirit increases your Joy is by helping you think My thoughts. The more you see things the way I see them, the better you can understand what's happening in your life. So learn what the Bible says, and keep repeating it to yourself over and over each day.

This world lies—all the time! It tells you that you're not important, that I don't matter, *even* that I'm not real. Fight these lies with My Truth. The most important truth is that I died to save all who follow Me, I rose from the grave, and I will come back again to take My followers home. You can be joyful always because of Me and My Truth.

READ ON YOUR OWN

1 Thessalonians 1:6; John 3:16; Philippians 4:4

A Delightful Way to Live

*This is what the L*ORD *says to the house of Israel: "Seek me and live."*
—Amos 5:4

To find even more Joy in My Presence, you need to think less and less about yourself. This is the secret to having the fullest, richest, happiest life possible. Forgetting about yourself is actually a delightful way to live!

Try to notice how much time you spend thinking about yourself. Take a look at what's inside your mind. Even though other people can't see your thoughts, *I* can. I see each and every one of them, and I want to help you. If a self-centered idea keeps popping into your mind, stop—and focus instead on a favorite Bible verse or a prayer. If you find yourself thinking about how much you don't like a certain person, remember what My Word teaches: *Forgive each other just as God forgave you.* Or try simply praying, "I love You, Lord." This forms a bridge for your thoughts—a bridge that takes you toward Me.

Thinking about Me instead of yourself will take practice, but don't give up. You are training your mind to *seek My Face,* and that makes Me happy. *Seek Me,* My beloved child, *and live* joyfully!

READ ON YOUR OWN

John 10:10; Ephesians 4:32 ICB; Psalm 27:8

I Am Your Rock

The Lord is my rock, my protection, my Savior. My God is my rock. I can run to him for safety. He is my shield and my saving strength, my high tower.
—Psalm 18:2 ICB

I am worthy of *all* your trust. I will *never* let you down. There are people and things in this world that deserve *some* of your trust, but only *I* deserve all of it. In a world that seems unsafe and is always changing, I am the Rock that never changes. You can build your life on Me. And more than that, I am *your* Rock. *You can run to Me for safety* because I am *your God.*

Don't let what's happening in your life and in the world decide how safe and secure you feel. Though it's natural to want to be in control, I can give you the power to live *super*naturally if you'll let *Me* be in control.

I am always ready to help you when trouble comes, and I am always right by your side. I'll help you face those changes you didn't want to happen—even the disasters in your life—without fear.

Instead of letting worries roam around in your mind, capture them by saying, "I trust You, Jesus. You will take care of me." Then bring those captured thoughts to Me. I'll take away their power to hurt you, because *whoever trusts in Me is kept safe.*

READ ON YOUR OWN

Psalm 46:1–2; 2 Corinthians 10:5; Proverbs 29:25

My Joy Is Yours

*Delight yourself in the L*ORD *and he will*
give you the desires of your heart.
—Psalm 37:4

I am the Joy that no one can take away from you. Just think about the wonder of this gift. Spend time with Me—lots of time—rejoicing in the blessing of My Joy. It is yours for all eternity.

A lot of things in this world can make you happy for a time, but none of those things lasts forever. In Me, you have a priceless and timeless Treasure—Joy in the One who never changes and never goes away. I am *the same yesterday, today, and forever*. I am faithful, and *no one can take My Joy away from you*.

Whenever you feel unhappy or unsatisfied, the problem isn't Me. I haven't changed or gone away, but perhaps you have. Are you thinking so much about other things in your life—good or bad things—that you've forgotten Me? It's an easy problem to fix: Remember that I am your *First Love*, and put Me first in your life by spending time with Me and obeying Me. Then, ask Me to open your eyes to see My Presence at work all around you. *Delight yourself* in being with Me, and My Joy will be yours.

READ ON YOUR OWN

John 16:22; Hebrews 13:8; Revelation 2:4

I Am Your Strength

I can do all things through Christ because he gives me strength.
—Philippians 4:13 ICB

I am *your Strength*! I make you strong. When you start your day feeling weak and tired, it's all right, because your weakness can remind you that you need *Me*. Remember that I'm with you always, ready to help as you go through your day. Take My hand, trust Me, and let Me guide you and make you strong. I delight in helping you, My child!

Whenever you feel you just can't do any more or you just aren't good enough, stop and think about Me. I am your Strength— and I never run out of anything. I never get tired. Work together with Me, and I'll give you everything you need to keep moving forward, one step at a time. You may not reach your goal as quickly as you'd like, but you will get there in My perfect timing. Don't be discouraged by delays or detours. Instead, trust that I know what I'm doing, and then take the next step. Keep moving forward and keep trusting in Me—that's a powerful combination.

READ ON YOUR OWN

Psalm 59:16–17; Isaiah 40:28–29

My Unfailing Love

He Himself is our peace.
—Ephesians 2:14 NKJV

*T*he mountains may disappear and the hills may come to an end. But My Love will never disappear. My promise of Peace will not come to an end.

There is nothing on this earth that seems quite as solid and unmovable as a mountain soaring high into the sky. When you stand on a mountaintop, breathing in that cool, crisp air, you can almost smell heaven. Yet My Love and My Peace are even *more* solid and unmovable than the biggest mountain on earth!

Think about *My unfailing Love*. "Unfailing" means My Love never makes a mistake, never quits, and never runs out. No matter how needy you are, or how many mistakes you make, or how often you sin, My supply of Love for you will never run low. Another meaning of "unfailing" is *constant* or *never changing*. It means I don't love you more on the days you do well, and I don't love you less on the days you mess up. I love you perfectly all the time.

I Myself am your Peace. When you stay close to Me—through prayer and praise and reading your Bible—you can have My Peace. Come to Me anytime. Sit with Me, My precious child, even when you're feeling bad about yourself. Remember who I am: *the Lord who has compassion on you*, who never stops loving you!

READ ON YOUR OWN

Isaiah 54:10; Isaiah 51:6

Good Plans for You

"I know what I have planned for you," says the Lord.
"I have good plans for you. I don't plan to hurt you.
I plan to give you hope and a good future."
—Jeremiah 29:11 ICB

Relax, My child. I'm in control, and I love you." Whisper these words to yourself, over and over again. Let them wash over you like soothing waves on a beautiful beach. You waste a lot of time and energy trying to figure things out all on your own. But I'm already working on those things, preparing the way before you. So be on the lookout for some wonderful surprises—things only *I* could have done.

Remember that I love you. I'm on your side, and I only want the very best for you. I am a generous and powerful God, and you can expect to receive great blessings from Me. *You* are loved by the King of the universe, and *I have good plans for you*. As you look toward the future, relax in knowing who you are—*the one I love*. Hold tightly to My hand, and go bravely through your days. As you and I walk together along *the path of Life*, trust Me. I will fill your heart with Joy and your mind with Peace.

READ ON YOUR OWN

Deuteronomy 33:12; Psalm 16:11

January 27

Joyfully Depending on Me

*My God will meet all your needs according
to his glorious riches in Christ Jesus.*
—Philippians 4:19

Walk with Me, trusting that I love you and joyfully depending on Me to take care of you. "Joyfully depending" on someone may not sound like a good thing. I know you're growing up, and you want to do things on your own. But depending on Me is different. It will bring you Joy because that's the way I designed you to live. And I'll never let you down.

The relationship I want to have with you will give you *glorious riches*—not of silver or gold, but of Love and Peace and Joy. I am right here with you, closer than the very air you're breathing. I rejoice when you choose to trust Me! Your trust makes our relationship stronger and builds more love between us.

You're connected to your family by much more than just who your parents are. You share experiences and create memories together that strengthen your love for each other and make you want to spend more time together. In the same way, as you and I share experiences and create memories, you'll want to spend more time with Me. I will fill your heart with loving memories as you *live in the Light of My Presence*, joyfully depending on Me.

READ ON YOUR OWN

Psalm 52:8; Psalm 89:15–16

A Taste of Endless Joy

You made man a little lower than the angels.
And you crowned him with glory and honor.
—Psalm 8:5 ICB

*I*made you a little lower than the angels. I crowned you with glory and honor.* You were made for greatness, My child. Never doubt how important you are to Me! *I created you in My own image*—in My likeness. I gave you an amazing brain that can talk to Me, solve problems, invent wonderful things, and so much more. *I made you to rule over the fish in the sea and over the birds of the sky* and *over every living thing that moves on the earth.* Out of everything that I created, only mankind is made in My image. This is both a wonderful gift and a great responsibility. It makes every moment of your life meaningful and important.

One of your greatest purposes in life is to give glory to Me. I *crowned you with glory* so that you could *reflect My Glory* into the world, just as a mirror reflects the sunlight. You were made to shine My Light into this dark world and help others come to know Me. I also want you to enjoy Me. I created you to find endless Joy in knowing Me. And this Joy that you find in spending time with Me now is only a tiny taste of the eternal Joy that waits for you in heaven.

READ ON YOUR OWN

Genesis 1:27–28; 2 Corinthians 3:18

Search and You Will Find Me

Let us run the race that is before us and never give up.
—Hebrews 12:1 ICB

*Y*ou will search for Me. And when you search for Me with all your heart, you will find Me!* I don't expect your search to be perfect—it's not about perfection at all. What pleases Me is that you're looking for Me. And when you keep looking for Me, especially when it's really hard, that pleases Me even more.

The fact that it's not easy is actually a good thing. Because as you search for Me, your thoughts are focused on Me. You may sometimes feel like you're trudging through a swamp of distractions, but your searching makes you more and more aware of Me. Even if you don't *feel* close to Me, you'll find yourself talking to Me. I want you to know that I'm right here beside you in your search. And because I'm with you, you'll feel more alive, more awake, and more real—as you look for Me.

Your willingness to pour yourself into this quest makes My heart sing. Because it *is* a long, difficult journey, you'll need to keep trying even when it's hard. But as long as you continue searching for Me, you're on the right path. And *you will find Me!*

READ ON YOUR OWN

Jeremiah 29:13–14; Romans 5:3; 2 Peter 1:5–6

I Will Make Everything New!

*The One who was sitting on the throne said, "Look! I
am making everything new!" Then he said, "Write this,
because these words are true and can be trusted."*
—Revelation 21:5 ICB

I am making everything new! This is the exact opposite of
what's happening in the world—where everything is getting
older and dying and wearing out. Every day that you live means
you have one less day left on this earth. The world sees this as
a sad thing, but for My followers, this is very good news! At the
end of each day, you can tell yourself, "I'm one step closer to
heaven."

This world is so broken that there is only one way to fix
it: *Make everything new.* So don't be frustrated or discouraged
if your efforts to make the world better don't seem to work.
All things, even these attempts to do good, are affected by sin.
I want you to keep trying to make things better—depending
on Me to help you—but this world needs much more than a
tune-up or repair. It needs to be made completely new! This is
something only I can do, and it will happen when I come back at
the end of time. You can believe this because My *words are true
and can be trusted*.

You have a good reason to be joyful, My beloved child. Someday I will make everything—including you—new and wonderfully
perfect!

READ ON YOUR OWN

Philippians 1:21 ICB; Romans 8:22–23

February 1

I See You

Christ had no sin. But God made him become sin. God did this for us so that in Christ we could become right with God.
—2 Corinthians 5:21 ICB

I am *the One who sees you*. I am more fully and wonderfully alive than you can even imagine. Someday you will see Me *face to Face* in all My Glory, and you will be amazed! Now, you only see a reflection of Me, as if you were looking at Me in a blurry mirror. Because of your sins, you cannot see Me clearly. But I see *you* perfectly. I know everything about you, even your most secret thoughts and feelings. I know when you're hurting. I know when you're tired and when you just don't feel strong enough to keep trying to do what's right. But I also remember that you're only human and made of dust. And I still *choose* to love you with a Love that never, ever ends.

The gift of My Love came at such a terrible price. I suffered indescribable pain as I died on the cross. But I did it to save you from an eternity of suffering. I never sinned, but *I became sin for you. I did this for you so that in Me you could become right with God.* Think about that wonderful truth: My righteousness—My perfection—is now yours! That is My gift to you when you decide to trust and follow Me—and it's priceless. Rejoice and be glad because *the One who sees you* perfectly is the also the Savior who loves you always!

READ ON YOUR OWN

Genesis 16:13–14; 1 Corinthians 13:12; Psalm 103:14

Come to Me in the Morning

*God is our protection and our strength. He
always helps in times of trouble.*
—Psalm 46:1 ICB

I always help you in times of trouble. How often do you crawl out of bed in the morning and just sort of stumble toward breakfast? You're not awake enough yet to think clearly, but you know you need food to get you going. In the same way, when your thoughts stumble toward Me, I can give you what you need to get you going. When you aren't sure what you should do, ask Me to clear away any confusing thoughts. Then you can *really* talk to Me—and listen. Talking with Me is an amazing ability—and you have it because I created you *in My own image.*

Come to Me first thing in the morning. As you sit with Me, I'll unscramble your thoughts and make it easier for you to go the right way through this day. I'm Lord over every moment of your life, so this is no problem for Me. You may think you don't have time to start your day with Me, but I can make things so much easier for you. I can stop problems before they start and show you ways to make your day go smoother. Spending time with Me will actually *save* you time—I'll bless you richly by helping you think clearly and by smoothing out the troubles in your life.

READ ON YOUR OWN

Genesis 1:27; Jeremiah 32:17; Psalm 33:20

On Holy Ground

*"Do not come any closer," God said. "Take off your sandals,
for the place where you are standing is holy ground."*
—Exodus 3:5

*G*lory in My holy Name. To "glory" in something means to
praise it and to give honor and respect to it. Jesus is *the
Name that is greater than every other name.* As My child, you can
whisper, shout, or sing My Name—and you can *know* that I am
listening. Just saying My Name brings you closer to Me and
helps you find strength in My Presence.

I'm delighted when you take time to look for Me because
you want to know Me better. Come to Me any time of the day or
night. Find Joy and Peace in My Presence. Remember that you
are on *holy ground*, just as Moses was when he stood before the
burning bush. Breathe in the sweet, pure air of My holiness.
Let go of troubles and worries while you rest in the wonder of
My Glory. Let My Presence wrap you up in Joy like a blanket—
warming you all the way through to your heart and soul. As you
delight in being near Me, time seems to slow down, helping you
enjoy Me even more. Thank Me for these sweet moments of
closeness with Me.

READ ON YOUR OWN

Psalm 105:3; Philippians 2:9–11; Philippians 4:4–5

Morning and Night

It is good to praise the Lord, to sing praises to God Most High. It is good to tell of your love in the morning and of your loyalty at night.
—Psalm 92:1–2 ICB

It is good to tell of My love in the morning and of My loyalty at night. Begin each day by stating how wonderful My Love is. This is so good for you, My child. Because when you declare the wonders of My Love and My Presence with you, you are encouraged and made stronger. These blessings only grow as you speak your words of praise out loud. Praising Me can fill you with a Joy that is too wonderful to describe!

Just think about My amazing Love for you: It never fails, it is priceless, and it's endless—reaching all the way *to the heavens*. My Love shines so brightly that it can light up your darkest day.

When you get to the end of each day, take time to think about My loyalty—My faithfulness that *reaches to the skies*. Look back over your day. Do you see how I helped you through it? The more problems you faced, the more help I gave you. It's good to speak of all I have so faithfully done for you—especially at night. Then you can *lie down and sleep in peace.*

READ ON YOUR OWN

1 Peter 1:8; Psalm 36:5–7; Psalm 4:8

No Matter What

Depend on the Lord and his strength. Always go to him for help.
—Psalm 105:4 ICB

The Joy I give you doesn't depend on what kind of day you're having. No matter what's happening in your life—whether wonderful or terrible—it's possible to be joyful with Me. The prophet Habakkuk had a whole list of horrible things that he was expecting to happen: no fruit on the trees, no grapes on the vine, no food in the fields, no sheep, and no cattle for the people. But he said, *"I will still be glad in the Lord. I will rejoice in God my Savior."* That is heavenly Joy!

I am teaching you to see your life from a heavenly point of view—through eyes of faith. So when things don't go the way you hoped they would, I want you to talk to Me. *Seek My help.* I will help you decide if you need to work to change things or just accept them. Either way, teach yourself to say, "I can still be happy in *You*, Jesus." These few words show that you have faith in Me and that you trust Me. As you practice doing this more and more, your Joy will grow. This training will also help you be ready to face the bigger problems waiting for you on your journey to heaven. *Be full of My Joy always*!

READ ON YOUR OWN

Habakkuk 3:17–18; Philippians 4:4

Not Guilty

*I am overwhelmed with joy in the Lord my God! For
he has dressed me with the clothing of salvation
and draped me in a robe of righteousness.*
—Isaiah 61:10 NLT

Be joyful because *I have dressed you with the clothing of salvation*. This *robe of righteousness*, a robe of My perfect holiness that saves you from your sins, is yours forever and ever! Your salvation can never be taken away from you because I am your Savior. This means you don't have to be afraid to face your sins and mistakes—and to deal with them. When you realize you've messed up, simply tell Me about what you've done wrong and I'll forgive you.

It's important that you also forgive yourself. Beating yourself up doesn't please Me, and it's very unhealthy for you. When you find yourself thinking about your sins and beating yourself up over them, stop. Think about *Me* instead and about how much I love you.

Since you are already precious in My sight, you don't have to prove to Me that you're worthy of My Love. I lived a perfect life for you because I knew you could not. No one can—except Me. Now I want you to live in the wonderful freedom of knowing that you're completely forgiven because you belong to Me. Remember that because you are Mine, *you are not judged guilty.*

READ ON YOUR OWN

Matthew 1:21; 1 John 1:9; Romans 8:1–2

February 7

Trust Me to Help

God is the one who saves me. I trust him. I am not afraid. The Lord, the Lord, gives me strength and makes me sing. He has saved me.
—Isaiah 12:2 ICB

I am with you. Don't be afraid. I will support you with My right hand that saves you. Let these words wrap around you like a warm blanket. Let them shelter you from the cold of fear and discouragement. When troubles seem to follow you wherever you go, hold tight to My hand and keep on praying. You can *trust* and not be *afraid; I will give you strength and make you sing* with Joy again. My powerful Presence is always with you. You never face anything alone! I promise that I will make you strong, and I will *help you.*

My strong hand holds on to you and lifts you up in both good and bad times. When things are going well in your life, it's easy to forget that I'm with you. But when *you are walking through the darkest valley* of troubles, you remember how much you need Me. During these tough times, hold tight to Me—this keeps you from falling. I will help you stand tall and take the next step. Even though your days are filled with troubles, I bless you with My Joy as you trust Me to help you.

READ ON YOUR OWN

Isaiah 41:10; Psalm 23:4

My Love Is Unshakable

*I pray that you and all God's holy people will have the
power to understand the greatness of Christ's love.
I pray that you can understand how wide and how
long and how high and how deep that love is.*
—Ephesians 3:18 ICB

My Love will never let you go! I will hold on to you forever!
You live in a world that's always changing. And it's not
always safe. As you look around, you see so many people who
have lied and broken their promises.

But My Love is a promise that will never be broken. *Though
the mountains be shaken and the hills be removed, yet My unfailing Love for you will not be shaken.* These words of the prophet
Isaiah paint a terrible picture of shaking mountains and dis-
appearing hills. But no matter *what* is happening, no matter
how bad things may be, My Love is unshakable. It will never be
taken away. You can build your life on this Love!

Sometimes My children believe that I care about them, but
they still find it hard to believe how much I love them. I want
you to *understand how wide and how long and how high and how
deep My Love is* for you. Ask My Spirit to show you this Love that
is too huge for you to completely understand. Let go of all your
doubts about whether or not you're good enough for Me. Try to
see yourself as I see you—beautifully wrapped in the glowing
light of My Love.

READ ON YOUR OWN

Isaiah 54:10; Ephesians 3:16–19; Isaiah 61:10

I Understand You

*For the L*ORD* takes delight in his people; he crowns*
the humble with salvation. Let the saints rejoice in
this honor and sing for joy on their beds.
—Psalm 149:4–5

I understand you completely. This is something to be incredibly happy about! And I love you with a perfect Love that never, ever ends.

So many people are afraid that if others really knew them, they wouldn't love them—or even like them. For this reason, they don't let anyone know who they really are. They only show the parts of themselves they think other people will like. Even though they might feel safer this way, it's a very lonely way to live.

Be thankful that there is no hiding from Me! I see right through all your pretending, and I know who you really are. In fact, I know absolutely *everything* about you—and I not only *love* you, I *delight* in you. You don't have to be perfect, and you don't have to earn My Love. The truth is, nothing could ever *stop* Me from loving you. You are Mine. I paid for you by dying for your sins, and I will treasure you forever. You need to tell yourself this truth over and over again. Keep saying it until it sinks into your heart and changes the way you look at yourself. Knowing that I'll always love you is the first step toward spending less time thinking about yourself and more time thinking about *Me*—and that's the way to find heavenly Joy!

READ ON YOUR OWN

Psalm 107:1, 43; 1 Corinthians 13:12; Ephesians 1:5–6

I Will Give You Rest

*"Come to me, all you who are weary and
burdened, and I will give you rest."*
—Matthew 11:28

Come to me, and I will give you rest. Come to Me boldly, dear child. You don't have to be afraid. I already know every-thing that is worrying you, and I understand perfectly. Tell Me all your troubles. Don't hold anything back. Let the Light of My Presence shine on those troubles and help you think clearly about what to do. Then rest with Me for a while. Breathe in My Presence just as you breathe in the air. You are safe in *My arms that will hold you forever.* As you spend sweet time with Me, let Me take away your worries and quiet your soul.

Your soul is the most important part of you because it is the part that is eternal—it lives forever! The New Testament Greek word for "soul" is sometimes translated "life." When you are *weary and burdened* with troubles, you may feel as if you just can't go on. But I will strengthen you and help you see things as I see them. Plus, *I will give you rest.* As I give you strength, just relax and let yourself rest. Your soul finds true rest only in Me.

READ ON YOUR OWN

Deuteronomy 33:27; Psalm 23:2–3; Psalm 62:1

February 11

Be Thankful Always

*Always be joyful. Never stop praying. Be thankful
in all circumstances, for this is God's will for
you who belong to Christ Jesus.*
—1 Thessalonians 5:16–18 NLT

*A*lways be joyful. Never stop praying. The way to Joy is to find happiness in your relationship with Me—every single moment of the day. I love you, and spending time with Me will comfort and encourage you. With Me, it's possible to be joyful even when everything seems to be going wrong.

Be thankful always—no matter what's happening in your life. When you pray, "Thank You, Jesus," I pour My Power into your life. These three little words are perfect for every situation. Even on the worst possible day, it's good to thank Me because of all I've sacrificed to save you. As soon as you notice something good in your life, praise Me for it. Practicing your praises will add sparkle to your blessings and increase your Joy.

When you're feeling sad or upset, it's still a good time to thank Me. This shows Me that you really do trust Me. To add to your thankfulness, think of those things about *Me* that delight you—I am always with you, I pour out My grace on you, and My Love never fails or quits. Thanking Me, on good days and bad days, makes our relationship stronger and helps you live more joyfully!

READ ON YOUR OWN

Romans 12:12; Ephesians 1:7–8; Psalm 143:8

Because You Believe

We love Him because He first loved us.
—1 John 4:19 NKJV

I offer you Joy *that cannot be explained* and *that is full of Glory.* This kind of heavenly Joy can only be found in Me. It's easy to slip away from Me and begin finding your happiness in the things of this world. Sometimes I do bless you with a taste of heaven's wonders here on earth, but I do this to make you hungry for heaven. This world you live in is so terribly broken. But you can still find Joy in My Presence—even while living in this broken world.

Someday you will see Me face to Face, but for now *you love Me without having seen Me. You believe in Me even though you do not see Me.* Your love for Me is not silly or foolish or unthinking. It's your response to My unending Love for you—a Love that I showed by dying on the cross and then proved by My resurrection, when I became alive again. You worship a living Savior who rose from the grave! Blessed are you because you *believe without seeing Me.*

READ ON YOUR OWN

1 Peter 1:8; Psalm 73:23–24; John 20:29

February 13

Pleasure Forever

*You will teach me how to live a holy life. Being with you will fill
me with joy; at your right hand I will find pleasure forever.*
Psalm 16:11 NCV

*B*eing with Me will fill you with Joy. As you sit in My Presence,
thinking about how powerful and wonderful I am, also think
about this amazing promise: *Nothing in the whole world will ever
be able to separate you from My Love.* Your relationship with Me
is solid and sure—and it has been ever since you admitted your
sins and asked Me to be your Savior. You are My beloved child,
and I delight in you. *My child* is who you really are, and who you
will always be.

You can find Joy even in this troubled world, because *I have
set eternity in your heart.* That simply means you can know—no
matter what happens in this world—I have a home in heaven
waiting just for you. As you learn to delight in spending time
with Me, I'll give you strength and help you relax. And as your
love for Me grows stronger, you'll want to help others come to
know Me and have My Joy in their lives. There is overflowing
Joy in heaven and on earth when your love for Me shines into
other people's lives! As you walk along the path of your life, I
will lead you—and I'll bless you with joyful *pleasure forever.*

READ ON YOUR OWN

Romans 8:39; Ecclesiastes 3:11; Psalm 37:4

I Comfort You

He is the God of all comfort. He comforts us every time we have trouble, so that we can comfort others when they have trouble. We can comfort them with the same comfort that God gives us.
—2 Corinthians 1:3–4 ICB

Let My unfailing Love be your comfort. One definition of "comfort" is a person or thing that makes you feel less upset or frightened during a time of trouble. Because you live in a world that is so full of sin, trouble is never far away. There are many things in this world that can comfort you—a favorite spot, a best friend, your mom or dad. But even family and friends aren't perfect, and there are times when they simply can't be with you. Only *I* am perfect. Only I can comfort you with My tender Love that never, ever fails. And only I am with you *all* the time.

My perfect Love is not just a *thing* that makes you feel better; it's also a *Person.* How is that possible? Remember, *nothing in all creation can separate you from Me.* And *I* can never be separated from My Love. I *am* Love.

Because you are My child, you can come to Me for comfort at any time of the day or night. Since you have the wonderful blessing of My comfort, I want you to be a blessing to other people. *You can comfort them with the same comfort that I give you.*

READ ON YOUR OWN

Psalm 119:76; John 16:33; Romans 8:38–39

I Am Your Shepherd

The Lord is my shepherd. I have everything I need.
—Psalm 23:1 ICB

I am your Shepherd; I will guide and protect you. A good shepherd cares about his sheep. He understands them and knows what they need. My care for you is complete because I love you with a perfect Love that will never, ever let you down. I know *everything* about you—the things you are good at and the things that are hard for you. I know when you struggle to do the right thing, and I know when you fail. Because I know all about you and I love you so much, I am just the right Shepherd for you.

When I created you, I designed you to need Me. As you walk through this world, I go in front of you and prepare the path for you to follow. I clear away many of the dangers and troubles from the road ahead—and the ones I don't remove, I help you face.

Even when you walk through the darkest valley, where the most difficult and scariest troubles are, you don't have to be afraid because I am right beside you. Talk to Me and enjoy being with Me, just as I love being with you. I will carefully guide you through this day and every day of your life. *I am your God forever and ever*, and *I will guide you from now on.*

READ ON YOUR OWN

Exodus 15:13; Psalm 23:4; Psalm 48:14

Before You Begin

*The Lord says, "I will make you wise. I will show you
where to go. I will guide you and watch over you."*
—Psalm 32:8 ICB

Before you begin any sort of chore or project or task—big or
small—pray about it first. By praying first, you admit that
you need Me and you trust that I will help you. Depending on
Me is a smart way to get your work done. I can guide your mind
as you think about things and try to figure out what to do. I can
help you make the best decisions. Just knowing that I am pointing the way for you will give you confidence. You won't be as
stressed. Thank Me often for My help—and keep asking Me to
show you where to go and what to do.

The Bible tells you to *never stop praying*, but I know that
sometimes you ignore these instructions. When you're in a
hurry, you think you don't have time to stop and pray. Instead,
you just dive in and start working. But if you stop to pray *before*
you begin, I can point you in the right direction—saving you
time and energy. I want to help you with everything, even the
simple things. Helping you brings Me Joy, because you are My
child and I love you.

READ ON YOUR OWN

Colossians 3:23; 1 Thessalonians 5:17; Song of Songs 6:3

February 17

Treasures in Your Troubles

When troubles of any kind come your way,
consider it an opportunity for great joy.
—James 1:2 NLT

You can find Joy in the most surprising places. But it takes a bit of work. You have to *search* for the good and not allow your troubles to blind you to your blessings. It's much easier to see the bad, but I'll help you find the good. I'll open your eyes so that you don't see only troubles—you'll discover the hidden treasures of blessings *in* those troubles. Just ask Me.

Living joyfully is a choice. Because you live in a world that's broken and full of sin, you must choose to be happy—and you have to make that choice many times each day. This is especially true when you're struggling through a hard time. When something happens that troubles you and takes away your happiness, it's a test. But that test can make your faith even stronger when you choose to trust Me.

Your faith is *more precious even than gold*. I'm training you to see troubles as *an opportunity for great Joy*. That may sound impossible, but it isn't—when you ask for My help.

I chose to *die on the cross* because of the never-ending Joy of *bringing My children into the Glory* of heaven with Me. You can choose to be joyful by *looking to Me* and searching for treasures in your troubles.

READ ON YOUR OWN

1 Peter 1:6–7; Hebrews 12:2; Hebrews 2:10

Safe and Secure

You, Lord, give true peace. You give peace to those who depend on you. You give peace to those who trust you.
Isaiah 26:3 ICB

W hen you are with Me, in My Presence, you will be *filled with Joy*, *perfect Peace*, and *My unfailing Love*. Walk beside Me along the path of your Life—enjoying My company and talking to Me every step of the way. Because I am always by your side, the Joy of My Presence is always there for you!

I will give you true and *perfect Peace* as you keep your thoughts on Me. Never stop talking to Me—with your words, your thoughts, and even with songs. Spend time every day reading My Word. Let it teach your heart and change the way you think and live. As you think about who I really am, My Light shines into your thoughts and helps you live in My Peace.

My child, I want you to grow stronger in My Presence—*like an olive tree thriving in the house of God*. Just as the sun nourishes a tree, the sunlight of My Presence nourishes *you* and makes you able to produce heavenly fruit such as Love, Joy, Peace. And the more you *trust in My never-failing Love*, the more you will understand just how completely safe and secure you are.

READ ON YOUR OWN

Psalm 16:11; Psalm 52:8

Keep Your Eyes on Me

*I have set the L*ORD *always before me. Because*
he is at my right hand, I will not be shaken.
—Psalm 16:8

*K*eep your eyes always on Me. I am at your right hand, close by your side. You can depend on Me to give you My Joy because you know I'm always near. Practice remembering that I am with you. The more you realize that My Presence is with you, the more Joy you will have and the safer you will feel.

Talking to Me—whether it's in silent prayer, in whispers, in out-loud prayers, or in shouts of praise—is the best way to *keep your eyes on Me*. I want you to be real with Me in your prayers. Don't pretend everything is just fine. You can talk to Me about whatever is on your mind. Tell me all your worries and troubles, and then trust Me to take care of them. I'll show you the best way—*My* way—to handle that person who's upset you or that problem that's worrying you.

Study My Word, taking time to really think about what you're reading. Let it fill your heart and mind so that it changes the way you think. Let the words and ideas from the Bible fill your prayers. As you stay close to Me, talking to Me all through-out your day, I give you the Joy of My Presence!

READ ON YOUR OWN

Psalm 71:23; Philippians 4:6; Psalm 90:14

Talk to Me

"The Lᴏʀᴅ your God is with you, he is mighty to save.
He will take great delight in you, he will quiet you with
his love, he will rejoice over you with singing."
—Zephaniah 3:17

Don't think of prayer as just another chore. Instead, think of it as talking to the One you love. *Take delight in Me*—in talking to Me. As you learn to do this, you'll want to spend even more time with Me. Remember all that I am and all I've done for you. I love you with a perfect, never-ending Love, and *I take great delight in you*. Let My tender Love wrap around you and convince you that you are loved. Be joyful because I am the One who will never let you go!

The easiest way to start talking with Me is to thank Me for being your Savior—forgiving all your sins—and for being your greatest Friend. You can also thank Me for family, friends, church, and all the things that are happening in your life. Your grateful prayers bring you to Me and help you to pray other kinds of prayers, such as prayers for help, for forgiveness, and for other people.

You can tell Me anything at all, since I already know everything about you and your life. I'll never turn away or think badly about you because I paid for all your sins when I died on the cross. Trust Me enough to *pour out your heart to Me, for I am your Refuge*, your safe place to hide in any storm.

READ ON YOUR OWN

Psalm 37:4; Psalm 118:28–29; Psalm 62:8

February 21

The Armor of My Light

Let us put aside the deeds of darkness and put on the armor of light.
—Romans 13:12

*P*ut on the armor of Light and *put aside the deeds of darkness.* That sounds complicated, but the meaning is simple: Stop doing the things you know are wrong, and cover yourself in My Light by trying to do the right things. Things like praying and loving Me and loving others. Living this way will protect you from being led down the wrong path by this sinful world you live in.

I want you to *live in My Light* by living close to Me. Know that My loving Presence is always with you. Just as you put clothes on your body, you can also *clothe yourself with Me.* This closeness to Me will help you make good choices—in your thoughts and in the way you live. Even so, sometimes you will still make bad choices, and you will sin. Don't give up when this happens. I died on the cross to forgive your sins and to keep you living in My Light. *If you confess your sins, I will forgive your sins and make you clean from all the wrongs you have done. You can trust Me. I will do what is right.* And I am happy when you live close to Me!

READ ON YOUR OWN

1 John 1:7; Romans 13:14; 1 John 1:9

Your Wonderful Counselor

A child will be born to us. God will give a son to us. He will be responsible for leading the people. His name will be Wonderful Counselor, Powerful God, Father Who Lives Forever, Prince of Peace.
—Isaiah 9:6 ICB

One of My names is *Wonderful Counselor*. A *counselor* is someone who helps you make the right choices—and I am *wonderful* at that. You see, I understand you, much better than you even understand yourself. So come to Me, and tell Me all your problems and worries. Ask Me to help you, and I will guide you. In the Light of My loving Presence you can see who you *really* are: My dearly loved child. No, you aren't perfect. Only I am perfect. All your life you'll struggle with your weaknesses and failures as well as the imperfections of others. Even so, you are still My beloved child. *Nothing in all creation can separate you from My Love*!

A good counselor helps you see what is true and how to live by that truth. *I was born to tell people about the truth. That is why I came into the world*. So be honest when you talk to Me. Fill your mind and your heart with My words from the Bible, which is completely true.

A *wonderful* counselor not only helps people but also brings them Joy. *Take delight in Me*—loving Me and enjoying Me—and *I will give you the desires of your heart*. I will give you Joy.

READ ON YOUR OWN

Romans 8:38–39; John 18:37; Psalm 37:4

The Word of Life

Before the world began, there was the Word.
The Word was with God, and the Word was God.
—John 1:1 ICB

I am *the Word of Life—eternal life* that never ends. I have always been. I have existed from the very beginning. I am divine—I am God. As the apostle John wrote, *"The Word was God."* And I, the Word, bring Life to all who believe in Me.

From the very beginning of creation, words have brought life. The earth was empty and dark and had no form. Then I said, *"Let there be light," and there was light.* I spoke and every-thing was created, including all the plants and animals. And then I spoke again and created man and woman.

The Life that I want to give you is *eternal*. It begins when you trust Me as your only Savior—but it never ends. You can live your life with sweet freedom, knowing that you are *not judged guilty* when you sin. I have set *you free from the law that brings sin and death*. Be grateful for this amazing gift! I love you perfectly *and* I love you forever. Let this fill you with Joy. And remember, I am always near you, even closer than the air you breathe.

READ ON YOUR OWN

1 John 1:1–2; Genesis 1:1–3; Romans 8:1–2

I Teach You to Listen

Every morning he wakes me. He teaches me to listen like a student.
—Isaiah 50:4 ICB

*E*very morning I wake you. I teach you to listen to Me. I'm always thinking of you. I never sleep, so I'm able to watch over you, even while you're sleeping. *When you wake up* in the morning, *I am still with you.* As you become aware of My loving Presence, I help you become more alert, more awake—smoothing out the tangled thoughts in your mind. This helps you see Me more clearly and find My way for you.

I want you to enjoy being with Me and feeding your soul with My Word. My Love calls to you, inviting you to come close to Me. When you do, I am delighted!

This time you spend with Me blesses you and makes you stronger. I will teach you what My Word means, helping you understand the Bible and how to use its words in your life. As you make plans for your day, I will help you know what I want you to do. Planning your day *together* with Me gives you the power to handle whatever comes your way. I am training you to *trust Me at all times*, no matter what happens.

READ ON YOUR OWN

Psalm 139:17–18; James 4:8; Psalm 62:8

The Light of My Glory

We all show the Lord's glory, and we are being changed to be like him. This change in us brings more and more glory. And it comes from the Lord.
—2 Corinthians 3:18 ICB

The Light of My Glory is shining down on you, My beloved child. Look up to Me with praises in your heart. Just as the sun shines down on you and warms your face, let My Love shine down on you and warm your soul—soaking deep down inside. Treasure these moments alone with Me. I am using them to make you more like Me. The more you think about Me and focus on Me—in quiet times *and* busy times—the better you can *show My Glory* to others.

Remembering to think about Me when you're busy can be hard to do. But I have created you with an amazing mind. It isn't like a train that can only run on one track at a time—your mind can be on two, three, or even more tracks, all at the same time. Let one of those "tracks" be thinking about Me. That's how you practice staying in My Presence.

This practice will bless you in many ways. When you know I'm with you, you'll be less likely to do or say things that don't please Me. When you're struggling or hurting, knowing that I'm with you will give you comfort and courage. I can use every single thing in your life for good—*changing you to be more and more like Me.*

READ ON YOUR OWN

Hebrews 12:2; Romans 8:28

Guard Your Heart

"God does not see the same way people see. People look at the outside of a person, but the Lord looks at the heart."
—1 Samuel 16:7 ICB

*P*eople look at the outside of a person, but the Lord looks at the heart. Being able to see is a great gift. I want you to use your eyes to see My Glory in the beauty of nature. Beautiful paintings, sculptures, and photographs can also give you glimpses of My Wonder and Glory. Celebrate these gifts, but do not become a slave to beauty. Don't judge things only by how they look on the outside. I am more interested in your heart, and I am working to make it more and more beautiful.

It is so important to nourish and feed your heart with My Word. I tell you that *above all else, guard your* heart—for everything you do flows from your heart. This means that if you fill your heart with thoughts about Me, My Life will flow through you. But if you fill your heart with evil and dark thoughts, then darkness will flow through your life. Guard and protect your heart by "feeding" it with Bible study and prayer.

When you don't like the way things look in your world, when there are just too many troubles, close your eyes and look at Me. Remember who I am. Remember that I am *Immanuel—God with you!*

READ ON YOUR OWN

Proverbs 4:23; Matthew 1:23

The Light of the Good News

*I have come as light into the world. I came so that
whoever believes in me would not stay in darkness.*
—John 12:46 ICB

I *have come as Light into the world. I came so that whoever
believes in Me would not stay in darkness.* I didn't just *bring*
light into the world; I am *the Light that keeps on shining in the
darkness.* Because I am all-powerful and never-ending, nothing can put out My Light!

When you decided to believe in Me and follow Me, you
became *a child of Light*, and My Light entered into you. This
helps you see things as I see them—both things in the world
and things in your heart. Sometimes though, seeing what's
inside your heart can be uncomfortable, especially when you
find anger or jealousy or hate there. But once you see those
things, you can ask Me to help you get rid of them and to fill
your heart with My Love instead.

Be glad of this new, brighter way of seeing things. *The devil
who rules this world has blinded the minds of those who do not
believe. They cannot see the light of the good news—the good
news about My Glory.* But because you are My cherished child,
you have *the Light that lets you know My Glory*, and it is shining
in your heart. Be glad! Rejoice!

READ ON YOUR OWN

John 1:5; 1 Thessalonians 5:5; 2 Corinthians 4:4, 6

I Have Always Known You

"I knew you before I formed you in your mother's womb."
—Jeremiah 1:5 NLT

You are no stranger to Me, dear one. *I knew you before I formed you in your mother's womb.* And I have known you every moment of your life. I delight in making you more and more into the person I created you to be, just as a potter delights in creating a masterpiece with his clay.

Because My Presence is always with you, you are never alone. *Never.* I'm training you to be more and more aware of Me. But I understand that you are human and your thoughts wander away from Me. Sometimes, especially when you're upset or suffering, you may feel as if you're alone or think that I've left you. But that is never true! *I* suffered all alone on the cross so that you would *never* have to be alone in your struggles. *I am always with you; I hold you by your right hand.*

The last enemy you will ever face is death, but you don't even have to fear that! I defeated death when I rose up alive from the tomb. Trust Me to guide you all through your life and to take you home with Me someday—to the Glory of heaven.

READ ON YOUR OWN

Psalm 139:16; Psalm 73:23–24

February 29

Out of Darkness

You are chosen people. . . . God chose you to tell
about the wonderful things he has done. He called
you out of darkness into his wonderful light.
1 Peter 2:9 ICB

I called you out of darkness into My marvelous Light. I not only brought you *out* of darkness, but I also brought you *into* My royal family. I wrapped you in My own *robe of righteousness—* covering all your sins with My perfection and making you a member of My kingdom. You are one of *My own special people.* You belong to Me, and I delight in you.

I know you aren't perfect, but I have still chosen you to praise Me and tell the world about Me. I know you can't do this as well as you want to. The truth is, without My help, you couldn't do it at all. There's a big gap between what I have called you to do and what you are able to do. But this gap is part of My plan—it lets you see that you need Me. I fill in the gap with My Power because you are My child.

Don't spend time worrying about the things you think you can't do. Think about Me! Try to depend on Me and My help in everything you do. Joyfully focus on all that *I* can do—forgetting about yourself and your worries. As you look to Me for help, your face will shine with the Light of My great Glory.

READ ON YOUR OWN

Isaiah 61:10; John 15:5; 2 Corinthians 3:18

MARCH

The Word was full of grace and truth. From him we all received more and more blessings.

—John 1:16 ICB

The Sparkling Gift of Joy

You will teach me God's way to live. Being with you will fill me with joy. At your right hand I will find pleasure forever.
—Psalm 16:11 ICB

I will give you Joy as you live out your days in this world. This sparkling gift isn't just a luxury or a special treat; it's something you really need. There will be bumps in the road ahead. And there will be sharp curves, steep climbs, and heart-stopping hills. Without My Joy in your heart, you will *get tired and stop trying.*

My Joy doesn't depend of what's happening in your life, good or bad. It's bigger than the events of this world. That's why poor people are often more joyful than rich people. And that's why sick—and even dying—people can have Joy. Because they are trusting in Me as their Savior, Lord, and Friend.

Spread Joy to the world around you. Let My Light shine through you—your smiles, your laughter, your words. My Holy Spirit will help you do this when you let Him work in your life. Ask Him to fill you with a Joy so big it just has to be shared! Then focus on staying close to Me in your thoughts and prayers. *I will teach you My way to live. Being with Me will fill you with Joy,* and *you'll find pleasure forevermore.*

READ ON YOUR OWN

Hebrews 12:3; Habakkuk 3:17–18

A Wonderful Mystery

How great are God's riches and wisdom and knowledge! How impossible it is for us to understand his decisions and his ways!
—Romans 11:33 NLT

It is impossible for you to understand My decisions and My ways. So come to Me with a humble heart, believing that I know all things. Let go of your demand to understand everything, and simply trust that there are many things you'll never make sense of. I am infinite and eternal, while you are finite and human, with a mind that can only know so much. So it's important to make room for mystery in the way you think about the world.

You're blessed because you already know many things that used to be a mystery—things that were *kept hidden since the beginning of time*. The New Testament is full of answers about spiritual truths that became clear through My life, death, and being raised to life again. You understand things that the people of long ago didn't understand. This knowledge is a priceless treasure!

Even so, the ways I work in your world are often beyond your ability to figure out. So you have a choice to make: Either be upset because My ways don't make sense, or bow before Me in wonder and worship. Be amazed at *My riches and wisdom and knowledge*—for they are greater than you could ever imagine!

READ ON YOUR OWN

Proverbs 3:5; Colossians 1:26

Chased by Love

Your beauty and love chase after me every day of my life.
I'm back home in the house of GOD for the rest of my life.
—Psalm 23:6 MSG

I chase after you with My Love *every day of your life*. So look for signs of My gentle Presence as you go through this day. I show Myself in many different ways—like when just the right words from the Bible pop into your mind exactly when you need them, or another person says something that helps you, or through "coincidences" that I have planned, or through nature's beauty, and so on. My Love for you doesn't just sit around and wait. It chases after you and jumps into your life. Ask Me to open the eyes of your heart so you can "see" My thousands and thousands of blessings—both small and great—that are all around you.

I want you to not only receive these blessings but to take some time to notice them. *Think about them* and treasure them in your heart. Thank Me for all the ways I show up in your life. Write them down in a diary or notebook so you can read and remember them over and over again. These signs of My Presence will make you stronger and help you get ready for any hard times that might be coming your way. Remember that *nothing in all creation can separate you from My Love.*

READ ON YOUR OWN

Psalm 119:11; Luke 2:19; Romans 8:39

Waiting on Tiptoe

Trust the Lord with all your heart. Don't depend on your own understanding.
—Proverbs 3:5 ICB

B *lessed are all those who choose to wait for Me!* I understand that waiting patiently isn't easy, but it *is* good for you. I know you like to plan everything out, decide what you think is best, and make things happen. There's a time for that, but this isn't it. Now is the time for simply sitting with Me, in My Presence, and trusting Me with all your heart and soul. This way of waiting will bring you many blessings.

Some of the gifts I want to give you aren't for now—they're for the future. And while you wait with Me, obeying Me, those future blessings are growing. Because they're hidden in the mystery of what will come to you someday, you can't see them clearly. Don't worry—there are other blessings for now.

The very act of waiting with Me and trusting in My timing is good. It keeps your soul on tiptoe—as you to look up to Me with hope in your heart. You know I'm in control, and you can trust My goodness. You may not understand why you have to wait, but I'll bless you as you choose to *trust Me with all your heart.*

READ ON YOUR OWN

Isaiah 30:18; Psalm 143:8

The Best Family Ever

Give all your worries and cares to God, for he cares about you.
—1 Peter 5:7 NLT

I am taking care of you. I know that you sometimes feel alone and frightened—as if the evils of this sinful world are out to get you. When you're feeling this way, stop and say to yourself: "Jesus is taking care of me." Reminding yourself of this truth can comfort you and help you relax. It'll keep you from worrying about the future and wasting time trying to figure out what *might* happen.

When things in your life are confusing and you're not sure what to do, remember that I'm watching over you. I know everything about you and everything that's going on. I also know what's going to happen in the future. Just as a child doesn't have to worry about how his parents will take care of him tomorrow, next week, or next year, you don't have to worry about how I'll take care of you.

With Me, you are in the best family you could ever imagine! My ability to help you and watch over you has no limits, My child. So bring Me all your needs and worries. Trust Me to handle them. Then you can live boldly, with confidence—as a child of the *King of kings*. Relax and be joyful, because I'm taking very good care of you.

READ ON YOUR OWN

Isaiah 58:11; Revelation 19:16

Even in the Darkest Valley

Even when I walk through the darkest valley, I will not be afraid,
for you are close beside me.
—Psalm 23:4 NLT

You don't have to be afraid, *even when you're walking through the darkest valley.* The Light of My Presence shines even in that deep, sunless valley—giving you strength, comforting and encouraging you. Because I never sleep, I'm able to watch over you all the time. And there is simply no pit, no problem, no place so dark that I cannot see all the way to the bottom of it.

Even if you wander away from Me and fall into a slimy pit of trouble, you can count on Me to rescue you. When you call out to Me, *I will lift you out of the mud* and *set your feet on a rock—* giving you *a firm place to stand.* Find comfort in knowing that I promise to help you, even when you mess up.

Whenever you start to feel afraid, remember that *I am with you.* I've promised that *I will never leave you.* I will go ahead of you, to smooth things out and to protect you. While you're walking through that valley of trouble, keep saying these comforting words over and over: *"I will not be afraid, for You are close beside me."*

READ ON YOUR OWN

Psalm 121:2–3; Psalm 40:1–2; Deuteronomy 31:8

Joy in My Name

God our Savior, help us so people will praise you.
Save us and forgive our sins so people will honor you.
—Psalm 79:9 ICB

*P*raise My goodness and *rejoice all the time in My Name.* My Name represents Me in all that I am and all that I do. Using My Name in good ways draws you closer to Me and helps you enjoy My Love. But many people use My Name as a swear word. Hearing their curses makes Me both angry and sad. However, as My child, you can lovingly say the name "Jesus" all day long—to praise Me or to ask for My help or simply to remind yourself that I am with you. *I am God your Savior, and I will help you so that people will honor My Name.*

I invite you to exult in Me and My perfect righteousness. "Exult" is a fancy word that means to delight in and celebrate, especially because of a great victory. Just before I died on the cross, I said, *"It is finished!"* I was declaring the greatest victory ever imagined, when I defeated sin and death for everyone who believes in Me. Through this great victory, My righteousness—My perfection—is given to you. It is yours forever. No one can take it away from you. I have covered you with the *robe of My righteousness*, which covers all your sins and mistakes. Wear My *clothes of salvation* with Joy and celebration!

READ ON YOUR OWN

Psalm 89:16; John 19:30; Isaiah 61:10

On Top of the World

He makes my feet like the feet of a deer; he
enables me to stand on the heights.
—2 Samuel 22:34

I help *you to stand on the heights*. "Heights" can mean different things. It can, of course, mean something that's very high up. It's the perfect word to describe mountaintops or the highest floors of skyscrapers. It can also mean the greatest of joys—that wonderful feeling of being "on top of the world." *Or* it can mean just the opposite, like when you feel the weight of all your responsibilities.

If you want to reach the "heights"—to be on top of the world, to be so successful that people notice what you've done—be ready for the responsibilities that come with it. But don't forget to enjoy the satisfaction of working with Me and doing important things for Me.

Because you're Mine, *you can stand strong*—even on the highest heights—*with the belt of truth buckled around your waist and wearing on your chest the protection of right living*. Everything I teach you is completely true, for *I am the Truth*. My Truth is a solid rock to stand on. The world may shift and change, but I won't. My perfect righteousness is yours forever—it covers all your sins and mistakes. No matter what trouble you face, My Truth and righteousness can help you stand strong and keep doing the right things.

READ ON YOUR OWN

Ephesians 6:14; John 14:6; Romans 3:22

The "Why?" Trap

So don't worry, because I am with you. Don't be afraid,
because I am your God. I will make you strong and will help
you. I will support you with my right hand that saves you.
—Isaiah 41:10 ICB

My ways are mysterious and sometimes hard to understand, but they are good. When you look at what's happening in the world—with so many bad things going on—it's easy to feel afraid and discouraged. You just cannot figure out why I would let such terrible things happen. The fact that's hard to understand is this: I am *infinite*. That means I have no beginning and no end. I have no limits in time or space—or in any way! But you are not infinite. Because of this difference between you and Me, there are things that are simply beyond your understanding. But don't give up. When things don't make sense, choose to *trust in Me*. Tell Me that you trust Me by talking to Me all the time through your prayers. Even simply whispering My name will keep you close to Me.

Don't get trapped in wanting to know "Why?" all the time. That's the wrong question to ask Me. The right questions are: "How do You want me to see the things that are upsetting me?" and "What do You want me to do right now?" You can't change what has already happened, so start with now.

Trust Me—one day, one moment at a time. *Don't worry, because I am with you. I will make you strong and help you.*

READ ON YOUR OWN

Proverbs 3:5; Ecclesiastes 8:17; Psalm 37:12–13

My Gift of Grace

I mean that you have been saved by grace because you believe.
You did not save yourselves. It was a gift from God. You cannot
brag that you are saved by the work you have done.
—Ephesians 2:8–9 ICB

*B*ecause *I am full of grace and truth, from Me you have received*
one gift after another. Stop for a moment, dear child, and
think about the incredible gift of salvation. *You have been saved*
by grace because you believe in Me.

You could not save yourself. But since you have My gift
of grace, your salvation is safe and secure. No one is perfect
enough to deserve this gift, which was bought for you with
My blood on the cross. Yet it is yours forever; you just have to
accept it.

My grace is priceless! So many blessings come to you
because of it. Feeling guilty for sins and mistakes melts away
like ice cubes in the sunshine. You are a *child of God*—this gives
your life a meaning and a purpose. You can love and forgive
others better because I love and forgive you.

The best way to respond to My amazing gift of grace is to
fill up your heart with thankfulness. Take time each day to think
about the blessings in your life and to thank Me for each one.
This will protect your heart from the weeds of *un*-thankfulness
that sprout up so easily. *Be thankful*, My child!

READ ON YOUR OWN

John 1:16; John 1:12; Colossians 3:15

Too Wonderful for Words

Thanks be to God for his gift that is too wonderful for words.
—2 Corinthians 9:15 NCV

Live in this day with Me! Your whole life is a gift, and it's made up of millions upon millions of moments. These moments of your life—countless, tiny gifts—can slip away so easily that you don't even notice them. The best cure for wasting them like this is to fill your moments with Me. Start in the morning with a prayer: "Thank You, Jesus, for this wonderful day of my life. Help me 'see' all the ways You are with me today."

Thanking Me keeps you in touch with Me, and it keeps you living in *this moment*. Worrying, on the other hand, drags your thoughts into the future, where you don't know what's going to happen. Worrying leaves you confused, upset, and sometimes even frightened. But you can always come back to Me by whispering, "Jesus, help me."

To keep living in this day, try being more thankful. Look around and search for the many gifts I place in your life—and thank Me in detail for each one you see. As you do this, your joy grows bigger and bigger, and you'll discover just how blessed you really are.

READ ON YOUR OWN

Psalm 118:24; Colossians 2:6–7; Psalm 13:5

Search for Me!

*"You will search for me. And when you search
for me with all your heart, you will find me!"*
—Jeremiah 29:13 ICB

The Joy you have in Me doesn't depend on whether good things or bad things are happening in your life. That's because *being with Me will fill you with Joy*, and you're never separated from Me! *Search for Me* as you go along your way today. I love to show Myself to you. Sometimes I do it in such big ways that you're certain it's Me—"coincidences" that are clearly the work of My hands. At other times, I show Myself in quiet ways. These are often just for you to see. Others may not even notice them, like your favorite flower blooming in the corner of the playground. Yet these quiet signs can give you a deep Joy that is yours alone.

The more you're watching for Me, the more you'll find Me in the moments of your day. So stay alert—be on the lookout for Me!

Fill your mind and heart with Scripture, because that's where I show Myself to you most clearly. Let My promises flood your thinking and keep you close to Me. *Listen to My voice. I know you, and you follow Me. I give you eternal Life; no one can snatch you out of My hand.* Rejoice and be glad as you search for Me!

READ ON YOUR OWN

Psalm 16:11; John 10:27–28

A New Thing

"Forget what happened before. Do not think about the past. Look at the new thing I am going to do. It is already happening. Don't you see it? I will make a road in the desert. I will make rivers in the dry land."
—Isaiah 43:18–19 ICB

*D*o not think about the past, My dear child. Yes, there are lessons you can learn from it, but don't let the past become the main thing you think about. You can't undo mistakes that have already been made, no matter how much you might want to. So instead of wishing for the impossible, come to Me and *tell Me all your problems*. Remember that *I am your Protection. Trust Me all the time.*

You can make your faith in Me stronger by saying: "I trust You, Jesus." Say it often. Those four words can brighten your day instantly. Dark clouds of worry are blown away by your trust in Me.

Be watching for *the new thing I am going to do in your life*! Ask Me to open your eyes—not just your physical eyes, but your mind and heart—to see all the possibilities I've placed throughout your day. Don't get into such a habit of doing the same old things over and over that you miss out on the new things I'm offering you. There will be times when what you need to do seems impossible, but *I can make a way for you where there doesn't seem to be a way. With Me all things are possible*!

READ ON YOUR OWN

Psalm 62:8 ICB; Matthew 19:26

Hear Me Sing!

You are the giver of life. Your light lets us enjoy life.
—Psalm 36:9 ICB

I will sing and be joyful about you. That means you fill Me with so much Joy that I just have to sing! Open up your heart, mind, and spirit, and let Me give you My best blessings. Because you're My child, bought with My blood, My Love for you is always flowing down from heaven's *throne of grace.* Look up to Me, follow Me, and receive all the gifts I have planned for you. Listen! Hear Me singing songs of Joy because *I am so happy with you.* Come to Me boldly and without fear, knowing you are *the one I love.*

The world tells you that love can change—because of what you do, what you look like, what you wear, or how famous you are. This is a lie. My Love doesn't change. But the world's lie is told so often—in movies, on the Internet, and even by the people around you—that it can still get inside your thoughts. That's why it's so important to focus your thoughts on Me. Fill your mind with My words, and let the Light of My Presence shine on you.

Set aside time to be alone with Me every day. The world will tell you that's weird, but do it anyway. Don't worry about what others say. Your whole life will be blessed by your time with Me. *For I am the Giver of life. My Light lets you enjoy life.*

READ ON YOUR OWN

Zephaniah 3:17 ICB; Hebrews 4:16; Deuteronomy 33:12

I Lift You Up

The Lord helps the fallen and lifts those bent beneath their loads.
—Psalm 145:14 NLT

I help the fallen, and I lift up those who are stumbling as they try to carry the heavy weight of their troubles. Sometimes you and I are the only ones who know you've messed up. When no one else knows, it's tempting to skip over the sinful things you've done, or the good things you haven't done. You may not be crushed by shame, but you do feel restless and upset—and a little guilty. Even at these times, I love you perfectly. Sometimes I show My Love for you in surprising ways. This can humble you *and* give you Joy, all at the same time.

It's humbling because you see how much I love you even when you sin and make mistakes. My unchanging Love makes you want to admit your sins and come closer to Me. When you do this, you start feeling peaceful instead of restless and upset. This is how I lift you up when you stumble and fall.

Remember that I can make *all things*—including your sins and mistakes—*work together for your good* because *you love Me*. That's part of My plan. Just knowing how much I treasure you, even when you're doing wrong, makes our relationship grow stronger. It also helps you relax and find Joy because *My Love* for you *never ends*.

READ ON YOUR OWN

Romans 8:28; Lamentations 3:22–23

Hold My Hand

*"I am the L*ORD* your God, who holds your right hand,*
and I tell you, 'Don't be afraid. I will help you.'"
—Isaiah 41:13 NCV

I am the cure for your loneliness. For *I am the L*ORD* your God, who holds your right hand, and I tell you, "Don't be afraid. I will help you."*

Close your right hand, just as if you were holding My hand. Doing this will help you remember that I really am with you. Whenever you start to feel lonely or afraid, you need to reach out for Me.

Tell Me what you're feeling and what you're struggling with. I already know, but it will help you to tell your troubles to Me. Spend time warming yourself in the Light of My Presence. Know that you are safe and secure in My Love for you. *I am with you* every second of your life. You are never alone!

Search for Me and ask Me to show you how *I* view what's happening in your life. Sometimes it's even good to write down your worries. This helps you think more clearly, and it gives you a record of your prayers, so you can look back at how I answer them. Writing down your problems also helps you let go of them and give them to Me. Take comfort in knowing that *I am watching over you* always.

READ ON YOUR OWN

Matthew 28:20; Psalm 27:4; Genesis 28:15

A Precious Promise

*God, your love is so precious! You protect people
as a bird protects her young under her wings.*
—Psalm 36:7 ICB

*N*othing in all creation can separate you from My Love. Just stop and think about how wonderful—how precious and priceless—that promise is! You live in a world full of separations: wives from husbands, children from parents, friends from friends. But there is one separation that's worse than any other—and that's being separated from Me. Happily, because you are My child, that's something you will *never* have to face.

I want you to hold on to Me tightly and confidently. This will give you the strength to face anything this broken and sin-filled world throws at you. Worries can attack your mind and fill you with fear if you forget that My Love will never fail you. When you feel afraid, hold My hand and trust Me completely. Rest in the safety and protection of My Presence. And remember that *My perfect love takes away fear*.

The greatest treasure on earth is nothing compared to the treasure of My Love—it's greater than any amount of money or jewels or gold. Yet My Love is a *free* gift to anyone who chooses to believe and follow Me. *How precious is My Love* that never fails you!

READ ON YOUR OWN

Romans 8:38–39; Isaiah 30:15; 1 John 4:18

Say No to Worry

*"Don't worry about tomorrow. Each day has enough
trouble of its own. Tomorrow will have its own worries."*
—Matthew 6:34 ICB

*D*o not worry about tomorrow—not one bit. Instead, live in today and keep your thoughts on the things of this moment. You'll have to work at this constantly, even struggle to do it. That's because it's so easy to slip into worrying about the future. But I want you to make looking for *Me* the main goal of your everyday life.

It's so very, very important to say no to the temptation to worry. You live in a world that's full of sin and struggles. So you'll never run out of things that you could worry about. But remember that *each day has enough trouble of its own*. I carefully measure how much trouble you will face in a day. I know exactly how much you can handle with My help. And I'm always right there with you, ready to make you stronger, encourage you, and comfort you.

Deciding to live close to Me is the best way to live in this present moment. If your thoughts wander to worries, bring them back to Me by whispering My Name. Come back to Me with Joy, My dear child. *I will be happy with you, and I will sing and be joyful about you.*

READ ON YOUR OWN

Isaiah 41:10; Zephaniah 3:17 ICB

Start with Me

*Lord, every morning you hear my voice. Every morning,
I tell you what I need. And I wait for your answer.*
—Psalm 5:3 ICB

*Y*ou can do all things—whatever I ask—because you are My child and *I give you the strength* you need. As you spend time with Me and rest in My Presence, I'll pour My Strength into you. Because you're a child of the King of kings, you're able to do so much more than you realize. To get the most out of being My child, however, you need to spend time with Me every single day. Learn to relax in My Presence. Open your heart to Me. This time we spend together will not only fill you with Joy, it will also fill you with My Power.

When you're busy and have so many things to do, it's tempting to rush through your time with Me and dive into your day. But just as eating a good breakfast starts the day off right, so does feeding your soul with a healthy diet of *Me* each morning. Read My Word, let it soak into your mind, and ask My Spirit to show you what it means. Treasure these words of Life! Our relationship is a living thing, growing stronger as you spend more time with Me. And I will help you start each day with confidence, knowing that *together* we can be ready for anything that comes your way.

READ ON YOUR OWN

Philippians 4:13 ICB; Psalm 37:4

Ask Me into Your Day

"Can all your worries add a single moment to your life?
And if worry can't accomplish a little thing like that,
what's the use of worrying over bigger things?"
—Luke 12:25–26 NLT

Stop worrying! Stop planning! Stop focusing your thoughts on *this* moment instead, because it is here in this moment that I am lovingly waiting for you. Search for Me with a smile in your heart, knowing that I love to be with you. Talk to Me about all your worries and all the troubles that are bringing you down. Call out to Me for help, and let Me show you what's truly important. Keep your thoughts on Me and on the things you need to do right now. Ask Me to walk with you through the activities of your day. This will not only bring you Joy, but it will help you do better at the things you need to get done.

When you need to take a break, remember that I am your resting place. My *everlasting arms* are always ready to hold you close and comfort you. When you relax with Me, waiting with Me for a while, this shows that you really do trust Me. Then, as you get ready to go back to your activities, ask Me to go with you. This will keep you from worrying. And it will help you stay close to Me, enjoying My Presence.

READ ON YOUR OWN

Psalm 62:5–6; Deuteronomy 33:27

Wait for Me

*Do not worry about anything. But pray and ask God for
everything you need. And when you pray, always give thanks.*
—Philippians 4:6 ICB

I am training you to not just get through your tough times
but to change them into something wonderful and glorious.
I know that sounds impossible. And it is *supernatural*—that's
why you need My all-powerful Spirit to help you. When your
problems are bigger than you can handle on your own, I see
you still searching for answers and trying to fix everything on
your own. But what you should do is stop and talk to Me. Ask My
Spirit to help you as you tell Me all about your problems. *Tell Me
what you need, and then wait for Me to answer.*

But remember that I may not answer your prayers quickly.
I am always doing something important in your life—something
much bigger than just solving your problems. That's because
your struggles are part of a much larger battle, a spiritual
battle. So the way you handle these struggles is very, very
important!

When you trust Me in hard times, and when you still pray
with a thankful heart, you give glory to Me. Keep on praying,
even when you don't seem to be getting any answers. Your
faithful, untiring prayers will—over time—make a big difference in *you*, My treasured child who is *crowned with Glory*.

READ ON YOUR OWN

Psalm 5:3 ICB; Psalm 8:5

Who You Really Are

He came to the world that was his own. But his own people did not accept him. But some people did accept him. They believed in him. To them he gave the right to become children of God.
—John 1:11–12 ICB

Rejoice and be glad! *Those who are in Christ Jesus are not judged guilty*, thanks to My death on the cross. I took away all your guilt: past, present, *and* future.

Being forever "not guilty" is a good enough reason to be happy each and every day of your life. Ever since Adam and Eve's first sin in the garden of Eden, sin has been a terrible problem for everyone. But My death on the cross solved this problem perfectly. I took away your sin—*I became sin for you*—and I gave you My perfect righteousness. *This* is the good news of the gospel, and it really is the best news of all!

I want you to learn to *enjoy* being not guilty. Through Me you are set free from your sins. This doesn't mean it's okay to just go out and sin as much as you want. It means that I want you to live joyfully, knowing you can ask Me to forgive you when you sin. And I always *do*—because you're My precious child. This is your true identity, and it makes every minute of your life important. Rejoice and be happy, because you know who you *really* are—a beloved *child of God*.

READ ON YOUR OWN

Romans 8:1–2; Genesis 3:6–7; 2 Corinthians 5:21

Do It All for Me

Whatever you do, do it all for the glory of God.
—1 Corinthians 10:31

I'm not some phony, false, dead god. I am the One who rose from the grave—your *living God*. Celebrate with Joy, because the Savior you serve is wonderfully and completely alive! What's more, I've promised to be with you *always*, for all time and throughout eternity. These truths will help you get through the greatest troubles and disappointments you'll ever face. So live boldly because I am by your side. Trust that I'm the One who never lets go of your hand.

Think about all that I want to give you: forgiveness for *all* your sins and Joy forever in heaven. These are such great and glorious gifts that you can't fully understand them. That's why worshiping Me is so important. It connects you to Me in powerful ways.

Worshiping Me says to the people around you that you know I am with you. You can praise Me in so many ways: singing, studying and memorizing My Word, praying alone and praying with others, or simply being amazed by the wonders of My creation. Serving, helping, and loving others with My Love is also a way to praise and worship Me. *Whatever you do, do it all for the Glory of God*—for the Glory of Me!

READ ON YOUR OWN

Matthew 28:5–6; Psalm 42:2; Colossians 2:2–3

Strong Enough

You will be strong as long as you live.
—Deuteronomy 33:25 ICB

No matter how helpless you may feel, you can always come to Me for help. You don't have to be in church or bow your head when you want to speak to Me. You don't have to use fancy words or do something special to make Me love you and listen to you. I'm always looking at you with Love because I see you wearing My perfect righteousness like a robe. I'm alive in you, and I already understand all that you're thinking. So just a single word, just a look up to heaven when you're trusting in Me, is enough to connect you to My help.

You waste so much time and energy trying to figure out whether or not you are strong enough for the work and troubles of this day. Stop checking *your* "battery power" and instead connect to *My* Power—which never runs out!

It's smart to simply say, "I need You today, Jesus," when you wake up each morning. Starting the day with this simple prayer tells Me that you're counting on Me to help you. And as you keep talking to Me throughout the day, I'll keep giving you My Strength. I've promised that *I will always help* you. I'll make sure you're able to handle whatever happens this day.

READ ON YOUR OWN

Psalm 105:4; Isaiah 61:10; Psalm 46:1

I Am the Way

"I am the way, the truth, and the life. No one comes to the Father except through Me."
—John 14:6 NKJV

I am the Resurrection and the Life. He who believes in Me will have life even if he dies. I said these words of truth to Martha when her brother Lazarus had died, and she believed Me. Soon after, I commanded Lazarus to come out of his tomb, and he did! Even though Lazarus did die again later, he knew he would rise again to Life in heaven—as all who follow Me will do.

Just a short time before My death on the cross, I taught My disciples that *I am the Way, the Truth, and the Life.* I'm every-thing you could ever possibly need—for this life and your life in heaven. I'm the Treasure that's greater than any other treas-ure. Knowing this truth can make your life so much simpler. That's because I'm the answer to every struggle, and I'm your Joy no matter what is happening in your life.

I can make hard times better and good times even more wonderful. So *come to Me* just as you are, My priceless child. Share more and more of your life with Me. Be happy as we walk along together. And remember, I am the Way to Joy, I am the Truth who always guides you, and I am the Life who gives you a never-ending future in heaven.

READ ON YOUR OWN

John 11:25, 43–44; Colossians 2:2–3; Matthew 11:28

More and More Grateful

I am like an olive tree flourishing in the house of God;
I trust in God's unfailing love for ever and ever.
—Psalm 52:8

Ask Me to make you more and more grateful. It will brighten your day and open your heart to Me. Search for signs of Me in your day—in whatever is happening—because My Presence *is* there with you. Be on the lookout for all the things that I do and the ways that I bless you.

Being grateful opens not only your heart but also your eyes. When you know Me personally, you can find Me in the tiny details of your life, as well as the big things. Take time to notice all My blessings, small and large, and thank Me for each one. This practice of thanking Me will help you enjoy My gifts even more.

And ask Me to help you trust Me more and more. The more you trust Me, the better you'll be at walking through tough times without stumbling. The harder your journey, the more often you'll need to talk to Me and depend on Me. Try praying, "Lord, *I trust in Your unfailing Love.* I know You'll never stop loving me." This short prayer will help you remember that I'm right there with you, I'm taking care of you, and I love you forever. You can depend on Me!

READ ON YOUR OWN

Colossians 2:6–7; Psalm 16:11

A New You

*You were taught to become a new person. That new person
is made to be like God—made to be truly good and holy.*
—Ephesians 4:24 ICB

Because *I rose from death*, you have *a new life* and *a living hope*. My work inside you is all about "newness." Because you belong to Me, you're *a new creation—you are made new. The old things have gone; everything is made new!*

The moment you first trust Me as your Savior, you are adopted into My royal family. And at that same moment, you are given the gift of eternal life. As My child, you have an inheritance—*blessings that are kept for you in heaven. They cannot be destroyed or be spoiled or lose their beauty.*

When you decide to follow Me, the Holy Spirit comes to live inside you. But becoming a Christian is only the beginning of the work I do. You need *to be made new in your heart and become a new person—becoming truly good and holy.* You will work on this your whole life, and it will prepare you for the Glory of heaven. So take on this assignment with courage, and be thankful for all I offer you. Stay alert, watching for all the wonderful things I'm doing in your life.

READ ON YOUR OWN

1 Peter 1:3–4; 2 Corinthians 5:17;
Ephesians 4:22–24; Romans 6:4

The Light of the World

Later, Jesus talked to the people again. He said, "I am the light of the world. The person who follows me will never live in darkness. He will have the light that gives life."
—John 8:12 ICB

The better you get to know Me, the more aware of your sins you will be. Then you'll face a choice: Focus on your mistakes and failures, or be joyful because of My wonderful gift of salvation that takes away your sins. When you keep your thoughts focused on all I did to save you from your sins, you'll live joyfully, knowing how much you are loved. There is *no greater Love than Mine*, and it is yours forever. The best way to thank Me for loving you so much is *to love Me with all your heart*.

Sadly, too many people think they don't have anything for Me to forgive. They think there is no real right or wrong. They believe good and evil depend on what they *think* instead of on what My Word says. They are wrong! And because they don't ask for My forgiveness, their sins are not forgiven. They have listened to the devil's lies instead of My Truth. But *I am the Light of the World*, and My Light can shine through you into their lives. Because you follow Me, you know the Truth and you can share it with others. You are forgiven. You never have to *live in darkness—you have the Light that gives Life*!

READ ON YOUR OWN

Psalm 13:5–6; John 15:13; Matthew 22:37–39

Walk in the Light

If we walk in the light, as he is in the light, we have fellowship with one another, and the blood of Jesus his Son cleanses us from all sin.
—1 John 1:7 ESV

*I*f you walk in the Light by living close to Me, *My blood cleanses you from all sin*. This cleansing doesn't just happen once. It's happening all the time. When you realize you've sinned, I want you to confess it—to tell Me about it. Ask Me to help you change so that you don't sin that way again. But your place as My child doesn't depend on how quickly you confess your sins or how well you tell Me about them. You are *always* My much-loved child because I gave you the gift of My perfect righteousness when you decided to follow Me. You are Mine always. And since you're Mine, beautifully clothed in *My robe of righteousness*, I invite you to come into My Presence with confidence and gladness.

Living in the Light of My Presence blesses you in so many ways. Good things become better and bad things are easier to handle when you share them with Me. As you find Joy in the Light of My Love, you can learn to love others better. You'll be less likely to stumble into sin, because the darkness of sin is so easy to see when you are living in My Light. Be happy and *rejoice in My Name all the time*. Enjoy simply being with Me and *praising My goodness*.

READ ON YOUR OWN

Isaiah 61:10; Psalm 89:15–16

Shining Down on You

*With the loving mercy of our God, a new day from heaven will shine
upon us. God will help those who live in darkness, in the fear of
death. He will guide us into the path that goes toward peace.*
—Luke 1:78–79 ICB

I am the Light *from heaven that will shine down upon you. I will
help those who live in darkness.* Sometimes the things that
happen in your life are so hard and confusing, it feels like
you're in a dark hole. Your mind thinks up all kinds of possible
answers, but nothing seems to work. So you worry and wonder what to do next. You feel helpless and tired and frustrated.
When it's been one of those days, look up and see My Light shining down on you. Keep your eyes on Me by praying and reading
My Word. Rest in My Presence. Stop trying to fix everything,
and stop struggling. *Be still and know that I am God.*

As you rest and relax in My Presence, remember that I am
the *Prince of Peace.* The closer you are to Me, the more Peace
you will have in your life. With each breath you take, think of
Me and breathe in the Truth that I am right here with you. After
you've rested for a little while, tell Me all about your troubles.
Trust Me to help you. Stay close to Me, dear one, and *I will guide
you into the path that goes toward Peace.*

READ ON YOUR OWN

Psalm 46:10; Isaiah 9:6

Written in Heaven

"Rejoice that your names are written in heaven."
—Luke 10:20

*R*ejoice—be happy—*that your name is written in heaven*. Your name is in My book of Life forever! Because you are My child, you have a Joy that doesn't depend on what happens to you. Your Joy depends on the Truth that you've been given eternal Life, an amazing gift that will *never* be taken away from you! *Those who are made right with Me* (through believing that I am their risen, living Savior) *are also glorified*. In a way, you are already *seated with Me in the heavens*—because by staying close to Me, your life is flooded with the heavenly Light of My Joy.

Joy is the blessing given to everyone who belongs to Me. You can have My Joy even in times of great sadness or terrible troubles. So come to Me each morning with an open heart and open hands, saying, "Jesus, I accept the gift of Your Joy." Then wait with Me while My Light and Love shine upon you, soaking deep down inside you. I will make you strong and get you ready for the day ahead.

As you walk through this day, keep coming back to Me to get more Joy—as often as you need it. I am a God who never runs out of good things, so I always have more than enough Joy for you!

READ ON YOUR OWN

Romans 8:30 ICB; Ephesians 2:6

APRIL

"May the LORD bless you and
protect you. May the LORD smile
on you and be gracious to you."

—Numbers 6:24–25 NLT

April 1

Sharper Than a Sword

God's word is alive and working and is sharper than a double-edged sword. . . . And it judges the thoughts and feelings in our hearts.
—Hebrews 4:12 NCV

I love to shine My Light into your life and change the way you see things. That's why I came to your world, even though I knew the terrible price I would pay on the cross. I came *to help the blind to see, to free those who are in prison, and to lead those who live in darkness out of their prison* and into My Light. Not all prisons have bars or locks on the door. There are prisons of sin, sadness, and anger. There's even the prison of being ungrateful for your blessings. If you find yourself in one of these dark places, ask Me to show you the way out.

You live in a world where people think they *deserve* to get whatever they want—the new game, the good grade, the spot on the team. Be different. *Be thankful.* Try keeping a list of all the things you're thankful for each day. This takes your thinking away from the stuff you wish you had, to the blessings you already have.

Filling your mind with My Word can help you see your life through My eyes. *My Word is sharper than a double-edged sword.* I use it to do spiritual surgery on *the thoughts and feelings in your heart.* As My Word lights up the way you see the world around you, it also sets you free from the prison of ungratefulness. And it releases you to experience the Joy of a grateful heart.

READ ON YOUR OWN

Isaiah 42:7; Psalm 119:105

Share My Truth

"I was born for this: to tell people about the truth. That is why I came into the world. And everyone who belongs to the truth listens to me."
—John 18:37 ICB

Believing in Me does so many good things for you, including filling you with *a Joy that cannot be explained. A Joy that is full of Glory.* My Joy is *inexpressible*—this means it's too great and too wonderful to be described! But you can experience it for yourself.

Come to Me, expecting to receive My Joy. Open up your heart for Me to fill it. My Joy is victorious and filled with the Glory of heaven. That's because I defeated sin and death once and for all time! This truth opens up the way to heaven for all who choose to believe in and follow Me.

No matter how many troubles you face, the goal of your faith is to save your soul. And your soul is safe and secure with Me. That's true for all people who truly trust Me. As you think about your future in heaven, let your own light shine *for other people*. My Spirit, the Spirit of Truth, will help you share My Truth with others. I came into this world *to tell people about the Truth*. And I want you to join Me in this quest—this great adventure. Help those *living in darkness* to find Me and walk in My *great Light*.

READ ON YOUR OWN

1 Peter 1:8–9; Matthew 5:16; Isaiah 9:2

April 3

I Live in Your Heart

I pray that Christ will live in your hearts because of your faith.
I pray that your life will be strong in love and be built on love.
—Ephesians 3:17 ICB

Look up to Me, dear one, for *My Face is shining upon you*. Be amazed by the glory of My holiness. Let the Light of My Love soak into your heart and soul. Remember that *I live in your heart because of your faith* in Me. I am the Master and Maker of the entire universe, which I created and control. I am also the Savior who lives inside you. My wonderful greatness and My gentleness come together to give you everything you need. You are rich beyond your wildest dreams—not in money, but in My Love and My Presence with you.

Because you live in a world so filled with sin, it can be hard to remember that you are royalty. You have been adopted into the family of the *King of kings*. Your journey through this world may take you down paths of problems or through deserts of sadness. Don't be surprised by the fiery trials that are coming. Instead, keep putting one foot in front of the other and doing the next right thing. Trust Me, the One who never leaves your side. At the end of your journey, I will take you into the Light of heaven, where there will be no more problems, no more sadness, and no more night.

READ ON YOUR OWN

Numbers 6:24–25; Ephesians 3:16–17;
Revelation 19:16; Revelation 21:25

Master of Time

I trust in you, O L<small>ORD</small>; I say, "You are my
God." My times are in your hands.
—Psalm 31:14–15

*Y*our times are in My hands. That means every moment of your life is under My control. My hands are completely able to take care of you and to meet your every need.

I want you to relax, knowing that I watch over you. Trust Me to do what's best. Because I am totally worthy of your trust, let me take care of the "whats" and "whens" of your life.

As long as you live on this earth, you have to face the reality of time. Days begin and end, whether you want them to or not. Birthdays won't come any faster just because you wish for them. And a tough test will not come any slower because you don't want to take it. Someone who is sick may long to be healthy again—and want it right now—but he must wait. I, however, live outside the rule of time. I am the Master of time. If you're struggling with having to wait for something, talk to Me about it. Ask Me to help you trust Me and My perfect timing. Don't fight against something you can't change no matter how hard you try. Instead, be glad because you know that I understand your struggles and troubles. And I love you *with a love that will last forever.*

READ ON YOUR OWN

Psalm 62:8; Jeremiah 31:3

The Living Water of Joy

"If a person believes in me, rivers of living
water will flow out from his heart."
—John 7:38 ICB

I want you *to receive your salvation with Joy. Take it as you would draw water from a well*—to satisfy a deep thirst. When you follow Me, I save you from your sins forever. Knowing this is like having a well of Joy in your life every day. Because you know for sure that I'm your Savior, you have *a spring of water flowing inside you. It will give you eternal life.* Just imagine how huge this amazing gift is—and be filled with Joy! When you get up in the morning, thank Me for all I've given you. And when you lie down to sleep at night, say thanks for all I've done.

My gift of salvation was given to bless you *and* the people around you. As you learn to trust in Me, *rivers of living water will flow out of your heart.* Ask My Spirit, who lives inside you, to use you to bless others. Ask Him to let the living water of My Love pour out of you and into the lives of others around you. One way to ask is to pray this: "Holy Spirit, think through me. Live through me. Love through me." While the rivers of living water are flowing through you into the hearts of people around you, I will fill both them *and* you with Joy!

READ ON YOUR OWN

Isaiah 12:3; John 4:13–14

I Guide Your Steps

*We can make our plans, but the L*ORD *determines our steps.*
—Proverbs 16:9 NLT

Even though your journey through life may seem unplanned and accidental, *your steps are directed by Me.* When you aren't sure where life is headed or what will happen next, the best thing to do is hang on to Me. Imagine that you're walking along a busy street in a strange city holding your mom's or dad's hand. You may feel overwhelmed by the noise and the unfamiliar sights. You may be afraid of getting separated from your parent and getting lost. But if you keep holding your mom's or dad's hand, you'll get where you're going—safe and sound. In the same way, hold on to My hand—ask for My help. I will guide you and keep you safe.

You may not always know which way to go, but you *do* know the One who is *the Way.* Because I am in control of your life, *I direct your steps* and guide you—even in those times when you feel lost. Talk to Me whenever you feel worried or afraid of making a wrong choice. And remember, the most important choice every moment is just to keep talking to Me. *That's* how you stick close to Me. And *that's* how you trust Me to guide you and keep you safe.

READ ON YOUR OWN

Proverbs 20:24; John 14:6; 2 Corinthians 5:7

Enjoy the Journey

"When you pass through the waters, I will be with you. When you cross rivers, you will not drown. When you walk through fire, you will not be burned. The flames will not hurt you."
—Isaiah 43:2 ICB

I give eternal life to you, and you will never die. And no person can steal you out of My hand. That's amazingly good news for everyone who knows Me as their Savior. I promise you an inheritance—eternal life in heaven—and it's far more wonderful than anything you could ever imagine! The gift of eternal life gives you a Light that shines in your heart even through your darkest and worst days. Let that Light lead you forward and protect you from being sad and discouraged. Don't let bad days or the wickedness of this world drag you down. Instead, think about the wonders of heaven that are waiting for you. Can't you imagine it—sparkling like a jewel in the faraway sky, just beyond what you can see?

There may be times when you feel as if you're drowning in troubles or in sadness. But remember, *when you pass through the waters, I will be with you. You will not drown.* Keep holding tight to My hand—with your thoughts and your prayers—and trust Me to take care of you. Know that I love you and *nothing will be able to separate you from Me.* Instead of worrying about tough times that might be coming your way, think about how much you can enjoy the journey of life because I am by your side.

READ ON YOUR OWN

John 10:27–28; 1 Peter 1:3–4; Romans 8:38–39

Be Ready!

*You must worship Christ as Lord of your life. And if someone
asks about your hope as a believer, always be ready to explain it.*
—1 Peter 3:15 NLT

*If someone asks about your hope as believer, always be ready
to explain it.* It's easier to follow this command of Mine when
you're feeling rested and your life is going great. It's much
harder to do when you're tired and worried and upset. Yet the
times when you're struggling may make your answer even
more powerful. That's because people will see you worshiping
Me and trusting Me *in* your struggle. So make it your goal to be
ready to tell others why you believe in Me.

You also need to be ready to explain to *everyone* who asks
you about why you have hope. Even people you don't like and
people you think will never believe in Me. Only *I* know their
hearts and what I have planned for their lives.

In order to be ready in this way, you must live in My
Presence—seeking Me, trusting Me, and knowing I'm with you
every moment of the day. This will help you face the ups and
downs of life. When you're struggling, encourage yourself by
thinking about what I've done and what I will do: I've saved you
from your sins, and I'll always love you. Keep your thoughts on
Me, for I am your Hope of heaven and your Joy for life.

READ ON YOUR OWN

Romans 5:5; Psalm 27:4

I Know What Your Heart Wants

*The LORD says, "I will guide you along the best pathway
for your life. I will advise you and watch over you."*
—Psalm 32:8 NLT

Be ready and willing to follow where I lead, My beloved child. Be open to the way I have planned for you, even if it looks very different from what *you* had planned. Don't become so stuck on what you want that you miss the things I've prepared for you. Relax and trust Me while *I change you*—from the inside out—*by a new way of thinking*. Trust Me enough to quit pushing for what you want. *Be still and know that I am God.*

Sometimes *you* keep yourself from the very things you dream of because you try too hard to get them on your own and you don't wait for My help. I know what your heart wants, and I know the best way for you to reach your goals. Instead of fighting to be in control so you can get what you want, *look for Me* instead. Tell Me about your hopes and dreams and plans. Rest with Me for a while. Then, when you are rested and feeling like new, ask Me to show you the way you should go. *I will guide you along the best pathway for your life. I will advise you and watch over you.*

READ ON YOUR OWN

Romans 12:2; Psalm 46:10; 1 Chronicles 16:11

Love as High as the Heavens

I will sing your praises among the nations. For your unfailing love is as high as the heavens. Your faithfulness reaches to the clouds.
—Psalm 57:9–10 NLT

*M*y unfailing love is as high as the heavens. My faithfulness reaches to the clouds. You can feel so wonderfully safe and secure in My Love because it has no limits and no end. My faithfulness also has no limits and no end.

Worship Me as you think about these amazing gifts. The more you praise Me, the more you can reflect My Glory to other people—just as a mirror reflects the sunlight. This is how the Holy Spirit works. He *changes you to be more like Me. This change brings more and more Glory* to Me. As you come closer to Me through worship, I change you in great and wonderful ways. I make you ready to share Me with others.

My Love is not only higher than the heavens, but it also fills the earth. Keep looking up to Me, My dear one. See Me smiling down on you. My endless Love falls upon you all the time, like heavenly snowflakes that melt softly on your face. No matter how bad a situation seems, My Love will get you through it. And someday, My Love will lift you all the way up to heaven. I am waiting for the day when I will take you home to live with Me forever!

READ ON YOUR OWN

2 Corinthians 3:18; Numbers 6:25–26; Psalm 73:23–24

Think Like Me

All of you holy brothers and sisters, who were called by God, think about Jesus, who was sent to us and is the high priest of our faith.
—Hebrews 3:1 NCV

Try to think like Me more and more often. Ask My Spirit to help you, because *if your thinking is controlled by the Spirit, then there is Life and Peace.*

When the worries of this world are beating you up, take time to think things out with Me. Rest with Me and breathe. Let Me wrap you up in My arms and cover you in My Peace. Take a break from worrying, and think about Me instead. Try sitting quietly for a while, then reading My Word, then praising Me, then sitting quietly again. You can use Bible verses as prayers to Me. When your thinking and your prayers are filled with My own words, you know you're praying good things!

I want you to be *changed by a new way of thinking—My* way of thinking. This world likes to keep you busy with beeping games and buzzing smartphones. Don't let these electronic gadgets control how you see the world. Instead, ask *Me* to change the way you think. As I do, your thoughts and values and attitudes will look more and more like Mine—and that's a joyful thing!

READ ON YOUR OWN

Romans 8:6; Deuteronomy 33:27; Romans 12:2

Exercise Your Trust Muscles

You know that when your faith is tested, your
endurance has a chance to grow.
—James 1:3 NLT

Your relationship with Me doesn't depend on what's happening in your life. That's why you can praise Me and enjoy
simply being with Me, even on your very worst day. To find Me in
tough times, though, you have to really put your faith to work—
but I'm always close by.

As a Christian, you actually live in two places at once.
One of those places is the world you can see, which is full of
trouble. The other is the supernatural world, where I am the
King of kings. To really *know* that I am with you—even in your
hard times—you'll have to use your "trust muscles," which
grow stronger every time you use them. Your hard times and
troubles can build up your faith as you discover just how much
you really can trust Me.

I want you to work on making your trust muscles stronger.
Like exercising your body's muscles, you need to exercise your
trust muscles every day. Do this by reading My Word, praising Me, and praying. Don't think too much about yourself and
your worries—keep bringing your thoughts back to Me. Make it
a habit to tell Me that you trust Me. Remember, your strength
comes from living close to Me. I'll make you strong and help
you be ready for anything and everything that comes your way!

READ ON YOUR OWN

James 1:2–3; Psalm 105:4; Philippians 4:13

Count on Me to Help

Remember the Lord in everything you do.
And he will give you success.
—Proverbs 3:6 ICB

Try to think about Me in more of the moments of your life. You can do this by joyfully trusting Me to take care of you. Remember, *I am with you, watching over you* all the time. There is nothing you do that I cannot see. No job or task is so small that you can't ask for My help. In fact, every breath you take depends on Me and My Power.

When you have a tough job to do, you usually remember to pray about it. You may pray before you start, and keep on praying while you're working: "Help me, Lord" or "Thank You, Jesus." Talking to Me that way encourages you to depend on Me and makes you grateful for My Presence with you.

But when the task you're facing is an easy one, you often forget to pray; you just dive into it. You may have some success anyway, though it would have worked out better if you had asked Me to help you. Or everything may flop—but it could have succeeded if you had just turned to Me. So count on Me and look for Me to help you in everything you do—both the big things and the small things—because I have blessings that I'm just waiting to give you!

READ ON YOUR OWN

Genesis 28:15; Hebrews 1:3

You Belong to Me

You should know that your body is a temple for the Holy Spirit. . . . You do not own yourselves. You were bought by God for a price. So honor God with your bodies.
—1 Corinthians 6:19–20 ICB

*Y*ou do not own yourself. You were bought by God for a price. And that price was a terribly high one—My Life! I went through horrible pain and shame as I sacrificed Myself on the cross to take away your sins. This was My priceless gift to you—because I love you. But the only ones who can receive the wonderful gift of My Love are those who see that they have sins and that they need *Me* to save them.

Hear Me calling out: *"Come to me, all of you who are tired and have heavy loads. I will give you rest."* Sin is a terrible and heavy burden that will crush you, but I have paid the price *in full* to take that burden away from you forever.

When you wake up each morning, say to yourself, "I do not own myself. I belong to Jesus." Then, all through the day, keep telling yourself Who you belong to—especially when it's time to make plans and decisions about what to do. Knowing that you belong to Me helps you keep your feet on *the path that goes toward My Peace*. Remembering that you're Mine takes away fear and worry—and fills you instead with feelings of safety and security. You are My child, and I love you very much!

READ ON YOUR OWN

Matthew 11:28; Luke 1:76–79

Trust Me

You know the grace of our Lord Jesus Christ. You know
that Christ was rich, but for you he became poor. Christ did
this so that by his being poor you might become rich.
—2 Corinthians 8:9 ICB

You can trust Me—the One who died to save you. In this world of lies and scams, it's hard to believe that anyone is really telling the truth. You've probably heard people say that others have to "earn" their trust. But *I* am the only One who has ever perfectly earned the right to be trusted.

So that I could save you, I left the amazing perfection of heaven and was born in a stable as a helpless baby. For the thirty-three years that I lived on this earth, I did not give in to any temptation. I did not sin—not even once—so that My death on the cross would pay for all your sins. I lived a perfect life, and then I willingly let Myself be spit on and beaten and nailed to a cross to pay the full price for sin. Because I died and rose to life again, *whoever believes in Me has eternal Life*!

I want you to trust Me—completely and with confidence. Trust Me not only as your Savior but as the God and Friend who takes care of you. I have already proven that you can trust Me. Now I invite you to rest and relax with Me, and tell Me all that is in your heart. Tell Me your hopes and fears and dreams. *Give all your worries to Me, because I care for you.*

READ ON YOUR OWN

John 3:36; 1 Peter 5:7

Share Your Day with Me

Lord, you have examined me. You know all about
me. You know when I sit down and when I get up.
You know my thoughts before I think them.
—Psalm 139:1–2 ICB

This is the day that I have made. I invite you to be thankful for it as you share it with Me. The more of Me you have in your life, the more joyful you will be.

Invite Me into the moments of your day by talking to Me about everything—what you're excited about, what's happening around you, what you're worried about—whatever is on your mind. These talks with Me will change the way you think. If there's some pesky little thing that keeps buzzing around in your mind, tell Me about it. I'll help you see how silly it is and get rid of it. If you're stuck on a mistake you made in the past, tell Me and let Me gently pull your thoughts back to today. Whatever you're facing—good or bad—I can help you handle it better.

Look for Joy in this day that I've made just for you. I've hidden small treasures all along your path. Search for them. And when you find one, thank Me! Many of these tiny treasures are things only *you* will see—that only *you* will find delight in. I know you so well that I can give you just what you need to make you smile. Be joyful, My beloved child!

READ ON YOUR OWN

Psalm 118:24; 1 Thessalonians 5:16–18

You Were Made for Joy

"I have told you these things so that you will be filled with my joy. Yes, your joy will overflow!"
—John 15:11 NLT

Look to Me to find your Joy. You were *made* for Joy—and I am the endless, overflowing Source of it.

I am infinite; I have no beginning and no end. So I never run out of anything. I always have more Joy to give. Everything else in your life only lasts for so long. There are things that can put a smile on your face for now, but soon the fun will run out. Friends are great, but they can have bad days. Games are a blast, but you can get tired of them. The more you make *Me* your focus, the less you will depend on other people or things to make you happy. You can still enjoy the gifts of friends and games and other things, but you don't have to hold on so tight to them. You don't have to try to squeeze every possible bit of fun out of them.

Learn to keep your eyes on Me even as the world parades by in front of you. Whisper My Name to remind you that I'm always near. Tell Me what troubles you. Thank Me for the things you enjoy—family and friends, food and a home, sunlight, starlight, and *especially* My Presence in your life. *Always come to Me for help*, and ask Me what I want you to do. *Depend on Me and My Strength*, and you will find Joy.

READ ON YOUR OWN

Hebrews 12:2; 1 Timothy 1:17; Psalm 105:4

I Am the Only One

Jesus is the only One who can save people.
No one else in the world is able to save us.
—Acts 4:12 ICB

Thank Me for the amazing gift of forgiving all your sins. I am your Savior God, the only One who can give you this blessing of forgiveness. I bought this gift at a terrible price—My death on the cross. You can receive My forgiveness and become My child by *receiving Me* and *believing in My Name*. My Name, Jesus, means *the Lord saves*. To get this gift of salvation, you must trust Me as your only hope, believing that I am the One who saves you from all your sins.

Those who follow Me are not judged guilty. I want you to enjoy the wonder of walking through your life as My follower—totally forgiven! Because I give you this gift, thank Me and try to please Me above anyone else.

You don't have to do good things to make Me love you. I *already* love you! Instead, do good things for Me because your heart is so grateful. Thank Me often—every day. That will help you stay close to Me, and you'll be ready to go wherever I lead you. Be joyful, dear child, because through Me you are set free from your sins!

READ ON YOUR OWN

John 1:12; Romans 8:1–2

My Love Will Last Forever

*"I love you people with a love that will last forever. I
became your friend because of my love and kindness."*
Jeremiah 31:3 ICB

*Y*ou love Me because I first loved you. I was watching over you
long before you even knew about Me. I noticed everything
about you and followed you everywhere. I placed situations
and events in your life to help you see that you needed Me. I
gave you people who taught you the truth about Me in ways you
could understand. And My Spirit worked to make you spiritually
alive—so that you would be able to *receive Me and believe in My
Name*. Why did I do all this? Because *I love you with a Love that
will last forever*!

The more you learn about how much I love you, the more
fully you can love *Me*. This helps you to grow, little by little,
into the person I created you to be. As you spend time in My
gentle Presence, it gets easier for you to find Joy in Me and
to show kindness to other people—even those who aren't your
favorites. When you are with others, ask Me to help you love
them better. Ask Me to help you love them with *My* Love—and
I will.

READ ON YOUR OWN

1 John 4:19 NKJV; John 1:12

The Gift of Today

Let those who seek the LORD be happy. Depend on the
LORD and his strength; always go to him for help.
—1 Chronicles 16:10–11 NCV

This day is a precious gift from Me. Treat it as a treasure by lifting it up to Me in prayer. Ask Me what I want you to do with this gift of another twenty-four hours. *Look for Me* to show you what is most important. When you're trying to decide what you'll do today, check with Me in prayer. Then keep checking with Me throughout the day to make sure you're still on the right path. This practice will help you make good choices. Then, at the end of the day, you can feel good about the things you've done—and also the things you have *not* done.

I want you to invite Me to be a part of everything you do. Even the quickest prayer—"Help me, Lord"—is enough to bring Me into whatever you're doing. I love when you admit that you need Me with you always. And I want *you* to love that you need Me. This links us together in the strongest possible way.

The world will tell you it's not good to need anyone else. But I tell you that needing *Me* is a wonderful way to live. And you'll find great Joy in knowing you're always in My Presence.

READ ON YOUR OWN

Psalm 118:24; John 15:5; Jude v. 24

April 21

A Thankful and Joyful Heart

The Lᴏʀᴅ has done great things for us, and we are filled with joy.
—Psalm 126:3

*T*he hope of those who are right with God is Joy. That means *you* can look forward to Joy—because you are My child. I lived a perfect life for you—without any sin. And I died in your place, taking all the punishment for your sins. This made it possible for Me to cover you in My own *robe of righteousness* and perfection. I want you to wear these *clothes of salvation* with so much Joy and thankfulness that your heart overflows.

A thankful, joyful heart will help you live a good life that makes Me smile. Starting off your day with this kind of positive attitude will make your Joy grow even more. And as your Joy grows, your thankfulness also grows, and so on . . . in a happy cycle that keeps going and going and going!

When you feel your Joy fading, give it a boost with some thanksgiving. Read verses from the book of Psalms, or sing songs and praises to Me. Making a list (in your mind or on paper) of the blessings in your life is another great way to give thanks. I want you to remember *the great things I have done for you*. Because this will *fill you with Joy*!

READ ON YOUR OWN

Proverbs 10:28 ɴʟᴠ; Isaiah 61:10; Psalm 13:6

Leave the Future to Me

"Seek first God's kingdom and what God wants.
Then all your other needs will be met as well."
—Matthew 6:33 NCV

*D*o not worry about tomorrow! Though this is a command that I want you to obey, it's a loving one, straight from My heart. You see, I understand you and your weaknesses. I know that you're human, that *you are dust*. My command not to worry isn't meant to make you feel guilty. It's meant to set you free from feeling stressed about the things of this world.

Just before I gave this command to My followers, I told them how to enjoy the freedom of not worrying. And I tell you the same thing: *Your heavenly Father knows what you need*. As you try to do *what God wants first*—because that's more important than anything else—your way of looking at life will change. The stuff of this world becomes less important than the eternal things, like adding more people to God's kingdom, God's family. So put more of your time and energy into growing your relationship with Me. Look for My Presence, but also look for My will—what I want you to do. Be ready to follow Me wherever I lead. I will guide you on great adventures that fill your life with meaning.

I created you to enjoy being with Me in this present day. Leave the future to Me—I'll take care of it. As you find your happiness in Me, *I will give you the desires of your heart*.

READ ON YOUR OWN

Matthew 6:32–34 NCV; Psalm 103:14; Psalm 37:4

Rescued!

*The Word became a man and lived among us. We saw
his glory—the glory that belongs to the only Son of the
Father. The Word was full of grace and truth.*
—John 1:14 ICB

I am *the only Son of the Father*. I am *full of grace and truth*. I came from God, and I returned to Him because I *am* God. I am the second Person of the Trinity—the Father, *Myself*, and the Holy Spirit.

I came to your world to make a way for you to have a relationship with your Father God. It's a relationship that's alive and will last forever. People who don't know Me say there are many different ways to get to God, but that's a lie! *I am the Way, the Truth, and the Life. No one comes to the Father except through Me.*

I come to *you*, dear child, *full of grace.* You have nothing to fear if you trust Me to save you from your sins. My death on the cross made this possible. You don't have to be afraid of messing up or failing or not being good enough. Because I am your Savior—the One who saved you when you couldn't save yourself—you are safe and secure in My grace. Be joyful and glad! I am faithful, and My death on the cross was enough to rescue you from the grip of sin.

No matter what troubles you have in this world, *you can have Peace in Me. Be brave! I have defeated the world*!

READ ON YOUR OWN

John 14:6; John 16:33 NCV

Your Protector

*God's way is perfect. All the L*ORD*'s promises prove true.*
He is a shield for all who look to him for protection.
—Psalm 18:30 NLT

I am a Shield for all who look to Me for protection. On some days you'll know you really need the shield of My Presence. On other days you may think you don't need Me. Even then, I'm still close by, watching over you all the time. The truth is, I love being your Protector. So you can always look to Me as your safe place.

One of the best ways to make Me *your Protection* is to spend time with Me. *Pour out your heart to Me.* Tell Me about all the things that have hurt you, and the unfair things people have said or done to you. I care for you, and I want to heal your hurts. And since I know the truth about everything, I don't listen to anyone's gossip or lies about you.

I understand you completely. Knowing this fact will help you heal. But it's also important to forgive the people who have hurt you. Forgiving can be hard, and it can take time. Keep asking Me to help you forgive a little more each day, until your anger is all gone. Then praise Me and be happy, dear one, for *I came to make you free*—free from sin, free from hurts, and free from the lies of this world.

READ ON YOUR OWN

Psalm 62:8; John 8:32

I Am the Truth

"Then you will know the truth, and the truth will set you free."
—John 8:32

I am the Truth—and My Truth *never* changes. So many people think that truth is *relative.* That's a fancy word that means their truth changes depending on what's happening, who they're with, and what day it is. Only *My* unchanging Truth gives you a solid rock to build your life on. Everything else is shifting sand. And like the foolish man's house that was built on sand, if you build your life on "relative" truths that are always moving, your life will come crashing down.

Because My Truth is perfect, *all the treasures of wisdom and knowledge are hidden in Me.* You can find everything you need in your relationship with Me. I am the rock-solid foundation to build your life on—and I Myself *am* Life. So the closer you live to Me in your thoughts and prayers and actions, the more alive you will feel!

People of all different ages struggle to figure out who they are and what they should do with their lives. But when you know Me and My Truth, then you know who you really are—you are My child. This gives your life meaning and hope. So take time to get to know Me. And *be prepared* to tell others about Me, the Savior who took away your sins and *set you free.*

READ ON YOUR OWN

John 14:6; Colossians 2:2–3; 1 Peter 3:15

No Night in Heaven

The city does not need the sun or the moon to shine on it, for the glory of God gives it light, and the Lamb is its lamp. . . . On no day will its gates ever be shut, for there will be no night there.
—Revelation 21:23, 25

There will be no night in heaven, *for the Glory of God gives it Light.* You won't need nighttime or darkness for sleeping, because your new body will always be full of energy. Getting tired is something you have to deal with in this world. You simply run out of energy and need to rest. But in heaven, you won't ever get tired, so you won't need to sleep.

The Light of heaven is perfect and brilliant. There isn't a speck of darkness in it. There will be no sin in heaven either—nothing to hide. You will see everything through new eyes, like nothing you've ever seen before. Colors will be brighter, and faces will shine with My Light. You will be able to look right into My Face. Even Moses didn't get to see My Face. He had to hide in the gap between rocks as My Glory passed by. He was only allowed to see My back, but in heaven *you will see Me face to Face*—in all My Light and Glory!

READ ON YOUR OWN

1 John 1:5; Exodus 33:22–23; 1 Corinthians 13:12

April 27

The Way I See You

Those who look to him for help will be radiant with joy;
no shadow of shame will darken their faces.
—Psalm 34:5 NLT

I know you worry about failure—messing things up or not doing things well enough—but My Love for you will never fail. Let Me tell you what I see when I look at you, dear child. You look royal, because I have clothed you in the perfection of My righteousness and *crowned you with glory and honor*. You are *radiant* and shining, especially when you are looking at Me. You are beautiful as you *reflect My Glory* to the world around you and back to Me. In fact, you give Me so much delight that *I rejoice over you with shouts of Joy*! *This* is how I see you.

Because I am infinite and never-ending, I can see you the way you are now *and* the way you'll be in heaven—all at the same time. I work with you and show you the things you need to change now. And I love you as if you were already the perfect "you" that you'll be in heaven.

Just as a pair of glasses can help you see things more clearly, I want you to learn to look at yourself and others through the glasses of My unfailing Love. As you learn to do this, you'll find it easier to love yourself *and* to love others.

READ ON YOUR OWN

2 Corinthians 3:18; Zephaniah 3:17 NASB

A Safe Place

*I will say to the Lord, "You are my place of safety
and protection. You are my God, and I trust you."*
—Psalm 91:2 ICB

*T*rust in Me at all times. Pour out your heart to Me, for I am your *refuge*—your safe place and your protection. The more you depend on Me, the better I can help you. Trust Me always, in all situations: in joyful and sad times, in times of peace and times of stress. Let those things that stress you out remind you to *look for Me*. Remember that I am with you, taking care of you, even when life is hard and it hurts. Talk to Me about your troubles, and then leave them with Me. Don't snatch them back so that you can worry over them again. Rest in My Presence while I go to work for you.

Tell yourself the truth about Me—don't listen to the world's lies. Use the words of the Bible to describe Me: "You are *my refuge and my fortress*. You are *my God, and I trust you.*

I *am* your refuge—a safe place in the storms of life. Saying these true things about me out loud, or even singing them, will pull you closer to Me. Your mind often has several different thoughts going through it all at once. So instead of just thinking about Me, speak to Me—out loud! This will chase away stray thoughts and help you focus on Me, the One you trust.

READ ON YOUR OWN

Psalm 62:8; 1 Chronicles 16:11; 1 Peter 5:7

You Can Trust Me

*The Lord is close to everyone who prays
to him, to all who truly pray to him.*
—Psalm 145:18 ICB

There are a lot of things in this world that you can't trust. But I am worthy of all your confidence and faith. Don't let what you hear on the news spook you. Instead, focus on trusting Me and looking for proof of My Presence in the world. Whisper My Name—*I am close to everyone who prays to Me*. I'll wrap you up in My Presence like a blanket and comfort you with My Peace.

Remember that I am both loving and faithful. *My Love reaches up to the heavens, My faithfulness to the skies!* This means you can never reach the end of My Love. It goes on and on, and it lasts forever. Nothing you do will make Me stop loving you. And My faithfulness—My loyalty to you—is like a rock that you can stand on. It won't shake or crumble. No matter what's happening around you, I can keep you safe.

People often put their trust in their own abilities, education, money, or the way they look. But all these things can change or be snatched away. Put your trust in Me—I never change and I never go away. I'm the Savior who died to take away your sins and who rose from death to open up the way to heaven for you!

READ ON YOUR OWN

Psalm 36:5; 2 Corinthians 4:17

I Fill the Empty Places

Fill us with your love every morning.
Then we will sing and rejoice all our lives.
—Psalm 90:14 ICB

*L*et Me fill you with My Love every morning. Then you will sing *and rejoice all your life.* People try to be "filled" with a lot of different things—with friendships, with work, with sports or food. They even try some things that can be very harmful, like drugs or alcohol. None of these things will ever really fill the empty places in your heart. Only I can do that. So come to Me each morning and spend time with Me—talking to Me and reading your Bible. Ask Me to fill you up with My Love. Think about *how wide and long and high and deep* My endless Love is, until your heart overflows with happiness.

Finding your Joy in Me above all other things gives you a solid foundation to build your life on. Building on this foundation—on Me and My perfect Love—will give you Joy and gladness. Yes, there will still be hard times and troubles because you live in a broken and sin-filled world. But as you trust Me, I will lovingly show you the way you should go. Then your life will have meaning, and you will find Joy as you travel with Me toward your goal of heaven.

READ ON YOUR OWN

Ephesians 3:17–19; Psalm 73:24

MAY

"I came to give life—life
in all its fullness."

—John 10:10 ICB

The Joy of Working with Me

*Work willingly at whatever you do, as though you
were working for the Lord rather than for people.*
—Colossians 3:23 NLT

This moment, the one you're in right now, is the point when time meets eternity. It's also the place and time where you can meet *Me*, your eternal Savior. So, as much as you can, think about the things of this day. Not yesterday or tomorrow. Enjoy being with Me here and now.

Invite Me to join you in whatever you're doing. Whether it's a school project or chores at home or giving a hand to a neighbor or friend, ask Me to help you *work willingly, as though you were working for Me.* Working together with Me makes your job easier—and helps you to do it better.

Share your work times with Me, but also your fun times—and thank Me for both of them. When something upsets you, don't let worried or frightened thoughts take over your thinking. Instead, tell Me about whatever is troubling you. Then *give all your worries to Me, because I care for you.*

If you ask Me, I will open your eyes and your heart so that you can see all the good things I have given you in this present moment. I love to meet with you when your heart is wide open! Remember that *I came to give life* to you—*life in all its fullness*—rich and overflowing with My Joy.

READ ON YOUR OWN

1 Peter 5:7; John 10:10

I Will Help

"For I am the LORD, your God, who takes hold of your right hand and says to you, Do not fear; I will help you."
—Isaiah 41:13

Trust Me. When everything around you seems to be falling apart, choose to trust Me instead of sinking into sadness or escaping into an electronic world that isn't real. When you're in the middle of a huge problem, it's hard to think clearly. Yet this is when it's most important to make good and wise decisions. Sometimes it's like being in the middle of a tornado—with choices swirling all around you. How can you know which is the right one to grab? There is one choice that's always right and that always works: *Trust Me with all your heart and mind.*

If you feel as if you're sliding into a pit of sadness—that there isn't any way out of the mess you're in—stop and say, "I trust You, Jesus." Whisper it, say it out loud, shout it! Then spend some time thinking about all the reasons you *can* trust Me. Remember that My Love for you is an endless and *unfailing Love.* Find Joy in this! Praise Me for it!

Maybe you've just been pretending everything is okay and there isn't really any problem at all. Declaring that you trust Me can help you face the truth. And the truth is that you don't have to face anything without Me by your side. Tell Me what's wrong, dear child. I already know, I understand everything, and I promise *I will help you.*

READ ON YOUR OWN

Proverbs 3:5; Psalm 52:8

See the Flowers

"The Lord bless you and keep you; the Lord make
His face shine upon you, and be gracious to you."
—Numbers 6:24–25 NKJV

It's only because of Me that anything ever works out right. When what you're doing pleases Me, I stand beside you and help you. Sometimes you can sense that I'm there, and other times you can't. But the more you turn to Me to guide and help you, the more I will pour my good gifts into your life. Some of those gifts will be for the work you're doing—making it go more smoothly and with better results. Other gifts will be for your heart—like peace and love and contentment. Knowing that I'm with you will make you feel safer and will fill you up with Joy.

I'm training you to look for Me all the time, no matter where you are or what you're doing. Sometimes, especially in bad times, you'll have to look *through* the stuff happening around you to find Me. It's like staring through a dirty window to see the bright, colorful garden on the other side. If you focus on the dirt on the window, you'll miss the beauty of the garden. But if you focus on the flowers, it's easier to look past the dirt. In the same way, try to look *through* the hard times to "see" *My Face shining upon you*. Look for Me everywhere, all around you, all the time!

READ ON YOUR OWN

Colossians 1:29; Acts 2:28

I Collect Your Tears

You have seen me tossing and turning through the night.
You have collected all my tears and preserved them in your
bottle! You have recorded every one in your book.
—Psalm 56:8 TLB

I know about every single one of your troubles and your tears. *I have collected all your tears in My bottle*. Don't be afraid to cry. And don't be afraid of the troubles that cause you to cry. I use them to make you stronger and more like Me. I want you to not only trust Me, but trust that I am in complete control. I know what I'm doing in your life.

Because I know *all* things—past, present, and future—My ways of working in this world are often impossible for you to understand. If you could know all that I know, then you would see how perfect My plan for you is. And you would sing My praises! But for now, it's as if *you're looking into a dark mirror* and can't see everything clearly. You must learn to trust Me and live with this mystery.

I have collected your tears in My bottle because you are so precious to Me. And someday, in heaven, *I will wipe every tear from your eyes. There will be no more death or mourning or crying or pain*. Be glad that this heavenly future is waiting for you!

READ ON YOUR OWN

1 Corinthians 13:12; Revelation 21:4

Stay Awhile

Remember the wonderful things he has done.
Remember his miracles and his decisions.
—1 Chronicles 16:12 ICB

I want you to stay awhile in your thankfulness. The Joy of My Presence warms you all the way through while you rest in this place of gratefulness.

So often, you pray and pray and pray until you get the answer you were looking for. When I give you what you want, you happily thank Me. But then you quickly forget and move on to the next thing. Instead of rushing through your thankfulness, spend some time in these joyful thoughts. Rather than just saying a short prayer of thanks, keep that happy, peaceful feeling flowing by remembering what I've done for you. One way to do this is to tell others about it. This not only encourages you and them, but it also makes Me smile. Another way is to write down a prayer of thanksgiving and put it someplace where you'll see it again and again.

Keep coming to Me with a grateful heart. You'll be blessed *twice*—once by the happy memory of the answered prayer, and then again by the delight of sharing your Joy with Me.

READ ON YOUR OWN

Psalm 95:2; 1 Corinthians 15:57

Lean on Me

*This is what the Lord says. He made you. He formed you when
you were in your mother's body. And he will help you. The
Lord says, "People of Jacob, my servants, don't be afraid."*
—Isaiah 44:2 ICB

*T*his is what I say—I formed you when you were in your mother's body. And I will help you. Don't be afraid. I have always been at work in your life, even before you were born. Because you are Mine, bought with My own blood on the cross, you can count on My promise to help you. That is how you can stop being afraid: by trusting Me and believing that *I always help in times of trouble*.

The trouble starts when you think too far ahead, trying to figure out what will happen and what you should do about it. Thinking too much about the future can easily turn into thinking too much about your problems. Then worries and fears sprout up in your mind like weeds in a garden. When you notice this is happening, turn away from your worries and turn to Me, the One who is already right beside you. Rejoice and be glad, because I will stay with you through every step of your journey. Lean on Me, trusting Me to help you today—and *all the days of your life*.

READ ON YOUR OWN

Psalm 46:1; Psalm 23:6

You Will See Me

Now we are children of God. We have not yet been shown what we will be in the future. But we know that when Christ comes again, we will be like him. We will see him as he really is.
—1 John 3:2 ICB

You are a child of God. Someday you will *see Me as I am*—you will be face to Face with Me in heaven. But until then, I am training you *to be made new in your hearts, to become a new person.* Even though your new self is thinking and acting more *like Me* each day, that doesn't mean you won't still be you. In fact, the more you become like Me, the more you will grow into the wonderful, one-of-a-kind person I created you to be.

You have been a member of My royal family since you first trusted Me as the One who saves you from your sins. That means you are an *heir with Me*—you will *share My inheritance,* living forever in heaven. But to enjoy this glorious gift, you must *share in my suffering* and remain loyal to Me when hard times come.

When you run into problems, look for Me. I'm right there with you, right in the middle of your struggles. After all, you are part of My royal family! So don't whine, give up, or throw a fit, but act like the prince or princess that you are—by being kind and doing the right thing, even when it's very hard. Every struggle you go through can help you become more like Me. And one day, you'll reach your greatest goal: *you will see My Face—and be satisfied!*

READ ON YOUR OWN

Ephesians 4:22–24; Romans 8:17; Psalm 17:15

Stay Alert!

*Pray with all kinds of prayers, and ask for everything
you need. To do this you must always be ready.
Never give up. Always pray for all God's people.*
—Ephesians 6:18 ICB

I save you from hell—crowning you with Love and mercy. I wrap you in goodness and renew you.

I give you these amazing gifts of salvation and Love and mercy because I delight in you. Let My delight soak deep down inside you, warming your heart and filling your soul. Yes, I still see all your sins and flaws, your faults and weaknesses. But My perfect Love for you never changes and never goes away. I see you as My beloved child, wearing a royal crown and wrapped in the beauty of My perfection.

I want you to think of yourself as My child first—not as a student or a soccer player or a trumpet player—but as My child. So often your thoughts get stuck on stuff that really doesn't matter, especially when your mind is not thinking about anything in particular. That's why I want you to stay alert—*always be ready* and *always pray.* Invite Me to share your thoughts, your feelings, and your decisions. Include Me in whatever is going on in your life. Talking to Me will help you think less about unimportant things and more about Me. While you wait with Me, I will make you strong. No matter how old you are, you're always stronger when you're with Me.

READ ON YOUR OWN

Psalm 103:4–5; Psalm 149:4; Isaiah 40:31

The Potter and the Clay

*O Lᴏʀᴅ, you are our Father. We are the clay, you
are the potter; we are all the work of your hand.*
—Isaiah 64:8

I will meet you in the place where you need Me most. Come to
Me just as you are. Don't pretend that you're okay or that you
have it all figured out. I see right through you. I know everything
about you. And because you are Mine—bought by My death on
the cross—My Love for you never ends and never fails.

Ask My Spirit to help you be honest with Me. Tell Me everything! Don't be ashamed of how much you need Me. Let your
need bring you even closer to Me. Ask Me to do what I know is
best in your life. Don't forget: I am the Potter, and you are the
clay. I hold and mold and shape you—even the weakest parts
of you—with My own hands, so that nothing about your life will
be wasted.

Your deepest need is to *lean on, trust in, and be confident in
Me*. Admitting that you're not strong helps you depend on Me
without any shame. I'm teaching you to trust Me *with all your
heart and mind*. You and I will work on this together your whole
life through. And the best way to *not be afraid* is to trust that I
am always with you and I am *your Strength*. I will help you be
strong.

READ ON YOUR OWN

1 Peter 1:18–19 ɪᴄʙ; Proverbs 3:5; Isaiah 12:2

Your Choices Matter

*We urge you in the name of the Lord Jesus
to live in a way that pleases God.*
—1 Thessalonians 4:1 NLT

Your choices matter, dear child. They are an important part of My work to make you more like Me. But you make so many of your choices alone—inside your own heart and mind. Remember: I am *Christ in you*! I know every thought before you think it, and every choice before you make it. Understanding that I already know everything that's going on inside you can protect you from careless, selfish choices. Seek to please Me, the One who knows you inside and out. This will change the way you think and live.

You may think that most of your choices aren't that important. After all, you're still so young. But that's not true. A good choice made today—even a small one—can set you on the path to doing something very big and important someday. In the same way, a bad choice, no matter how small, can cause a terrible failure or loss in the future. Your choices do matter! But remember, even when you make a bad choice, you are *not judged guilty*, because you are My child. I am your Savior, and I am God. I see all your sins and flaws and failures—yet I love you with a beautiful, bright *Love that never fails*.

READ ON YOUR OWN

Colossians 1:27; Romans 8:1–2; Psalm 13:5

Your Brother and Your Friend

He is Lord of lords and King of kings.
—Revelation 17:14 ICB

I am your Brother and your Friend. I'm *the Firstborn of many brothers*, and you are being changed to be *like Me*. This is an amazing gift! Some children are blessed to have a strong and loving big brother who helps them and watches out for them. But you have the perfect big Brother, because I am so powerful and I am always looking out for you. Even the best family member or friend can't be with you every second of the day, but I can! I *never* leave your side. I am *the Friend who sticks closer than a brother*.

Don't take My constant Presence with you for granted though. Remember that your big Brother and faithful Friend is also the *King of kings*. If you could see just a glimpse of Me in all My heavenly Glory, you would understand why the apostle *John fell at My feet* when he saw Me. *I am the First and the Last. I am the One who lives. I was dead, but look: I am alive forever and ever!* I want you to bow before Me because I am your Savior God. Remind yourself again and again that the gift of salvation is yours forever—and then honor Me by telling Me how thankful you are for this wonderful gift.

READ ON YOUR OWN

Romans 8:29 ICB; Proverbs 18:24; Revelation 1:17–18

Much, Much More

With God's power working in us, God can do much,
much more than anything we can ask or imagine.
—Ephesians 3:20 NCV

Praise Me for being with you always. No matter what's going on, it's good to say, "Thank You, Jesus, for being *with me* right here, right now." You may not feel My Presence with you, but I have promised that I am—and My promise is enough!

An important part of your job as a Christian is to trust and believe that *I am with you always.* Talk to Me about your thoughts and feelings, your struggles and joys—sure that I am listening to you. Know that I care for you so much, and that I hear your every prayer. Boldly ask for My help, and be confident that I will answer. Watch for all the ways I'm working in your life—inside you and through you to help others. Be glad that you and I can work together *to do much, much more than anything you could ask or imagine. My Power is at work within you*—and it works even better when you admit how much you need Me.

Remember that *nothing is impossible with Me.* No matter how tough things get or how big your problems are, don't be scared. Instead, praise Me for My Presence right by your side—and for the help you know I'm going to give!

READ ON YOUR OWN

Psalm 42:5; Matthew 28:20; Luke 1:37

Speak Up!

*We will speak the truth with love. We will grow up
in every way to be like Christ, who is the head.*
—Ephesians 4:15 ICB

*S*top judging by the way things look! Be fair, and judge by what is really right. I said this at the temple in Jerusalem to teach that judging can be good *or* bad. I was talking to people who had judged Me only by the words of the Old Testament Law, ignoring the heart and spirit of the Law. Once, when I healed a man's hand on the Sabbath—the Jewish day of worship—the Pharisees started making plans to kill Me. They said I was wrong because the Law ruled that no one should work on the Sabbath. But where was their kindness and concern for others? That kind of judging is wrong, but not all judging is wrong. *Do* decide between right and wrong, good and evil—and use My words in the Bible to do it. But *don't* decide what other people are worth based on how they look or how smart they are or how popular they are.

Today you often hear the word *tolerance*. It means you're supposed to accept what people do, even if I've said it's wrong. This causes many of My followers to stay quiet when they see things that aren't right. But I want you to be brave and speak up. Tell *the truth*, but do it *in love*, with words that are kind and gentle. To prepare yourself, search your heart to make sure you have the right attitude. Search the Scriptures too, so you can be very sure about what I say in the Bible. Then ask My Spirit to work through your words—just as He loves others through your actions.

READ ON YOUR OWN

John 7:24; Matthew 7:1

Joy Always

God is strong and can help you not to fall. He can bring you
before his glory without any wrong in you and give you great joy.
—Jude v. 24 ICB

God is strong and can help you not to fall. I know how weak you are. I know how easily you would stumble and fall into sin if I weren't holding on to you. You are *growing in grace and knowledge of Me*, but you'll never be completely free from sin as long as you live in this world. That's why you need My help all the time.

I can bring you into My glorious Presence, *without any wrong* or spot of sin *in you*, because *I have covered you with clothes of salvation* and *a coat of goodness* and righteousness. I want you to wear these royal clothes of Mine with confidence. Because of them, your salvation is complete. But remember that it's *My* goodness and righteousness that save you, not your own.

You and I will both have overflowing Joy. I delight in you now, but you will bring Me much, much greater Joy when you join Me in heaven. And the Joy you will have in heaven is too great for words to describe—beyond anything you could ever feel here on earth! Nothing can steal this gift that is waiting for you. This treasure is yours forever, and it can never *be destroyed or spoiled or lose its beauty*!

READ ON YOUR OWN

Jude vv. 24–25; 2 Peter 3:18; Isaiah 61:10; 1 Peter 1:3–4

Joy Rubs Off

May all who search for you be filled with joy and gladness in you.
May those who love your salvation repeatedly shout, "God is great!"
—Psalm 70:4 NLT

As you *search for Me, I want you to be filled with Joy and glad-ness in Me.* Take time to praise Me with songs and the words of My psalms. Think about who I am: I live in *glory, maj-esty, power, and beauty.* Then think about how I left the wonder of heaven and came to live in this world—so I could save you and one day bring you to heaven with Me! Remembering all this will help you *be joyful in Me, your Savior.* This Joy brings you closer to Me, which will give you even more reason to rejoice and be glad!

Being joyful blesses not only you but the people around you. Your joy will rub off on your family and friends. You can also bless people who aren't as close to you. Even people who don't know Me will want to know why you're so happy and at peace. And that will give you a chance to tell them about Me. Joy is like a light in dark room: People can't *not* see it. And some of those people will ask you about it. *Always be ready to answer everyone who asks you to explain about the hope* and happiness *you have.*

READ ON YOUR OWN

Psalm 96:6; Habakkuk 3:18; 1 Peter 3:15

Power Made Perfect

But the Lord said to me, "My grace is enough for you. When you are weak, then my power is made perfect in you." So I am very happy to brag about my weaknesses. Then Christ's power can live in me.
—2 Corinthians 12:9 ICB

When you start your day, or any sort of work or chore, feeling like you're not good enough, remember this truth: *My grace is enough for you*. That word "is" means that My wonderful grace goes on and on, moment after moment—it's always there for you. So don't waste time or energy thinking about how weak you feel. Instead, be glad that feeling weak reminds you of how much you need Me. Come to Me for help, and delight in the fact that I never get tired! *When you are weak, My power is made perfect in you*—My power and your weakness work very well together.

As you work, joyfully and happily depend on Me to help you. You'll be surprised by how much you can get done. And what you do will be better because we've worked together. Think about how amazing it is to be able to live and work with Me—the Creator of the universe, *the King of kings and Lord of lords*.

Try to live in a way that you know will please Me. Don't live selfishly by always putting yourself first. Instead, put loving Me and loving others first. This is a *living sacrifice to Me*. It's a way to worship Me, and it makes Me very happy. Living this way also helps your life make sense in more and more ways. And it gives you just a tiny taste of the great Joy that's waiting for you in heaven—a Joy that no dictionary has the words to describe!

READ ON YOUR OWN

Revelation 19:16; Romans 12:1; Jude v. 24

My Shoulders Are Strong

*Give your worries to the Lord. He will take care
of you. He will never let good people down.*
—Psalm 55:22 ICB

*G*ive your worries to Me. I will take care of you. Carrying
around all your own worries and cares will wear you out.
Your shoulders weren't made to bear such a heavy load. Let Me
carry it for you.

The first step is to notice that some worry is weighing you
down. Next, carefully think about that worry for a moment. Is it
yours or someone else's? If it isn't yours, just let it go and leave
it behind. If it's your problem, talk to Me about it. I'll help you
see it more clearly, and I'll show you what to do about it.

Be ready to do something about your problem if I tell you
to, but don't let it become the only thing you think about. Decide
to give it to Me—My shoulders are strong enough to carry it!
Then simply and joyfully depend on Me to handle it while you do
the next right thing.

My promise to take care of you is a wonderful blessing—it's
good news to your heart. Trust Me; I won't ever let you down.
I will use My wonderful riches to give you everything you need. I
promise.

READ ON YOUR OWN

Isaiah 9:6; Philippians 4:19

Forgetting Yourself

But you are not ruled by your sinful selves. You are ruled by the Spirit, if that Spirit of God really lives in you. But if anyone does not have the Spirit of Christ, then he does not belong to Christ.
—Romans 8:9 ICB

To see more and more of Me in your life, you must learn to forget yourself. I didn't create you to think only about yourself. But when Adam and Eve sinned in the garden of Eden, selfishness became a natural part of all people.

Selfishness is a deadly trap, but I give you the power to escape it. You have had My Spirit living inside you ever since you asked Me to save you from your sins. My Spirit can help you break free from selfishly thinking only about yourself and what you want. Pray, "Help me, Holy Spirit," as often as you need to.

One thing that keeps you trapped is worrying too much about how you look—either in the mirror or in what others think of you. Instead, pay attention to Me and the people around you. Ask My Spirit to help you really see what others need. Remember that you are safe in *My arms*; they *will hold you up forever.*

When you're with Me, you are wonderfully complete because I give you everything you need. So focus your thoughts on trusting and loving Me—the One who is always with you.

READ ON YOUR OWN

Genesis 3:6–7; John 15:26; Deuteronomy 33:27

Beautiful Blessings from Ugly Things

The Light shines in the darkness. And the darkness has not overpowered the Light.
—John 1:5 ICB

Look for Me in the hard places and hard times of your life. It's easy to find Me in the good times, when I've answered your prayers the way you wanted. It's easy to find Me in beautiful and happy things. But I'm also in the difficult things. In fact, your problems are like a rich soil for My Love and My grace to grow in. So search for Me—in the dark times you've already been through and the ones you may be going through right now.

If old memories are hurting you, then look for Me in them. I know all about what happened, and I'm ready to take away the power of those memories to hurt you. Ask Me and I'll turn all the ugly pieces into a beautiful blessing. Perhaps the blessing is a lesson you learn or being able to help someone who's struggling through the same kind of problem.

If you're living through a tough time right now, hold My hand—tight! The Light of My Presence shines like the sun in the darkest times. This Light comforts you and shows you the way you should go. Walk close to Me, and I'll guide you forward one step at a time. I'll bless you by holding you closer and closer to Me.

READ ON YOUR OWN

Psalm 139:11–12; Psalm 73:23–24

A Little + Me

I cling to you; your strong right hand holds me securely.
—Psalm 63:8 NLT

I am the Door. The person who enters through Me will be saved. I'm not a locked door. I'm an open door for you and for everyone who chooses to follow Me. *I came into this world to give you life—life in all its fullness.*

A full life means different things to different people. So as you try to live a full life, don't compare your life to others. Even if you don't have as much money or as many fancy things as your neighbor, you can still have a good life.

Serving God makes a person very rich, if he is satisfied with what he has. This simply means that I want you to be satisfied and happy with what I give you. If you have food and clothes—the basic needs of life—be happy with that. If I give you more, be thankful and joyful. But don't hold on to your stuff so tightly that you forget about Me. And don't want more stuff so much that you forget about all I've given you. The only "thing" you can always hold on to without hurting your soul is *Me*. No matter how much or how little you own in this world, remember this simple bit of heavenly math: A little (or a lot) + Me = everything!

READ ON YOUR OWN

John 10:9–10; 1 Timothy 6:6–8; John 3:16

Treasure Me

"But the Helper will teach you everything. He will cause
you to remember all the things I told you. This Helper is the
Holy Spirit whom the Father will send in my name."
—John 14:26 ICB

Treasure Me above all else. This will fill your heart and mind with Joy. It will also bring Me honor, causing others to want to praise and worship Me!

When you treasure something, you hold on to it because it is worth a lot to you. I'm training you to hold on to Me, your Savior and Friend. Knowing that I never leave your side will increase your Joy and Peace in so many ways you can't count them. And cherishing Me as your Savior will make you want to live close to Me—in the way that I know is best for you.

When you treasure Me above all other things, those other things become less important. One way to figure out what you're treasuring is to notice what you think about when your mind is resting. Is it Me? Or stuff? Or even things you know will make Me unhappy? If you don't like where your thoughts go, you can teach yourself to think more about Me. One way that's helpful is to memorize Bible verses. Try putting verses about My Love in the places you often look—on your bedroom dresser, on your notebook, on the door as you leave the house, and even in your locker at school. And remember to ask My Spirit to help you. He loves finding ways to point you back to Me!

READ ON YOUR OWN

Matthew 13:44; Philippians 3:8–9; John 16:14

Love Made Perfect

Dear friends, if God loved us that much we also should love each other. No one has ever seen God, but if we love each other, God lives in us, and his love is made perfect in us.
—1 John 4:11–12 NCV

I want you to know how deep and how wide My Love for you is. *It's a Love that's greater than you can ever know.*

There's a huge difference between knowing Me and just knowing *about* Me. In the same way, spending time in My loving Presence is hugely different from just memorizing facts about who I am. To help you really know Me and enjoy being in My Presence, you need My Spirit. Ask Him to *give you the power to be strong in your own spirit* so that can know how big My Love for you really is.

Since the moment you chose to follow Me, I have been alive in your heart. The more room you make for Me there, the more I can fill you with My Love. There are several ways to open up more room for Me in your heart. First, spend time with Me—just enjoy being with Me and studying My Word, the Bible. Then, talk to Me. That's so very important! The apostle Paul wrote, *Never stop praying.* Talking to Me will not only give you Joy; it will also keep you close to Me. And last, let My Love flow through you to others by blessing them with your loving words and actions. When you live this way, *My Love is made perfect in you.*

READ ON YOUR OWN

Ephesians 3:16–19; Acts 4:12; 1 Thessalonians 5:17

You and I Together

Depend on the Lord and his strength. Always go to him for help.
—Psalm 105:4 ICB

When the way ahead of you just seems too difficult to keep going, turn to Me and say: "I can't, but *we*—You and I together—*can*." Telling Me that you can't handle things on your own is a good thing, since it's the truth! But that's only part of what you need. Because feeling that you can't handle whatever's coming can cause you to freeze up and not do anything. The most important thing is to remember that I am with you and I will help you.

Pour out your heart to Me—tell Me everything. Ask Me to carry your troubles for you and to show you the next step to take. Don't waste your energy worrying about things that you can't control. Instead, use that energy to reach out to Me—in prayer and in praise for the help you know is coming.

Always come to Me for help. And be ready to follow wherever I lead, doing whatever I ask. Trust Me to walk ahead of you, clearing the way for you.

Dare to see your troubles as a door to My Presence. Look upon this journey as an adventure that you will share with Me. Keep talking to Me—all the time—and enjoy being with Me as we walk through this tough time together, side by side.

READ ON YOUR OWN

Philippians 4:13; Psalm 62:8

Don't Forget Me

*"But I have this against you: You have left
the love you had in the beginning."*
—Revelation 2:4 ICB

Look for Me as you go through this day—I'm waiting for you to find Me! I watch over you all the time; you're never out of My sight. But sometimes I am out of *your* sight, though these times don't usually last for long. Perhaps you get distracted by a problem, or even by something wonderful. It's an easy thing to fix. Just remind yourself that I am with you.

A much bigger problem is *forgetting the love you had for Me in the beginning* of our relationship. If you notice this has happened, tell Me how sorry you are and run back to Me in your thoughts and prayers. Tell Me the things that have pulled you away from Me. Did you get too busy with school or friends? Did some sin make you forget about Me? Tell Me. Come back to Me, and I will forgive you. Then take time to thank Me for My forgiveness. Work on putting Me first in your life again. As you spend time with Me, remember who I am: King of the universe and *Light of the world*. Soak up My Light so you can shine it into the lives of others. And while you delight in being with Me, I'll fill you up with *Love, Joy, and Peace*.

READ ON YOUR OWN

Psalm 121:8; John 8:12; Galatians 5:22–23

Joy in Troubles

You will have many kinds of troubles. But when
these things happen, you should be very happy.
—James 1:2 ICB

I want you to thank Me for *all* things, even the hard times and challenges. They're gifts from Me. They give you a chance to grow stronger in your faith and to learn to depend on Me more and more. Most people think that the stronger they get, the less help they'll need. But it's different in My kingdom. In My kingdom, being strong and depending on Me go together. That's because I created you to walk close to Me as you travel through your life. Hard times point out just how much you need Me, and they help you depend on My endless Strength.

When you stand up and face the hard times by trusting in Me, you are blessed. And when you make it through struggles you didn't think you'd get through, it feels so wonderful. Best of all, knowing you made it because you had My help brings you even closer to Me.

Getting through those difficulties makes you feel safer and more secure in Me. You realize that you and I can handle whatever this world throws at you—because we're together. *You can do all things*—anything—*through Me because I give you Strength.* Be glad and celebrate, because I am always strong enough to help you.

READ ON YOUR OWN

Psalm 31:14–16; Philippians 4:13

Praise My Goodness

In your name they rejoice all the time. They praise your goodness.
—Psalm 89:16 ICB

I am your *God, your Joy and your delight*. I want you to find Joy in being with Me and in reading My Word. Because I am the living Word. I have always been, and I will always be. So you can always find Me in My written Word, the Bible.

Take time to think about and memorize the words you read. They'll help you get through the tough times and worries that keep you awake at night. And as more and more of My Word soaks into your heart, you'll find that you're able to enjoy My Presence more and more.

When you know that I'm *your Joy*, you don't whine and moan because you're having a hard time. And you aren't jealous of friends who are having an easier time. Because I am always with you, you can always have Joy with Me. *Rejoice in My Name all the time*—and you'll find Joy. Simply saying My Name, "Jesus," as a prayer can lift your spirits and make you smile. A wonderful way to find Joy in Me is to *praise My goodness*, which I have filled your world with. And *I have covered you with a coat of goodness*; it covers over *all* your sins—perfectly and completely—forever!

READ ON YOUR OWN

Psalm 43:4; John 1:1; Isaiah 61:10

I've Already Won

"I told you these things so that you can have peace in me. In this world you will have trouble. But be brave! I have defeated the world!"
—John 16:33 ICB

*M*y kingdom is not of this world. It can never be destroyed, and it lasts forever. When you see all the evil around you, don't give up. When I was being arrested in the Garden of Gethsemane, I told My disciples that *I could ask My Father, and He would give Me more than twelve armies of angels*. But this was not the plan My Father and I had made. I needed to die on the cross—so that I could save *everyone who calls on My Name*.

Remember that you are part of My kingdom of Life and Light. The darker this world gets, the tighter you need to hold on to My promise of hope and heaven. No matter how bad things look, I'm in control. I'm working in ways and doing things you cannot understand. Even though this world is full of sin, it's still possible for you to live in it with Joy and Peace in your heart. I tell you the same thing I told My disciples: *Be brave! I have defeated the world!* I've already won. And because you belong to My kingdom, *you can have Peace* and Joy with Me.

READ ON YOUR OWN

John 18:36; Matthew 26:53; Acts 2:21

I Am the Vine

And this is the secret: Christ lives in you.
—Colossians 1:27 NLT

I am the Vine, and you are the branches. If you remain in Me and I remain in you, then you will produce much fruit. But without Me you can do nothing.

Think about this amazing truth: I am alive inside you! Just as the life-giving sap flows from a vine down through its branches, so My Life flows through you. I am perfect and unending, yet I *choose* to live inside you. This is an incredibly rich gift! I know your every thought. I know your every feeling. I know how weak you are, and I'm ready to fill you with My Strength.

When you work together with My Spirit inside you, asking Me to be in control, you can produce a lot of fruit in your life, such as love, joy, peace, and kindness. And not just in your own life, but in the lives of others around you. But if you ignore Me and try to do things using only your own strength, you'll probably fall flat on your face. And anything you *do* make happen will be worthless in My kingdom—because you did it without Me. So stay close to My Spirit. Strengthen and cherish your closeness with Me by spending time in prayer. Find Joy in My loving Presence!

READ ON YOUR OWN

John 15:5; 2 Corinthians 12:9; Deuteronomy 33:12

Thank Me with Joy

Praise be to the God and Father of our Lord Jesus Christ!
—1 Peter 1:3

Joyfully thank Me for forgiving *all* your sins—the past, present, and future ones; the ones you know about and the wrongs you don't notice you've done. You need forgiveness more than anything else. And I've given you what you need—perfectly and forever!

I am *the eternal Life that was with the Father and has appeared to you*. Because you believe in Me as your Savior and God, you have everlasting Life. Let this amazing promise fill you with Joy and chase away any fear of the future. Your bright future is completely safe with Me. It's an inheritance of *blessings that cannot be destroyed or be spoiled or lose their beauty. They are kept for you in heaven*. Thank Me for this priceless, never-ending gift.

The more often you thank Me, the more joyful your life will be. So be watching for things that feed your gratitude. Thank Me in silent prayers, in whispers, shouts, or songs. Say your thanks out loud or write them down. Just doing this will lift you above your troubles and increase your Joy. Another way to tell Me how much you love Me is to read the Psalms out loud. Be happy and rejoice in Me, dear child, for *nothing can separate you from My Love*.

READ ON YOUR OWN

1 John 1:2; John 3:16; 1 Peter 1:3–4; Romans 8:38–39

I Am God

Do not worry about anything. But pray and ask God for everything you need. And when you pray, always give thanks. And God's peace will keep your hearts and minds in Christ Jesus. The peace that God gives is so great that we cannot understand it.
—Philippians 4:6–7 ICB

I am God, and you are *not*. That may sound harsh, but this truth is actually a blessing. In the garden of Eden, Satan tempted Eve with the sin of wanting to *be like God*. That's the very same sin that caused Satan to be thrown out of heaven. Eve gave in to that temptation, and so did Adam. Ever since that time, the sinful nature of people keeps them trying to act as if they are God. They try to control everything—and then they blame Me when things don't turn out the way they want.

Remembering that you are *not* God helps you live free— free from the burden of worrying about things you can't control (which is almost everything). And because you don't try to take control of those things, *that* frees you up to be better at the things you *can* control, like your thoughts and your words. Pray about everything in your life, trusting that I am Ruler over all of it. Bring Me your prayers *with thanks. Ask Me for everything you need.* Living this way will protect you from worry and bless you with *a peace so great that you cannot understand it.*

READ ON YOUR OWN

Luke 10:18; Genesis 3:5

Building Blocks of a Joyful Life

Keep your roots deep in him and have your lives built on him. Be strong in the faith, just as you were taught. And always be thankful.
—Colossians 2:7 ICB

*C*ontinue to live in Me. Keep your roots deep in Me—and always *be thankful*. The relationship you have with Me is not like any other. You live *in* Me, and I live *in* you. You never go anywhere without Me! Our connection is amazing, and it gives you a rock-solid foundation for your life. Keep building on that foundation, living with Joy because you know I'm with you always.

Being thankful gives you some very important blocks for building your life. The more of these blocks you use, the better your life will be. Thankfulness creates even more room in your heart for Joy. It also helps you get through really hard times without giving up or feeling sorry for yourself.

No matter what's happening in your life or in the world, you can always thank Me for two things: saving you and loving you. These blessings *never* change. Other blessings *can* change. Friends move away, money is lost or spent, and people get sick. So I want you to count *both* kinds of blessings: the ones that never change and the ones that can change. Keep counting, and I'll keep blessing. And your heart will overflow with joyful thankfulness!

READ ON YOUR OWN

Colossians 2:6–7; Colossians 1:27; Psalm 13:5–6

JUNE

He will protect you like a bird spreading its wings over its young. His truth will be like your armor and shield.

—Psalm 91:4 ICB

You Delight Me

In Christ, he chose us before the world was made. In his love he chose us to be his holy people—people without blame before him.
—Ephesians 1:4 ICB

I *approve* of you, My child, because you are Mine. I adopted you into My royal family, and now I see you through the eyes of My loving grace. *I chose you before the world was made. I chose you to be holy and without blame before Me.*

I understand that you aren't perfect. I know you sin and make mistakes every single day. But in My eyes, you are holy and without any blame because you are part of My forever family. Of course, I'm not happy with everything you do, just as I'm not happy when you choose not to do good things. But I still accept you. And I'm pleased with your true self—the child I created you to be.

I know how much you want to be sure that I love you just as you are. I also know how hard it is for you to believe this. I want you to learn to see yourself through My eyes of grace. As you do, you can focus on what is good and right instead of what is bad and wrong. You'll learn to work together with Me and be glad about what I'm doing in your life—which is *changing you to be like Me, bringing more and more glory.* Dear one, I approve of you and accept you as you are—I even *delight* in you!

READ ON YOUR OWN

Philippians 4:8; 2 Corinthians 3:18; Psalm 149:4

What You See

*So we set our eyes not on what we see but on what
we cannot see. What we see will last only a short
time. But what we cannot see will last forever.*
—2 Corinthians 4:18 ICB

*S*et your eyes not on what you see but on what you cannot see. You spend far too much time and energy thinking about things that don't really matter—things that have no value in My kingdom. Your sense of sight is a wonderful gift from Me, but it can actually make you a slave if you use it in wrong ways.

There are so many mirrors around to you show you exactly what you look like. And there are so many fake images on television and in movies and magazines of "perfect" people, "perfect" rooms, and "perfect" lives. It's tempting to think only about how you look and how the people and things around you look. But don't do that! Appearances don't last. Instead, think about the things that *do* last. Focus on the lasting Joy of knowing Me.

When you spend time with Me, you get to enjoy being with the only perfect Person who ever lived. Yet My perfection wasn't about how I looked. It was about a life lived completely free of sin. I'm the One who can love you with a perfect Love that never, ever fails. And I'm the One who can give you perfect Peace. Don't waste time thinking about stuff that doesn't matter. Instead, keep thinking about Me, and I'll give you My Peace.

READ ON YOUR OWN

Psalm 36:7; Isaiah 26:3

See My Beauty

I ask only one thing from the Lord. This is what I want:
Let me live in the Lord's house all my life. Let me see the
Lord's beauty. Let me look around in his Temple.
—Psalm 27:4 ICB

I invite you to *see My beauty* and to *search for Me* more and more. This is a very wonderful and happy invitation! You can see little bits of My beauty in the wonders of nature, but these are only tiny, weak hints of My endless Glory. And as great as those glimpses are, the best is yet to come—when you see Me face to Face in heaven. For now, seeing My beauty in the world around you means you must focus the eyes of your heart on My unseen Presence. You can do this by praying and by reading and memorizing My Word.

The most important thing to remember when you're searching for Me is that I'm constantly with you, every second of every day. I'm always tuned in to what you're thinking and feeling. And I'm training you to be aware of Me more and more. Remind yourself that I'm with you by putting notes in your room like, "Jesus is here!" Tuck favorite verses into your books or your pockets. Whisper My Name to remind yourself I'm close by. Sing praises to Me. Read the Bible out loud, listening to the words. Find friends who also want to know Me better—and remind each other that I'm with you. *When you search for Me with all your heart, you will find Me!*

READ ON YOUR OWN

1 Corinthians 13:12; Jeremiah 29:13

No Bad Days

The Lord himself will go before you. He will be with you. He will not leave you or forget you. Don't be afraid. Don't worry.
—Deuteronomy 31:8 ICB

I am your Joy! Let these words echo in your mind and sink into your heart and soul. I—your Friend who *will never, ever leave you*—am an endless source of Joy. If you really believe this is true, then you can believe that every day of your life is a good day. So don't say you're having a "bad day," even when you're struggling. Your life may be really hard at the moment, but I'm still with you, *holding you by your right hand.* That means there's good to be found in *this* day and in every day because I'm always by your side, always loving you.

This world may say you aren't rich, but you are—you're rich in My precious, unfailing Love. No matter what's happening, My Love promises that you can *find shelter in the shadow of My wings*, just as a baby bird hides beneath its mother's wings. And this Love gives you the right to come to *My river of delights*, which is My Presence. When your world feels anything but delightful, turn to Me. Drink deeply from the river of My Presence. *I* am your Joy!

READ ON YOUR OWN

Psalm 73:23; Psalm 36:7–8

Leave the Rest to Me

*I trust you. Show me what I should
do because my prayers go up to you.*
—Psalm 143:8 ICB

Do what you can do, and then leave the rest to Me. This is wisdom that is worth more than all the money in the world!

When you're stuck in the middle of a tough situation, *pour out your heart to Me*. Tell Me everything, knowing that I hear you and I care. Depend on Me to help you, trusting that I'm always with you. Don't let your problem become all you think about, no matter how much you want to fix it. When you've done everything you can do, then it's time to simply wait for Me to act. Rest and refresh yourself in My Presence. Don't believe the lie that you can't enjoy your life until the problem has been solved. That's just not true. *In this world you will have trouble*, but *you can have Peace in Me*—even in the middle of a mess!

Your relationship with Me is all about us working together. Ask Me to help you and guide you. Do whatever you can to make things better, but then trust Me to do what you can't do. Instead of trying to force your own quick answer to a problem, relax and ask Me to *show you the way you should go*. I will—in *My* perfect timing. Until then, trust Me and hold tight to My hand, knowing I'll take care of everything. And enjoy the journey with Me, My beloved.

READ ON YOUR OWN

Psalm 62:8; Psalm 46:1; John 16:33

The Royal Road to Joy

Let us come before His presence with thanksgiving;
Let us shout joyfully to Him with psalms.
—Psalm 95:2 NKJV

Thankfulness is My royal road to Joy—so encourage yourself to be thankful. The truth is that no pleasure, no good thing, is really complete until you tell Me how thankful you are for it. It's great to thank the people who bless you and help you, but remember that all blessings really come from Me. So praise Me often throughout your day. This feeds your soul, and it helps you to be full of Joy. Thankfulness also makes our relationship better and brings you closer to Me.

As My precious child, you've been given My wonderful and shining gift of grace. You didn't earn it, and you don't deserve it. Yet this grace can never be taken away from you. No one can steal it, and no trouble can take it from you. You belong to Me forever! *Nothing in all creation will be able to separate you from My Love.*

When you wake up each morning, say, "Thank You, Jesus, for the gift of this new day." As you walk through your day, be watching for the blessings and little gifts of Joy that I scatter along your path. Though the greatest treasure you'll ever have is My Presence with you—I am the *indescribable Gift* that is simply too wonderful for words!

READ ON YOUR OWN

Ephesians 2:8–9; Romans 8:38–39; 2 Corinthians 9:15

You Are My Masterpiece

For we are God's masterpiece. He has created us anew in Christ Jesus, so we can do the good things he planned for us long ago.
—Ephesians 2:10 NLT

I am your Savior, Lord, and Friend. If you have Me, you have everything that really matters. You may not be rich or famous, but don't let that upset you. As I told My disciples, *"It is worth nothing for a man to have the whole world if he loses his soul."* Nothing in this world is as good as the priceless treasure of eternal Life with Me!

Imagine it this way: *A man was looking for fine pearls. One day he found a very valuable pearl. The man went and sold everything he had to buy that pearl.* My kingdom in heaven is like that—a treasure worth giving up everything else for. So no matter what else you may feel you're missing, learn to be happy and satisfied because you have Me, dear child.

So much of your unhappiness comes because you compare yourself to others. Don't do that! You are My unique creation. This means there's no one else on earth like you. I have bought you with My own blood, by dying for you on the cross. You are more precious to Me than gold or diamonds or anything money can buy. I'm the Savior who loves you more than you can imagine! And I'm working inside you to make you more and more into the *masterpiece* I designed you to be.

READ ON YOUR OWN

Matthew 16:26; Matthew 13:45–46; 1 Timothy 6:6

Set Free

You were made free from sin, and now you are slaves to goodness.
—Romans 6:18 ICB

The power of My Love is so great that it has made you My slave. You think of a slave as a terrible thing to be—and in this world, it is. But to be a slave to Me is a *wonderful* thing; it actually *sets you free*.

You are not your own. You were bought at a price—the price of My precious blood. The more you love Me, the more you will want to serve Me. This service can fill you with heavenly Joy as you give yourself to Me more and more.

Because I am perfect in every way, you can trust yourself to me completely and never fear that I will use you or take advantage of you. Becoming a slave to Me is what makes you truly free—free from worry, free from fear, *free from sin*. I have invaded your heart and your soul, and My Spirit is taking over more and more of you. *Where the Spirit of the Lord is, there is freedom*. I want you to *show My Glory*, shining it into the lives of those around you. *I am changing you to be more and more like Me.* Be happy because you are free in Me. Joyfully offer your life to Me and My Love!

READ ON YOUR OWN

1 Corinthians 6:19–20; 2 Corinthians 3:17–18

I Am in This Place

Surely the Lord is in this place. But I did not know it.
—Genesis 28:16 ICB

Without Me you can do nothing. On days when there are just too many tasks and chores for you to handle, remember this: I am with you and ready to help. Take a moment to rest in My loving Presence. Whisper, *"Surely the Lord is in this place."* Relax and take a deep breath. It's okay; you weren't made to do everything on your own.

I designed you to depend on Me. So *come to Me* just as you are—there's no point in pretending you don't need Me. And don't be ashamed of needing Me. That's a *good* thing. Talk to Me about everything you're facing and how it makes you feel. Ask Me to show the way to go. Instead of just rushing ahead on your own, take small steps with Me, talking to Me and trusting Me to lead you.

I am the Vine, and *you are one of My branches.* As long as you stay connected to Me—like a branch is connected to its vine—My Life flows through you. This is what makes your life grow spiritual "fruit," like Love and Joy and wanting to help others. Don't worry about being famous or popular in this world. Producing fruit for Me means *doing the good things I planned for you long ago.* So live close to Me, ready to do whatever I ask, and I will help you.

READ ON YOUR OWN

John 15:5; Matthew 11:28–29; Ephesians 2:10

I Give You My Strength

I ask the Father in his great glory to give you the power to be strong in spirit. He will give you that strength through his Spirit.
—Ephesians 3:16 ICB

Let Me *strengthen you with My own great Power.* When problems just won't go away, don't give up. Don't frown and do nothing, thinking there's just no point in trying. This kind of attitude is not the way I want you to handle hard times.

I am King over everything in your life. So I've placed the possibility for good in *every* moment of your life—even the difficult ones. Don't be like *the man who hid his master's money in the ground* because he was afraid of what his master might do if he didn't make more money. That man gave up and didn't even try; he blamed his tough situation instead of making the most of this chance he'd been given. The truth is this: The tougher your situation, the more you can gain through it.

I gladly give you My great Strength. It's incredibly powerful because the Spirit Himself gives it to you—making you strong in your heart and spirit. It's My unlimited Strength that makes you able to keep going through the hardest times. And because My Power is so great that it never runs out, there's more than enough of it to also fill you with Joy.

READ ON YOUR OWN

Colossians 1:11; Isaiah 40:10; Matthew 25:25

My Ways Are a Mystery

*The L*ORD *gives strength to his people;*
*the L*ORD *blesses his people with peace.*
—Psalm 29:11

*M*y *Presence will go with you, and I will give you rest*. Wherever you are, wherever you go, I am with you! This is an incredible thing to say, but it's completely true. My unseen, invisible Presence is more real than the people around you that you can see and hear and touch. But you must learn to "see" Me with the eyes of your heart and talk to Me through prayer. Trust that I really do hear and care.

I promise that your prayers do make a difference. You may not always understand how, and it may not happen as quickly as you would like. But I listen to the prayers of My children, and I consider those prayers as I decide how I will work in the world. The ways I work in your life will not make sense to you every time, but remember: *My thoughts are not like your thoughts. My ways are not like your ways*.

Because what I do is often a mystery to you, it's important to spend time with Me. *Be still and know that I am God*. Your trust in Me will grow as you sit quietly in My Presence. Breathe in My Peace, dear child, and I will give you rest.

READ ON YOUR OWN

Exodus 33:14; Isaiah 55:8–9; Psalm 46:10

I'm on Your Side

*So what should we say about this? If God
is for us, then no one can defeat us.*
—Romans 8:31 ICB

If I am for you, then no one can defeat you. And, dear child, I am most *definitely* for you—I am on your side—because you are My follower. Of course, this doesn't mean that no one will ever be against you. You may still have some people who fight against you. But it *does* mean that having Me on your side is the most important fact of your life. That's because no matter what happens to you, you're on the winning side! I've already defeated sin with My death, and defeated death with My resurrection. I am the forever Winner, the eternal Champion, and you share in My victory no matter how much trouble you face on your road to heaven. Nothing and no one can keep you down because you belong to Me forever.

Knowing that you never have to doubt your future with Me can change how you think and live. Instead of living in fear, trying to protect yourself from any hurt or pain, you learn to follow Me bravely wherever I lead you. I'm training you to not only *search for Me* and follow My lead, but to enjoy the adventure of living with Me by your side. Remember: I am your *ever-present Help in trouble*. I will always be at your side.

READ ON YOUR OWN

Psalm 27:8; Psalm 46:1

June 13

You're Never Alone

*"You can be sure that I will be with you always.
I will continue with you until the end of the world."*
—Matthew 28:20 ICB

Let My Peace protect your mind and your heart. Remember that I am near—always. And you can find Joy in My Presence—always. Spend time with Me. Not just a minute here or there, but *real* time. *Ask Me for everything you need. And when you pray, always give thanks.* That's the way to My Peace, a peace *so great you cannot understand it.* That's also the way I protect *your heart and mind.* This life is about you and Me working together. You never face anything alone!

For Christians, being alone is an illusion, a dangerous lie that can lead to sadness or self-pity. The devil and his servants work hard to keep you from enjoying My Presence. That's why it's so important for you to realize what they're doing and stand up to their attacks. Fight back with My powerful Word, which is *alive and working*—always. Read it; think about it; memorize it; say it out loud—its truths can make you strong and sure and brave.

Even if you're feeling alone, you can talk to Me, trusting that *I am with you always.* The longer you talk to Me, the more certain you'll be that I am near. *Stand against the devil, and the devil will run away from you. Come near to Me, and I will come near to you.*

READ ON YOUR OWN

Philippians 4:4–7; Hebrews 4:12; James 4:7–8

Learn to Be Patient

Love is patient and kind. Love is not jealous,
it does not brag, and it is not proud.
—1 Corinthians 13:4 ICB

*L*ove is patient. First Corinthians 13 was written by Paul and is often called the "Love Chapter." Notice that the very first word he uses to describe love is "patient." *Patience* is a quality I treasure in My children, even though you'll hardly ever hear the people around you describe love in this way.

Patient people are able to stay calm while they're waiting, or while dealing with difficult people or tricky problems. I want you to take a look at your own life: How do you handle waiting? How do deal with annoying or mean people? This will tell you how patient and loving you are.

Patience is also the fourth fruit in Paul's list of *the fruit of the Spirit*. My Spirit will help you grow in this important "fruit," especially when you ask Him to help you. Some Christians are afraid to pray for patience. They're afraid I'll answer their prayer by making them go through even harder times, making them suffer worse things. But suffering has an important purpose in My kingdom, and hard times are simply a part of life on this earth. When you hold tight to Me in tough times, those tough times *prove that your faith is pure*. And a pure faith will bring *praise and glory and honor* to Me!

READ ON YOUR OWN

Galatians 5:22–23; 1 Peter 1:6–7

A Love That Lasts Forever

The Lord appeared to his people. He said, "I love you
people with a love that will last forever. I became
your friend because of my love and kindness."
—Jeremiah 31:3 ICB

Come to Me, precious child. Every moment of every day, I am inviting you to come closer to Me. Be still with Me and *think about Me*. Relax and listen as I whisper My Love into your heart: *"I love you with a Love that will last forever."* Think about the wonderful truth that *I am with you always*. You can build your whole life on these rock-solid promises!

The world you live in is always changing. Like the shifting sands on a beach, you won't find any solid ground to stand on there. So I challenge you to stay aware of Me—of My Presence with you—as you go through your day. You won't be able to do this perfectly, but keep practicing. I'll help you if you ask Me. You can pray: "Jesus, make me aware that You are here with me." Let these words echo through your heart and mind over and over again. Your thoughts will sometimes wander to other things, but this simple prayer will bring you right back to Me.

The more of Me you have in your life—staying close to Me in your prayers and thoughts—the more Joy you will have, and the more I can bless others through you.

READ ON YOUR OWN

Hebrews 3:1 CEV; Matthew 28:18–19

Trust Me and Be Happy

I will be content as if I had eaten the best foods.
My lips will sing. My mouth will praise you.
—Psalm 63:5 ICB

I have good plans for you. They may be very different from what you wanted or expected, but they are still good. *I am Light; in Me there is no darkness at all.* So look for My Light in every moment of your life. I am with you, fully and tenderly with you, in every moment. Your job is to be open to Me and to My ways. This may mean you'll need to give up some of your own plans or dreams at times. But remember and believe that *My way is perfect*, even when it's hard.

I am a shield to those who trust Me. When you're feeling attacked or afraid, come to Me and say: "Lord, I trust You." I won't shield you from the things that are part of My plan for you, because you have an important part to play in this world. But I do protect you from more dangers and troubles than you could ever imagine. So try very hard *to live the life I've given you to live.* You can do this by joyfully depending on Me. As you trust Me, *you will be content*—peaceful and happy.

READ ON YOUR OWN

1 John 1:5; Psalm 18:30; 1 Corinthians 7:17

Follow My Lead

Do not be foolish with your lives.
But learn what the Lord wants you to do.
—Ephesians 5:17 ICB

Try to become more and more open to following Me and My ways. I am always at work in your life. So instead of trying to force Me to do what you want *when* you want it, stop and look for what I'm already doing. Then live in a trusting way—willing to wait for Me and My timing. *I am good to those who put their hope in Me* and *to those who look to Me for help.* Ask Me to open your eyes to the things I have prepared for you. Seeing what I am doing will strengthen your faith in Me and help you live ready to do My will.

So often, My followers don't notice the many blessings I rain down on them. They're so busy looking for other things that they miss what's right in front of them, or what's on the way. They forget that I am God and My timing is perfect.

I want you to trust Me enough to let Me lead you. When you play Follow the Leader, only one person leads. If everyone tries to lead, the game gets confusing and stops being fun. Follow Me, dear child. Follow your Leader as I guide you through your life.

READ ON YOUR OWN

Lamentations 3:25; Psalm 71:6; Psalm 28:6

Being Still in a World That Never Stops

God says, "Be still and know that I am God. I will be praised in all the nations. I will be praised throughout the earth."
—Psalm 46:10 ICB

It's hard to be still in this world that never stops. You have to fight to find time for Me. When you start to sit quietly with Me, distractions and interruptions seem to come from everywhere. Electronics beep, friends want to play, chores are waiting. But our time together is worth fighting for, so don't give up! Pick out a time to spend with Me each day when you won't be interrupted. Read a favorite Bible verse and think about what it means to you. Sing your favorite song from church. Talk to Me about your day. Thank Me for all the good things I am doing in your life. I am *Immanuel— God with you*. Relax and rest in My peaceful Presence. Let all your worries slip away. *Be still*, dear child, *and know that I am God*.

The longer you spend with Me, the more Joy you'll find in My majesty—and the more you'll trust My control. So *if the earth shakes, or if the mountains fall into the sea*, I will still be your safe place, your shelter. I will help you stand even when the storms of life blow all around you. As you think about how magnificent My Power and Glory are, your problems will seem smaller. *In this world you will have trouble. But be brave! I have defeated the world!*

READ ON YOUR OWN

Matthew 1:23; Psalm 46:1–2; John 16:33

June 19

I Am Your Guide

I am guiding you in wisdom. And I am leading you to do what is right.
—Proverbs 4:11 ICB

I *am guiding you in the way of wisdom and leading you to do what is right.* Wisdom is being able to make a good decision based on what you know and what you've done before. So it's important to learn what is true and to use that truth to help you make decisions. Because *I am the Way, the Truth, and the Life*, I'm the best Guide you could ever imagine. I am also *the Word, who was with God* from the very beginning, and who *is God*. My written Word, the Bible, is filled with wisdom to guide you through your life. There's nothing you'll ever face that My Word can't help you with. So study the Bible and stay close to Me—in your thoughts and prayers—as you go through this life.

Look for the straight paths that I've laid out for you, and follow them. I'm not promising these paths will always be easy. But if you walk close to Me, your journey will be less troubled. When you view the road ahead, you may see confusing twists and frightening turns. But if you look back at where you've already traveled, you'll see that I've been with you every step of the way. I've protected you from dangers and moved many troubles out of your way. I make your path straighter as you let Me lead you.

READ ON YOUR OWN

John 14:6; John 1:1

When There Is Evil

Trust the Lord and do good.
—Psalm 37:3 ICB

*D*on't worry about evil people who prosper and get rich. Don't worry or *fret about their wicked schemes* and plans. Because of the Internet and TV and smartphones, not only do you hear about evil people and their wicked plans, but too often you see all the terrible details. These images have a powerful effect on your mind: Too many images of war, sickness, disaster, and evil can make you feel worried and afraid.

I want you to pray about the terrible things happening in the world and to try to do what helps others. But you need to understand that there are many things you cannot change. Worrying about what you can't control just steals your energy and makes you sad. *Think about Me* instead. I am with you, and I'm on your side. *Delight yourself in Me*!

Remember that I know everything, and I'm a God who loves justice. In My own perfect timing, I will make all the wrongs be right. So *be still in My Presence. Trust Me* with all your heart while you *wait for Me to act*.

READ ON YOUR OWN

Psalm 37:7; Hebrews 3:1 CEV; Psalm 37:3–4

I Am Everything You Need

Jesus has the power of God. His power has given us everything we need to live and to serve God. We have these things because we know him. Jesus called us by his glory and goodness.
—2 Peter 1:3 ICB

I live in you! I am everything you could ever possibly need in a Savior God—and I am alive inside you. I fill you with shining Life and Love. I want My Life to fill you up so much that it overflows into the lives of the people around you. As you talk and play with others, ask Me to live through you and to love them through you. When you and I work together that way, My Light will shine from your face and My Love will be heard in your words.

In Me you have a full and complete life. Everything you need to be saved, and everything your spirit needs to grow, is found in Me. Through *My divine Power* you have all you need to live the never-ending Life I've given you. *You have these things because you know Me.* I want you to open up and share with Me whatever you're thinking and feeling—both your struggles and your joys.

Because I died on the cross, you can find rest in Me. Be happy that I have made you safe and secure forever. Let your heart and soul be satisfied and joyful by living close to *Me,* your loving Savior and forever Friend.

READ ON YOUR OWN

Galatians 2:20; 2 Corinthians 3:18; Colossians 2:9–10

You Will Be Joyful Again

"Now you are sad. But I will see you again and you will be happy. And no one will take away your joy."
—John 16:22 ICB

Whenever you're feeling sad, I want you to think about feeling joyful again—because you will! Sadness likes to pretend it's bigger than it is. It likes to make you think you'll always be unhappy. But this is a lie. The truth is, *all* My followers have endless Joy ahead of them, and it's promised for all eternity! *No one can take this away from you.*

Your path through this world will have many ups and downs. The times of trouble are hard, but there's a good reason for them. Pain and struggles and sadness help you grow stronger as you learn to trust Me. It's a bit like running a race—a long race, not a hundred-yard dash. It's not easy, and there will be times when your legs hurt and it's hard to breathe. You may even want to give up. But as you keep going and get closer to the end, you start to get excited about the joy of reaching the finish line. Then, when at last you *do* reach the end, there's the wonderful prize waiting for you—the joy of knowing you made it, you finished the race. So while you struggle through your earthly troubles, keep your eyes on the promised prize: endless Joy in heaven! And remember that I run this race right beside you. Even now you can become more aware of My Presence, which will give you My Joy as you run your race.

READ ON YOUR OWN

John 16:21; Psalm 16:11

Your Home in Heaven

*Our homeland is in heaven, and we are waiting for our
Savior, the Lord Jesus Christ, to come from heaven.*
—Philippians 3:20 ICB

Your citizenship—*your true homeland*—*is in heaven.* Someday I will change your earthly body and make it like My heavenly body. Then you'll have forever to enjoy this perfect version of you. So don't worry so much about how you look and feel right now. Too many of My followers focus so much on this that they forget about Me. And yet, your earthly body won't last forever, so try not to worry about it. Once you reach heaven, you won't worry about *anything.* You'll experience a Joy so great that it will be like nothing you could ever imagine!

Your times are in My hands. I have planned out all your days, and I know exactly how many there are. Since your body is a holy home, *a temple of the Holy Spirit,* I *do* expect you to take care of it, but I don't want you to think about it too much. This will steal your thoughts away from Me. Instead, accept each day as a precious gift from Me. Look for both the joys and the tasks I've placed in your path. Hold My hand, trusting Me as we walk along together. I am always by your side.

READ ON YOUR OWN

1 Corinthians 2:9; Psalm 31:15; 1 Corinthians 6:19–20

Be Made New!

If anyone belongs to Christ, then he is made new.
The old things have gone; everything is made new!
—2 Corinthians 5:17 ICB

I am making you *new in your heart* and mind. Living close to Me is all about change and being made new. And I am changing you *by a new way of thinking*. This is a huge project—you'll be under construction until the day you come to live with Me in heaven. However, unlike the bricks and wood that builders use to build houses, you are a living, breathing "material." I've given you the amazing ability to think things out and make important choices. I want you to use this godlike ability to work together with Me as I change you. This means *leaving your old self* behind—your old way of thinking and doing things—and putting on the new self, which is *My* way of thinking and doing things.

To make good and godly choices, you need to know Me—really know Me. Search for Me in My Word, the Bible, and ask My Spirit to show you what it means. He will shine His Light so that My words come alive to you. The more you choose to think and do things *My* way, the more you'll become like Me—and the more you'll enjoy *living in the Light of My Presence*.

READ ON YOUR OWN

Ephesians 4:22–24; Romans 12:2; Psalm 89:15

Praise and Trust

Give thanks whatever happens. That is
what God wants for you in Christ Jesus.
—1 Thessalonians 5:18 ICB

Don't worry, My dear child. Throw away those worried thoughts and fill your mind with trusting, thankful thoughts instead. Increase your faith in Me while you praise Me for all that I am and all that I've done. This combination of praise and trust is a powerful one. It chases away fear and the powers of darkness. It also makes your relationship with Me even stronger. You may have real troubles to deal with, but I'll help you handle them. As you feel more at peace and less stressed, you'll be able to look at your problems in the Light of My Presence, knowing I am with you. Ask Me what you should do. Read My Word and let its verses fill your heart and mind— because I often speak to you through the Bible.

Take time to thank Me for the many good things in your life. I want your prayers, your words to others, and your thoughts to be filled with thankfulness. I always know what you're thinking, and I'm so happy when your thoughts are grateful ones. You can even thank Me for the things you wish were different. This tells Me you have faith in Me and that you believe I'll work everything out for your best. Thankfulness gets rid of unhappy thoughts and feelings and opens you up to Joy. So *give thanks whatever happens. This is what I want for you.*

READ ON YOUR OWN

Psalm 31:14; Psalm 32:8

I Am for You

"May the Lord watch over you and give you peace."
—Numbers 6:26 ICB

*I*f *I am for you, who can be against you?* It's so important that you understand: I truly *am* for you. I'm on your side. This is a promise for all My followers. When things aren't going your way and the people you've trusted turn against you, it's easy to feel as if I have left you too. In those times, you must tell yourself the truth: I am not only *with* you always, I'm also *for* you all the time. This is true on days when you do well and on days when you seem to mess up everything, on days when people are kind to you and when they are not.

If you really understand and totally believe that I am on your side, then your fears will fade away and you can face troubles calmly. Knowing that I'll never turn against you will give you the courage to get through hard times. I want you to know that I think good things about you because you're My beloved child! It's *My* opinion of you that counts—not anyone else's. And it's *My* opinion that will matter in heaven too. No person and no thing *will be able to separate you from My loving Presence.*

READ ON YOUR OWN

Romans 8:31; Romans 8:39

Seek Me

Look to the LORD and his strength; seek his face always.
—1 Chronicles 16:11

I am present everywhere in this world around you. I'm in the Bible, and I'm in your heart through My Spirit. Ask Me to open the eyes inside your heart so that you can "see" Me—because I'm always right by your side, loving you every second of your life.

It's so important to set aside time to *seek My Face*—not just a minute here or there, but blocks of time to spend with Me. Choosing to think about Me will take practice. That's because pulling your thoughts away from the distractions and the stuff of this world isn't easy. Remember that I am the living Word, so you can always find Me when you search for Me in the words of the Bible.

I created all the beauty of this world, and I did it to point you to the One who made everything. *Without Me, nothing was made that has been made.* Whenever you're enjoying something beautiful, thank Me. This not only pleases Me, it increases your Joy. And even when you're faced with tough and ugly things in this broken, sin-filled world, I want you to trust Me enough to thank Me then too. Keep looking for Me in both your good times *and* your hard times. You'll find hope and comfort in knowing that *all your times are in My hands.*

READ ON YOUR OWN

John 1:3; Psalm 31:14–15

Every Breath

*The Lord God took dust from the ground and formed
man from it. The Lord breathed the breath of life into the
man's nose. And the man became a living person.*
—Genesis 2:7 ICB

Everything you have is a gift from Me—even the air you breathe. I rain so many blessings on you that it's easy to take some of them for granted, ignoring them or not thanking Me for them. Most people don't notice the wonder of constantly breathing in My Life. Yet the first man, Adam, *became a living being* only when I breathed *the breath of Life* into him.

As you sit in My Presence, try thanking Me silently each time you breathe in. Then, as you breathe out, tell Me you trust Me. While you're taking time with Me, I'll help you see the good gifts of Mine that you often miss—like the skies and trees, lights and colors, family and friends, and hundreds of tiny, wonderful, "everyday" things. The list is endless! As you keep looking for good things in your life, you will see more of My many, many blessings.

Of course, your greatest blessing is *eternal Life* in heaven with Me, and it's yours because you *believe in Me*—your Savior. This precious gift will fill you with a *Joy in My Presence* that just keeps growing and growing forever.

READ ON YOUR OWN

John 3:16; Psalm 16:11

With Shouts of Joy

*Those who plant in tears will harvest with shouts
of joy. They weep as they go to plant their seed,
but they sing as they return with the harvest.*
—Psalm 126:5–6 NLT

*T*hose who plant in tears will harvest with shouts of Joy. Don't hate your tears, My child. They are precious to Me. Someday, in heaven, *I will wipe every tear from your eyes*. But for now, you live in a world that is often full of tears. Yet just as water is needed for seeds to grow into plants, your tears help you grow into a more joyful Christian. When you're willing to share in the sadness of this sin-filled world, you learn to feel tenderness and compassion for those around you. This opens your heart for more Joy as you learn to enjoy Me in good times and hard times.

Shouts and songs of Joy have been your right ever since you became My child. Don't ignore this wonderful way of worshiping Me. Even though it may seem strange or even weird to sing praise songs when you're feeling sad, it's a powerful way to lift your heart to Me. As your Joy in Me meets with My Joy in you, you can dance in the Light of My Presence. This is *the Joy of the Lord*!

READ ON YOUR OWN

Revelation 21:4; Isaiah 62:4; Nehemiah 8:10

I Make You Sing

God is the one who saves me. I trust him. I am not afraid. The Lord, the Lord, gives me strength and makes me sing. He has saved me.
—Isaiah 12:2 ICB

Trust Me and don't be afraid. The stories you see on the news or in the papers show only tiny bits of world events, but they leave out the most important fact of all—*My Presence in the world*! As reporters dig through huge amounts of information, they toss out everything about Me and what I'm doing on the earth. Their reports aren't completely true because they talk as if I don't exist.

Whenever your world starts feeling like a scary place, remember that I am with you and talk to Me. Follow the example of King David in the Bible, who *found strength in Me* even when his own men were threatening to *kill him with stones*. When you're feeling upset or afraid, you can find courage by remembering who I am. Think about My awesome Glory and Power. Delight in My Love that will never fail you. Rejoice and be glad that you're on an incredible adventure with Me—and your last stop is the wonders of heaven. Your fears will fade away and Joy will grow inside you as you keep your mind on Me and enjoy the rich friendship I offer you. Trust Me with all your heart, dear one, because *I give you strength and make you sing.*

READ ON YOUR OWN

Exodus 33:14; 1 Samuel 30:6

JULY

"Even if that were possible, I would not forget you! See, I have written your name on the palms of my hands."

—Isaiah 49:15–16 NLT

You Are My Treasure

I will go to the altar of God, to God who is my joy and happiness. I will praise you with a harp, God, my God.
—Psalm 43:4 ICB

I have written your name on the palms of My hands. This is a sign of My forever-promises to you—to love you, to never leave you, and to bring all those who follow Me to heaven.

The words a jeweler engraves on a gold ring are meant to last forever. But over time, those words can wear away or be scratched off. A ring itself may be lost or stolen or melted down. Your name written on My hands is different. It can never be erased, for you are My treasure, bought with My own blood on the cross. So put Me first, dear child. Gold and silver have some value in this world. But they are like *worthless trash compared with the greatness of knowing Me* forever!

Since your name is engraved on the palms of My hands, you can be sure that I always see you. People sometimes write notes on their hands to remind themselves of something important. I have written your name on *My* hands because you are important to Me—for all eternity. Be joyful and glad, treasuring *Me* above all else! I, the King of the universe, consider you to be more precious than any treasure on earth!

READ ON YOUR OWN

Isaiah 49:15–16; Philippians 3:8–9

I Know the Way

God lives forever and is holy. He is high and lifted up,
and he says . . . "I give new life to those who are humble.
I give new life to those whose hearts are broken."
—Isaiah 57:15 ICB

*W*hen you are afraid, I, your Lord, *know the way out* of that fear. This is actually one of the blessings of fear. It proves to you that you can't find your way out of trouble without My help. If you're feeling afraid, or tired, or confused, you can choose to turn away from those feelings and look to Me instead. Pour out your heart and tell Me all that you're thinking. Then rest in My Presence, the One who *knows the way out* of your trouble—and your way *to* heaven.

Keep looking to Me even when you feel strong and confident. In fact, that's when you're in the most danger of going the wrong way, because it's easy to think you don't need Me. So don't just say, "Oh, this isn't hard; I know what to do." Train yourself to ask Me to guide you. Remember that *My ways and thoughts are higher than yours, just as the heavens are higher than the earth*. Let that truth remind you to seek and worship Me—*the One who is holy and lives forever*, and who reaches down from heaven to help you.

READ ON YOUR OWN

Psalm 142:3; Isaiah 55:9

My Love Surrounds You

Let your unfailing love surround us, L<small>ORD</small>, for our hope is in you alone.
—Psalm 33:22 NLT

I am the Lord your God, who takes hold of your right hand and says to you, Do not fear; I will help you.

It's so important for you to see—and to believe—that I'm not only your Savior, but I'm also *your God*. Many people try to say that I was just a good person—someone who sacrificed Himself and gave up everything for others. Yet if I were only a man, you would still be spiritually *dead because of your sins*.

I am the Living God! I am the One who holds your hand and takes away your fears. Celebrate with Joy as you think about this great truth. Delight in the mystery and wonder of the Trinity—the Father, Son, and Holy Spirit, who are one God.

Take time with Me, telling Me your troubles. *Pour out your heart to Me*; then listen to Me say, "Do not be afraid, beloved child. I am here, and I'm ready to help you." I know that you're afraid sometimes, and I understand. But I want you to trade those fears for hope and trust in Me. As you put your *hope in Me, My unfailing Love will surround you*.

READ ON YOUR OWN

Isaiah 41:13; Ephesians 2:1; Psalm 62:8

You Are Already a Winner!

The city does not need the sun or the moon to shine on it. The glory of God is its light, and the Lamb is the city's lamp.
—Revelation 21:23 ICB

To every person who wins the victory, I will give the right to eat the fruit from the tree of life. This tree is in the garden of God in heaven.

Dear child, you are already a winner! That's because for all those people (like you!) that *I planned to be like Me, I also called. And those I called, I also made right with Me.* I brought you out of the darkness of sin and into My kingdom of Light. That means you're on your way to the Glory of heaven. The victory over sin has been won through My death on the cross.

But there will still be struggles for you while you live in this world. There will be troubles and temptations that show just how weak and sinful you can be. You may feel sad and discouraged when you fail to live as I want you to. You may even feel as if you don't belong to Me anymore—but don't believe it! Instead, hold tightly to Me and My promises. Trust that the joyous wonders of heaven really are your inheritance—future gifts waiting for you from Me. When your way seems dark, remember that the Light of heaven shines bright because *the Glory of God is its light, and I am its Lamp.*

READ ON YOUR OWN

Revelation 2:7; Romans 8:30

Live in My Light

Let your face shine on your servant; save me in your unfailing love.
—Psalm 31:16

*L*ive in the Light of My Presence. This is a wonderful way to walk through each day. It means *rejoicing in My Name all the time* and *praising My goodness*.

To truly praise Me is to be excited about Me, even shouting and clapping sometimes! When you rejoice in My Name, you find Joy because of all that I am—your Savior and Shepherd, your Lord and God, your King, your Friend. I am the One who loves you with *an unfailing Love* that never ends. You can celebrate My goodness because I have shared it with you. Yes, you'll still sin and mess up in this life, but My perfect righteousness is always yours. I forgive all your sins because you're My child.

As you live in My Light, *My blood constantly makes you clean from every sin*. When you admit that you need forgiveness for your sins and you try to live the way I want you to, then My holy Light makes you pure. I look at you as if you'd never done anything wrong. This blessing is for all who believe in Me—and it allows My followers to *share a rich fellowship*, a special friendship, with each other. So live in the Light with Me, My friend. Enjoy spending time in My bright, loving Presence.

READ ON YOUR OWN

Psalm 89:15–16; Romans 3:22; 1 John 1:7

Get to Know Me

*Through his power all things were made—things in
heaven and on earth, things seen and unseen, all powers,
authorities, lords, and rulers. All things were made through
Christ and for Christ. Christ was there before anything
was made. And all things continue because of him.*
—Colossians 1:16–17 ICB

I was there before anything was made. And all things continue because of Me. I have always been and will always be.
*Through My power all things were made—things in heaven and on
earth, things seen and unseen.* I am Lord over creation, over the
church, over everything! Worship Me as your *living God.* I want
My children to thirst for Me, just as *a deer thirsts for a stream
of water*, and just as you thirst for a cool drink of water on a hot
summer's day.

Don't be happy with just thinking about Me or knowing Bible
stories about Me. Thirst for the *experience* of Me in your life. You
can find Me in My Word and also by spending time with Me. Try
to learn a little more of My Love each day—it is *greater than any
person can ever know.* You'll need My Holy Spirit's help to do this.

You must *be made stronger by My Spirit, who lives in your
heart and mind.* Ask Him to give you His power and to guide you
in this adventure. And remember that *I* am the goal; make Me
the focus of your quest. *When you search for Me with all your
heart, you will find Me!*

READ ON YOUR OWN

Psalm 42:1–2; Ephesians 3:16–19; Jeremiah 29:13

The Only Way

The Lord will rescue me from every evil attack and
will bring me safely to his heavenly kingdom.
—2 Timothy 4:18

I am the Door. *The person who enters through Me will be saved.* I am the only Way to *the path of Life*, which leads to eternal Life in heaven. If you don't go through Me, you will never be saved from your sins.

Some people think of their journey to heaven as climbing up a mountain. They imagine that there are different paths leading to the top, and that all the climbers will end up at the same place. People who think this way believe there are many paths to heaven. But that's just not true! You can get to heaven *only* through Me, the one true Door.

Once you've come through My door, then you can enjoy walking along the path of Life with Me. I'm not promising it will be an easy journey, but I do promise to be with you every step of the way. No matter what troubles or hard times come, *there is Joy to be found in My Presence*, in being with Me. And each step you take brings you closer to your goal: your home in heaven.

READ ON YOUR OWN

John 10:9; Psalm 16:11; Matthew 1:21

Here in This Moment

I love you, Lord. You are my strength.
—Psalm 18:1 ICB

I am close to you right now, in this moment. Search for Me and enjoy My Presence in the present. Trusting Me and being thankful for My gifts will help you in this quest to find Me.

When you struggle with the past or worry about the future, it's harder to see Me *right here*. But the more you trust Me, the more fully you can live in the present, where I'm always waiting for you. Talk to Me often. Tell Me, "I trust You, Jesus." Say to Me, "*I love you, Lord. You are my strength.*" These short prayers keep you close to Me—boldly trusting that I'm watching over you with Love.

It's important that you not only trust Me more, but also learn to be more thankful. You need a grateful heart if you want to live close to Me. When you aren't grateful, it hurts and insults Me. And it drags down both your heart and your spirit.

Remember that *you have a kingdom that cannot be shaken*, no matter what's happening in your life or in the world. This means you always have a reason—a rock-solid, unshakable, unchanging reason—to be thankful. Like a boat anchored to the safety of the shore, stay anchored to Me. Enjoy being with Me *by giving thanks whatever happens*.

READ ON YOUR OWN

Hebrews 12:28–29; 1 Thessalonians 5:18

The Center of Your Life

Be strong and brave. Don't be afraid of them. Don't be frightened. The Lord your God will go with you. He will not leave you or forget you.
—Deuteronomy 31:6 ICB

As you *seek Me* and search for Me more and more often, I become the center of your life—and this gives you Joy. When you look at the world today, there are so many terrible things trying to steal your attention away from Me. If you think about these things too much, you'll become very sad and discouraged. But I am the One who *is always with you*, and I'm calling out to you: "I'm here! Look for Me, and find Joy in Me!"

My Presence can bless you every moment of every day, even when I'm only in the background of your thoughts. The amazing brain I gave you is able to do several different things, all at the same time. So even when you're busy with something that needs a lot of thought, like homework, you can train yourself to stay aware of Me. Remembering that I am with you will quietly comfort and encourage you.

In spite of what some people say, making Me the center of your life isn't running away from the real world. Staying close to Me actually gives you the strength and courage to deal with the hard things that happen! The more you look to Me, the better you'll be at everything you do. You'll also be much, much happier.

READ ON YOUR OWN

Psalm 105:4; Psalm 73:23

More Like Me

I will sing to the Lᴏʀᴅ because he is good to me.
—Psalm 13:6 ɴʟᴛ

I am the King of Glory, and I love you! You are *more than a conqueror and a victor* through Me.

No matter what's happening in this broken and sinful world—or in your own life—you win! That's because *I* won the Victory for you by dying on the cross and rising from the grave. *My unfailing Love* made this defeat of death and sin possible. It also made you much, much more than just a winner. It made you an heir of My kingdom of never-ending Life and Light.

Nothing will be able to separate you from My Love! Just think about what it means for Me to love your soul every moment, forever and ever. Your soul is the part of you that never dies, the part that can never be separated from Me. You don't see it in the mirror, but it is the "real you," and it *brings more and more Glory* to Me. So don't get discouraged when you do something wrong. Instead, remember that I'm still working in you, and then rejoice because I'm *changing you to be more like Me*.

READ ON YOUR OWN

Romans 8:37–39; Psalm 13:5; 2 Corinthians 3:18

No Room for Bragging

I do not mean that we are able to say that we can do this work ourselves. It is God who makes us able to do all that we do.
—2 Corinthians 3:5 ICB

I am the One who makes you able to do all that you do. That means there's no room for bragging about what *you've* done. It also means you can do much, much more than you think you can. Your natural talents added to My supernatural Power is a mighty thing. I want you to depend on Me—with happiness in your heart. Don't be afraid to ask Me for help. Search the Bible for how I want you to live, and *seek Me* in prayer. Older Christians can also help guide you. I will show you what to do and where to go.

Ask My Spirit to go with you on the path I've chosen for you. My Holy Helper will make you strong and give you everything you need to succeed in what I've asked you to do. Thank Me for everything: the talents and abilities I've given you, the opportunities you have, and My Spirit's help in doing important things for My kingdom. Pay attention to Me as you travel along the path of Life. *Being with Me will fill you with Joy.*

READ ON YOUR OWN

1 Chronicles 16:10–11; 1 Thessalonians 5:16–18;
Psalm 16:11

I Will Be Your Song

*You will receive your salvation with joy. You will
take it as you would draw water from a well.*
—Isaiah 12:3 ICB

I want you *to receive your salvation with Joy* in the same way *you would draw water from a well*. This well is deeper than you could ever imagine, and it's filled to the top with My blessings. The value of your salvation is priceless. It's greater than all the earth's treasures put together—the treasures of the past, present, and future.

When your life in this world ends, you'll live with Me forever in a perfect heaven that's filled with My dazzling Glory. You and all My followers will worship Me. You'll love each other as brothers and sisters—and you'll love Me with an even greater Love than ever before. You'll also receive so much Love from Me that you won't be able to measure it!

The promise of this future Joy in heaven can help you get through your struggles in this world. I understand all the troubles you're facing, but remember: *I give you strength and make you sing*. I am strong enough to carry you when you're too tired to go on. I can even help you want to sing with Me—on good days *and* hard days. I will be *your Song*, and I will fill you with Joy!

READ ON YOUR OWN

Isaiah 12:2; 2 Corinthians 8:9; Psalm 16:11

I'll Show You the Way

God wanted them to look for him and perhaps search all around for him and find him. But he is not far from any of us.
—Acts 17:27 ICB

Sometimes you need help *asking* for My help. When you try to do more than one thing at a time, you have to move faster and faster to keep up. Then, while you're trying to do one thing, like studying for a test, you get interrupted by something else. Those interruptions can stress you out. The best way out of this stress is to STOP everything. Take a few deep breaths and whisper My Name, *Jesus.* Admit that you need Me to guide you through your day. I will lovingly and gently lead you down *the paths that are right—for the good of My Name.*

You usually take time to ask for My help when you're getting ready to do something hard. But with everyday things, you often jump right in—as if you can handle it all on your own. It's so much better to depend on Me in *everything* you do! Whenever you find yourself about to "jump in," ask Me to help you stop—and look for Me. Because *I will show you where to go,* and *I will watch over you.*

READ ON YOUR OWN

Psalm 23:3; Psalm 32:8

Be Still and Wait

*Be still in the presence of the L*ORD*, and wait patiently for him to act. Don't worry about evil people who prosper or fret about their wicked schemes.*
—Psalm 37:7 NLT

*B*e still in My Presence, and wait patiently for Me to act. "Being still" almost never happens in this world. In fact, many people decide whether or not they've had a good day by how much they've done. For them, resting in My Presence usually doesn't count as something they've accomplished—yet so many blessings can be found in this holy rest with Me!

Wherever I am, Peace and Joy are overflowing. But it takes time for them to soak into your heart and mind. It also takes trust. Instead of getting upset or angry when your plans don't work out, wait patiently for Me to show you *My* plans. You can *look to Me for help* because I am *God your Savior*. I *will* hear you. I may not answer as soon as you'd like, or in the way that you'd like, but I always answer your prayers in the way that's best for you.

Don't worry about evil people or their wicked plans. They don't worry Me, because I know their future; *I see that their day of judgment is coming.* Rest in Me, beloved child. *Be still, and know that I am God.*

READ ON YOUR OWN

Micah 7:7; Psalm 37:13; Psalm 46:10

There's No Limit to My Love

Your unfailing love is better than life itself; how I praise you!
—Psalm 63:3 NLT

*M*y unfailing Love is better than life itself! There's no limit to it—My Love never runs out or disappears. It's better than *anything* this world could ever give you. And it's yours. *How priceless is My unfailing Love!*

Think about the parable of t*he merchant looking for fine pearls* from Matthew 13. *When he found one of great value, he sold everything he had and bought it.* My Love is like that pearl: so valuable that it's worth giving up everything else you own in order to get it and keep it forever.

My Love is more precious than life. In fact, many people have sacrificed their lives to share the good news about it. The gift of My Love makes each day brighter and gives you a solid rock to build your life on. It also improves your relationships with others as you learn to love like Me. Knowing that you're perfectly loved helps you become the person I created you to be. *Understanding how wide and how long and how high and how deep My Love is* makes you want to joyfully celebrate My Presence in your life. *This* is how you and I grow closer: through your worship of Me!

READ ON YOUR OWN

Psalm 36:7; Matthew 13:45–46; Ephesians 3:17–18

Go and Tell About Me

Sing to the Lord and praise his name. Every day tell how he saves us. Tell the nations of his glory. Tell all peoples the miracles he does.
—Psalm 96:2–3 ICB

*E*very day tell others *how I saved you.* And repeat this truth every single day: *You have been saved by grace because you believe. You did not save yourselves. It was a gift from God. You cannot brag that you are saved by the work you have done.*

This truth is the exact opposite of what the world says. The world says you have to work at being good enough. And if you're not careful, your own heart and mind—which live in this sinful world—will agree with that lie. That's why My Word warns you to *be alert.* The devil is *the accuser* of My followers. He likes to steal your hope by pointing out every wrong you do and every mistake you make. But I say, don't listen to the devil's lies! Remind yourself that I have rescued you by taking the punishment for your sin.

The best thing you can do is thank Me for My gift of grace, which sets you free—and then do what I ask. It's important that you not only remind yourself how I saved you, but that you also tell the world. *Tell the nations of My glory!* Share this good news everywhere you can—both near (to family and friends and kids at school) and far (to other countries and cultures). *All peoples* need to know the truth about Me. Let your thankfulness encourage you, breathe new life into you, and fill you with Joy!

READ ON YOUR OWN

Ephesians 2:8–9; 1 Peter 5:8; Revelation 12:10

Learn to Praise Me

Happy are the people who know how to praise you.
Lord, let them live in the light of your presence.
—Psalm 89:15 ICB

*B*lessed are those who have learned to acclaim Me. "Acclaim" means to praise with Joy and excitement. This kind of praise won't come naturally to you. It's something you'll need to learn—and practice.

Start with your thoughts. Instead of thinking of Me in the same, boring ways over and over, think about My greatness! I spoke and the world appeared—with light and sound and animals and *you*! I made people in My own likeness, and I gave them souls that will live forever. I created beauty in this world and all throughout the universe. I'm smarter than the greatest genius who ever lived. My wisdom cannot be understood, and My Love never fails. Learn to think magnificent thoughts about Me and to praise Me with excitement and Joy. The Psalms are a really good place to start learning.

To "acclaim" Me also means to praise Me to other people. *You are the light of the world* because you know that I'm your Savior and God. I want you to *let your light shine before men*. Tell them the wonders of who I am and all I have done. This is how you *declare the praises of Him who called you out of darkness into His wonderful light*.

READ ON YOUR OWN

Romans 11:33; Matthew 5:14–16; 1 Peter 2:9

Be Joyful Always

Rejoice always.
—1 Thessalonians 5:16 NKJV

*R*ejoice always*! This is one of the shortest verses in the Bible, but it shines with heavenly Light. I made you *in My own image*—My likeness—and I created you with the ability to *choose* Joy in every moment of your life, even the most difficult ones. When your mind is stuck in unhappy, gloomy thoughts, change your thinking with this command: *Rejoice always*! Then see how many times each day you can remind yourself to be joyful.

Not only is it important to have Joy, but it's also important to think about *why* you're joyful. You can rejoice because I give you what you need—like food, a home, and clothes. Your family and friends can be a source of Joy. And because you're Mine, our relationship is always a reason to be filled with happiness. These thoughts will light up your mind and heart, and they'll help you see even more reasons for rejoicing in your life.

Choosing Joy will bless you *and* everyone around you. It will also make our relationship stronger as you delight in your life with Me.

READ ON YOUR OWN

Genesis 1:27; Philippians 4:4

Your Help and Your Shield

So our hope is in the Lord. He is our help, our shield to protect us.
—Psalm 33:20 ICB

I am your Help, your Shield to protect you. Pay extra attention to that word *your*. I am not just *a* Help and *a* Shield. I am *yours*—for all time and throughout eternity. This is a promise that I'll keep forever. Let it cheer you up and make you stronger as you walk with Me through this day. *I will never leave you or forget you*. You can always count on Me!

Because I am your Help, you don't have to worry about what you can or can't handle. When a task looks too big for you, be glad that I'm right beside you, ready to give you a hand. It's okay to admit you can't do it alone. But don't stop there—trust Me to give you what you need. You and I *together* can do anything—as long as it's My will for you.

You definitely need Me as your Shield. I protect you from so many dangers—dangers to your body, your heart, and your soul. Sometimes you can see what I'm protecting you from, but often you don't. Find comfort in knowing that My powerful Presence is always watching over you. *Do not be afraid*, My precious child, *because I am with you.*

READ ON YOUR OWN

Deuteronomy 31:8; Philippians 4:13; Psalm 23:4 ICB

Stay Close to Me

These troubles come to prove that your faith is pure.
This purity of faith is worth more than gold.
—1 Peter 1:7 ICB

*S*tay close to Me; I will support you *and hold you up* with My right hand. When you hold on to Me—just as you would hold on to your mother's or father's hand—you show that you trust Me. I won't let your struggles be wasted. I'll use them to make your faith purer and to prove that it's real. As you stay close to Me in times of trouble, your faith gets stronger and you are comforted. After you've gone through trials and hard times, you can then face future problems with courage, knowing that I'll always help you, just as I did in the past.

Whether it's the middle of the night or the middle of your worst day, remember that My right hand holds you up. My hand is so strong that there's no limit to how much I can do for you. When you're feeling as if you just can't take any more, don't give up! Instead, *look to Me and My Strength*. My powerful hand is righteous; it's good and fair. So *don't be afraid. I will make you strong and I will help you. I will support you with My right hand that saves you*.

READ ON YOUR OWN

Psalm 63:8; Psalm 105:4; Isaiah 41:10

Shine Your Light

"Be a light for other people. Live so that they will see the good things you do. Live so that they will praise your Father in heaven."
—Matthew 5:16 ICB

*T*hose who look to Me are radiant and shining with Joy. That's because I'm the Sun who's always shining, even when your life is hard and the future looks dark. Because you know Me as your Savior, you have a source of Light that chases away the darkness. I created you to *show My Glory*. You do this by looking to Me—turning your face toward My Light. Take time to be quiet with Me, soaking up My Joy. The longer you stay in the Presence of My Light, the more I can bless you and make you stronger.

While you're resting with Me, whisper these words that Jacob said so long ago: *"Surely the Lord is in this place."* I am everywhere at every time, so these words are always true. Even if you don't feel Me with you, I am there.

Taking time to soak up My Light and My Love will make you more aware of My Presence. You'll learn to see more of Me in your world. And this time spent with Me will help *you* be a bright light—shining My Love to everyone around you.

READ ON YOUR OWN

Psalm 34:5; 2 Corinthians 3:18 ICB; Genesis 28:16

A New Life

"I and My Father are one."
—John 10:30 NKJV

I gave you a new life. I gave you a living hope because I rose from *death*. I died on the cross for all My followers, to take the punishment for their sins. But if I had stayed dead in the grave, your faith *would be useless*. You would be spiritually dead forever—and *still guilty of your sins*. Of course, it was impossible for Me to stay dead because I am God! As I said to everyone who questioned Me, *"I and My Father are one."*

My resurrection—My rising up from the grave—is a historical fact. This miracle opened up the way for you to have *a new life* with Me.

By confessing that you have sinned, and by trusting Me as your Savior, you became a part of My family. And one day you'll walk with Me in heaven. Even your walk here on earth is full of *living hope*—because I'm your living Savior. No matter how hard things get, I'll *always* keep My promises! The Light of My loving Presence shines on you all the time, even in your most difficult times. Look up to Me, precious child. Let the shining Light of My Love chase away the darkness of trouble and fill your heart with Joy.

READ ON YOUR OWN

1 Peter 1:3; 1 Corinthians 15:17; Ephesians 2:1

Safe with Me

He won't be afraid of bad news. He is safe because he trusts the Lord.
—Psalm 112:7 ICB

I am *God your Savior*. No matter what's happening in the world, you can *be glad in Me*. Your planet has been in a terribly sinful and broken-down condition ever since Adam and Eve first disobeyed Me. They lost their first two sons, Cain and Abel, in a horrible way. Cain killed his younger brother Abel because he was jealous of him. Then God punished Cain by sending him away to a life of *restless wandering on the earth*.

Adam and Eve's sin is often called "the Fall"—and it has made this world a dangerous and uncertain place. Each day, your challenge is to find Joy in the middle of the sin and brokenness. Tell yourself often: "Jesus is with me and for me. *Nothing can separate me from His Love.*" Put your energy into enjoying My Presence and looking for the good that can still be found on this earth. Use your gifts to shine My Light into all the places I lead you. *Don't be afraid of bad news*, because I can make good things happen out of evil things. Train your heart to trust Me, your Savior. *You are safe* because of Me.

READ ON YOUR OWN

Habakkuk 3:18; Genesis 4:12; Romans 8:39

I Am in Your Future

*Now let your unfailing love comfort me,
just as you promised me, your servant.*
—Psalm 119:76 NLT

*D*o not be afraid. Do not be discouraged. You're looking ahead at the future—at things that are uncertain—and feeling worried. Fear and sadness are just waiting to walk with you into the future if you let them. So don't let them! Remember, *I am always with you, holding you by your right hand.* Because I live outside of time, I'm also in your future, on your path ahead. I'm shining My Light to show you the way and calling your name. Hold tightly to My hand, walking right past fear and gloom. Don't let them tag along with you. Focus instead on My shining Presence. That's where you'll find My *unfailing Love* and endless encouragement.

You can be brave because I am both here with you now *and* already in your future, getting everything ready for you. Listen as I call out words of wisdom and words of warning, words of courage and hope: *Don't worry, because I am with you. Don't be afraid, because I am your God. I will make you strong and will help you. I will support you with My right hand that saves you.*

READ ON YOUR OWN

Deuteronomy 31:8; Psalm 73:23; Isaiah 41:10

A Feast of Joy

The Lord's loved ones will lie down in safety. The Lord protects them all day long. The ones the Lord loves rest with him.
—Deuteronomy 33:12 ICB

It's in the present moment that you'll find Me close to you. My Presence in the present is an endless source of Joy for you—*a continual feast*, like Thanksgiving dinner every day!

I am training you to *rejoice in Me always*. This is a choice you'll have to make every moment. It's possible to find Joy with Me even in your worst times. I'm *always* near, so I'm *always* ready to help you. And when you face something really hard—so hard that you think you just can't go on—that's when I pick you up and carry you through it.

Imagine the perfect best friend—someone you love and want to be like. Just thinking about spending time together makes you happy. When you think of this person, even your troubles don't seem so bad. Nothing can take away the excitement of being with your friend. In the same way, remember that I'm the very best Friend you'll ever have—and I'll be your Friend forever. Even in the toughest times, you can find happiness and excitement in being with Me. As I fill up your soul with My Presence, you'll also find it easier to love other people. Enjoy being with Me, and you'll be able to bless others with your Joy.

READ ON YOUR OWN

Proverbs 15:15; Philippians 4:4–5; Psalm 63:5

A Wide Path

*About three o'clock Jesus cried out in a loud voice,
"Eli, Eli, lama sabachthani?" This means, "My God,
my God, why have you left me alone?"*
—Matthew 27:46 ICB

I give you a wide path on which to walk. Your feet have not slipped. This shows how much I care about the journey of your life. I know exactly what's waiting for you in the future, and I can change the path ahead of you to make it easier. Sometimes I let you see what I've done for you. Other times, I save you from troubles you never knew about. Either way, My work to widen the path ahead of you lets you see my deep Love for you and how much I'm working in your life. I won't let you slip and fall.

My work is often a mystery to you. I don't protect you—or anyone—from *all* trouble. *I* wasn't shielded from hard times during My thirty-three years in your world. In fact, I chose to suffer horrible pain, shame, and torture on the cross, just so I could save you! When My Father in heaven turned away from Me for taking the world's sins on Myself, I went through suffering so terrible that you can't imagine it. But because I was willing to be separated from My Father until the victory over sin was won, you *never* have to suffer alone. I have promised: *I am with you always!* And I always keep My promises.

READ ON YOUR OWN

Psalm 18:36; Matthew 28:20

Father, Son, and Holy Spirit

*Let everything that has breath praise the L*ORD*. Praise the L*ORD*.*
—Psalm 150:6

*W*hoever believes in Me is really believing in the One who sent Me. Whoever sees Me sees the One who sent Me.* It's true that I came into this world to be your Savior, but I also came to help you see God the Father more clearly. He and I always work together, and we always agree perfectly. I declared this when I was teaching in the temple in Jerusalem: *"I and My Father are one."* So when you try to live close to Me—*looking only to Me*—you aren't ignoring Him.

The Trinity is made up of Father, Son, and Holy Spirit. It's a great gift to you. It's also a mystery far beyond what you can understand. This blessing of three Persons in one can make your prayer life so much richer. You can pray to the Father in My Name. You can also speak right to Me. And the Holy Spirit is always with you to help you pray. Don't be worried by the mysteries of the Trinity. Instead, let these wonders give you another reason to praise and adore Me!

READ ON YOUR OWN

John 12:44–45; John 10:30; Hebrews 12:2

I Delight in Forgiving You

He has removed our sins as far from us as the east is from the west.
—Psalm 103:12 NLT

I am the living Lord who always sees you. I see all the way into your heart and mind. Not one single thought escapes My view. My perfect knowledge of you and everything about you means you're never alone—not in good times or in hard times. It also means I want to wash away any sinful thoughts you might have.

As soon as you notice yourself thinking in a selfish or hurtful way, admit it to Me. Ask Me to forgive you *and* to change you. You don't need to keep repeating it over and over again, as if you had to talk Me into forgiving you. I went through the torture of the cross and of being separated from My Father so that I could *remove your sins as far from you as the east is from the west*. I delight in forgiving you!

Even now I see you dressed in My own shining robes of perfect righteousness. And I already see you as the wonderful, perfect creation you'll be when heaven becomes your home.

READ ON YOUR OWN

Genesis 16:14; Psalm 139:1–2; 2 Corinthians 5:21

I'm Polishing Your Heart

If we are God's children, then we will receive the blessings
God has for us. We will receive these things from God
together with Christ. But we must suffer as Christ suffered,
and then we will have glory as Christ has glory.
—Romans 8:17 ICB

I am training you to wait with patience. This lesson isn't easy. But it *is* a rich blessing—and one part of sharing in My kingdom and My suffering.

Because My kingdom lasts forever, it has infinite, priceless value. And sharing in My suffering is needed so that you can *have Glory as I have Glory*. Also, sharing in My suffering shapes you into the person I created you to be.

Learning to wait with patience can only happen during hard times and struggles. I know it sounds crazy, but try to welcome the very problem you dread. Bring it to Me with a thankful heart. Tell Me you're willing to push through it as long as I think you need to. Ask Me to take that dark, ugly problem and change it into something lovely and wonderful. I can weave bright, golden strands of My Glory into the most terrible situation. It may take a long time to see the beauty, but waiting for it will build your patience. Rejoice and be glad, My loved one, because I'm polishing your heart so that it shines with the Light of My Glory!

READ ON YOUR OWN

Revelation 1:9; Philippians 2:14–15

My Overflowing Blessings

So the Lord must wait for you to come to him so he can show you his love and compassion. For the Lord is a faithful God. Blessed are those who wait for his help.
—Isaiah 30:18 NLT

Dearest child, *My love never ends. My mercies never stop. They are new every morning.* So you can start each day with courage and confidence, knowing that My pool of blessings is always overflowing. This knowledge helps you *wait for Me*, trusting Me to take care of all your unanswered prayers. I promise that not one of those prayers has slipped from My mind and been forgotten. I want you to come to Me and drink deeply from My well of unlimited Love and never-failing, tender compassion. As you wait with Me, My Love and compassion will satisfy the thirst of your soul.

Although many of your prayers are not yet answered, you can find hope in *My great faithfulness.* I keep all My promises, every single one, in My own perfect way and perfect timing. One of those promises is to *give you Peace* that will take away all the trouble and fear in your heart. If you get tired of waiting, remember that I wait too—*I wait for you to come to Me so I can show you My Love and compassion.* I wait until you're ready to receive the things I have so lovingly prepared for you. *Blessed are all those who wait for My help.*

READ ON YOUR OWN

Lamentations 3:22–24; John 14:27

While You're Still Praying

"I will answer them before they even call to me. While they are still talking about their needs, I will go ahead and answer their prayers!"
—Isaiah 65:24 NLT

I will answer you before you even call to me. While you are still talking to Me about your needs, I will go ahead and answer your prayers.

I know that sometimes you feel as if you're all alone in the dark! You keep praying because it's the right thing to do, but you wonder if your prayers even make a difference. If you feel this way, stop and remember who I Am—*the King of Glory*! I am bigger than time. The past, present, and future are all the same to Me. That's why I can answer your prayers before you finish saying them.

I hear every one of your prayers—and I always reply to them. But sometimes My answer is "No" or "Not right now." Other times, I answer your prayers in ways you can't see yet. *My wisdom has no end.* And *no one can understand My ways.* Just think about all the wonders of My limitless knowledge and intelligence: I know absolutely everything that's ever been, everything that is, and everything that will ever be. Then take Joy and delight in knowing that My Love for you has no end. As you keep thinking of these things and thanking Me for My Love, you'll know without a doubt that you are *never* alone. You are Mine!

READ ON YOUR OWN

Psalm 24:10; Romans 11:33

AUGUST

You will teach me God's way to live.
Being with you will fill me with joy.

—Acts 2:28 ICB

Run to Me

Fill us with your love every morning.
Then we will sing and rejoice all our lives.
—Psalm 90:14 ICB

Run to Me with excitement—because I am excited to be with you. Invite me to *fill you with My unfailing Love*. The best time to spend time with Me is *in the morning*, soon after you wake up. When you start your day with Me, the whole rest of your day goes so much better.

My endless Love will help you feel whole and complete. You'll know that you are treasured and important, that you matter to Me. Time with Me reminds you that *together* you and I can handle anything that comes your way today. And knowing that you are loved forever will give you the energy and the courage you need to power through even the toughest things.

Coming into My loving Presence first thing in the morning will make you feel like singing. Think about the amazing honor of meeting—right in your own home—with the One who made the stars, the *King of kings and Lord of lords*! Rejoice and be glad that your name is written in *My Book of Life*—with ink that can never be erased. Enjoy simply being with Me. Praise Me; sing to Me; read My Word and pray. Celebrate the wonderful truth that *nothing in all creation can separate you from My Love*!

READ ON YOUR OWN

Revelation 19:16; Revelation 21:27; Romans 8:39

My Promises to You

[Jesus] is able to save completely those who come to God
through him, because he always lives to intercede for them.
—Hebrews 7:25

I am your living Lord, your Rock, your Savior and God. Take some time to think about My greatness and My promises to you—promises that I *will* always keep. You live in a world where many people are afraid to make a promise. And so many of those who *do* make promises later decide to break them. I don't do that, and I won't ever do that. I am your forever Friend and the One who loves you always. You are completely safe and secure in My Love!

Instead of thinking about the troubles in your life and in your world, remember who I Am. Not only am I your living Lord and your Rock who never changes, I am also *God your Savior*. And because I am the everlasting God, My death on the cross for your sins *saves you completely*! You never need to worry that I'll stop loving you because you messed up or you aren't good enough. It's *My* goodness and *My* sinless perfection that keep you safe and secure in My Love. Let My promise of neverending Love give you comfort as you journey through this trouble-filled world. And remember that someday you'll live with Me in paradise. That's My promise to all who follow Me, and I *will* keep it!

READ ON YOUR OWN

Psalm 18:46; 2 Corinthians 5:21

I Will Make You Strong

*Wait patiently for the L*ORD*. Be brave and*
*courageous. Yes, wait patiently for the L*ORD*.*
—Psalm 27:14 NLT

Wait with Me in My Presence. So many good things come from spending time with Me—good things for your body, your mind, and your spirit. Yet many of My children think that spending time with Me is something they don't have time for! They want peace and rest, but they stay way too busy.

I want *you* to schedule your day so that you have quiet times with Me. Show Me that I'm important to you by making time for Me. When you do, I'll refresh your soul, and I'll give you strength for the day ahead.

Be brave and courageous. You have to be brave to live in this sinful, broken-down world. And since bravery isn't easy, you'll need My help. No matter what terrible things are happening in the world, you don't have to be afraid or worried or discouraged. Train yourself to *think about Me* again and again and again! Be comforted by My promise to *be with you wherever you go.*

Keep trying to be brave. Keep trying to be courageous— and ask Me to help you. Because I *will* make you strong!

READ ON YOUR OWN

Joshua 1:9; Hebrews 3:1 CEV

JESUS ALWAYS FOR KIDS

The Power of Prayer

*"If my people, who are called by my name, will humble themselves,
if they will pray and seek me and stop their evil ways, I will hear
them from heaven. I will forgive their sin, and I will heal their land."*
—2 Chronicles 7:14 NCV

Never forget the power of prayer! People who are feeling hopeless or discouraged will often say something like, "There's nothing left to do but pray." They say this as if prayer is their last hope, as if prayer is a weak choice. But that's not true!

I created you with the ability to talk to Me. Remember who I Am: *I am the King that rules forever! I cannot be destroyed.* I created the universe and all that is in it—so talking to Me is an amazing honor and blessing. Even when Adam and Eve disobeyed Me and the human race became stained with sin, I didn't take away mankind's ability to talk to Me. That's because I knew how much you need My help—all the time!

When you pray with all your heart, and you keep praying to Me, I will bless you. I will also bless your family, friends, church, and even your country. Ask My Holy Spirit to help you pray. And find other people who will pray with you. As you pray together, call upon Me with a humble heart. Ask Me to *heal your land.*

READ ON YOUR OWN

Colossians 1:16; 1 Timothy 1:17; Matthew 14:23

Your Soul's Best Friend

*God made the name of Christ greater than every
other name. God wants every knee to bow to Jesus—
everyone in heaven, on earth, and under the earth.*
—Philippians 2:9–10 ICB

*D*epend on Me and My strength. Always come to Me for help. Let your heart *be happy*—especially when you come to Me! Imagine two best friends. When one goes to visit the other, the friend doesn't open the door and just say, "Oh, it's you." And he doesn't look past his friend as if he were invisible and ask, "Did you bring anybody else with you?" Instead, they are thrilled to get to spend time together. You are *Mine*, and I am the best Friend of your soul. Be happy in the amazing Love I have for you! Rejoice and *glory in My holy Name*—it's holy because it stands for *Me*. My Name is *greater than every other name*, yet you can joyfully use it anytime in your prayers and worship.

You're blessed to be able to talk to Me so easily. Some people find glory in their wealth, their success, their beauty or fame. But I invite you to find glory in Me—your Savior, Lord, and Friend. Praising Me will give you strength and delight. It will bring Power to your prayers and Joy to your heart.

READ ON YOUR OWN

1 Chronicles 16:10–11; 2 Corinthians 11:2; John 15:13

The Joy of My Presence

*You have shown me the way of life, and you
will fill me with the joy of your presence.*
—Acts 2:28 NLT

When problems and plans about what to do fill your thoughts, turn to Me and whisper My Name, *Jesus*. Then let the Light of My Presence shine on you as you soak in *My unfailing Love*. Thank Me for always watching over you and loving you. Tell Me you trust Me and that you are Mine. Then ask *Me* what to do about your problems and plans. I'll help you sort out what needs to be done today—and what can wait. Yes, you should deal with the problems as they come along, but don't let worry or fear of what might happen next take over your mind.

Keep returning your thoughts to Me as often as you can, and I'll show you the world the way I see it. Fill your mind and heart with My Word—read it, study it, and memorize the verses that are most helpful to you. *My Word is a lamp to your feet and a Light for your path*.

If you follow these guidelines that I give you—to think about Me often and fill your life with My Word—you'll see your worries about problems and planning fade away. This will leave room in your life for more of *Me* and more of *the Joy of My Presence*.

READ ON YOUR OWN

Psalm 107:21–22; 1 Peter 5:7; Psalm 119:105

A Light in the Darkness

The Light shines in the darkness. And the
darkness has not overpowered the Light.
—John 1:5 ICB

I am the One who *gives light to your lamp. I brighten the darkness around you.* Sometimes, when you're *tired and have heavy
loads* to carry, you may feel as if the light of your lamp is about
to go out. It seems to be flickering and sputtering—almost out
of fuel. Whenever this happens, call on Me for help. Take some
deep breaths in My Presence, and remember that I'm the One
who keeps your lamp glowing. I am *your Strength*!

I am also your Light. Keep turning to Me, letting My Glory
soak into you. My shining beauty will brighten your life and
change how you see the world. When you turn away from Me
and forget that I am with you, your world looks very dark. It's
true that there is a lot of darkness in this world. But I am *the
Light that shines in the darkness.* So don't be afraid, My child.
Trust Me with all your heart—no matter how gloomy things
may look—and I will *turn your darkness into Light.*

READ ON YOUR OWN

Psalm 18:28; Matthew 11:28; Psalm 18:1

Let Me Set You Free

The fear of man is a snare, but the one
who trusts in the Lord is protected.
—Proverbs 29:25 HCSB

The fear of man is a snare. A snare is a kind of trap—something that tangles you up and makes it hard to escape. "Fear of man" is worrying too much about what other people think of you. This is both unhealthy and ungodly. It creates a kind of fear that can hurt and even destroy you. It's full of lies, because other people see you *through* the lens of their own sin and weakness. Besides, it's almost impossible to know what another person really thinks about you. When you see yourself through other people's eyes, you add your own mistaken ways of seeing things to theirs. As you struggle to be the person you think others want you to be, you get trapped—you're not able to be who *I* want you to be.

When "fear of man" starts controlling what you think and how you act, come to Me. I'll forgive you for trying to please other people instead of trying to please Me. Just ask. I'll help you break free from this trap you're caught in. Tell Me you trust Me, and then enjoy some time with Me. Forget about what others might or might not think of you. The more you focus on Me—the Lord who loves you—the freer you will be!

READ ON YOUR OWN

1 John 1:9; 2 Corinthians 3:17

Put Me First

In everything you do, put God first, and he will
direct you and crown your efforts with success.
—Proverbs 3:6 TLB

Come and rest with Me, dear one. I know that you have so much to do—homework and chores and practices and friends. But what you need most is to *be still* in My Presence. Take some deep breaths, and turn your eyes and your thoughts to Me. As you give Me your attention, let your worries roll off like water off a duck's back. This helps you relax and enjoy My nearness to you. I'm never far away!

Search for Me in the words of the Bible, and then think about those words. Let their grace and truth soak into the deepest parts of your soul. Let them pull you closer to Me. *My Word is alive and working* in your life and in this world. It can fill you with more life, more energy and strength.

When it's time to get back to all those things you need to do, bring Me those activities through prayer. Include Me in your plans. Ask Me to help you solve your problems. I'm an important part of everything you do, say, and think. Whisper My Name, and remember that I am near. *In everything you do, put Me first*—because I am the Lord of your life.

READ ON YOUR OWN

Psalm 46:10; Hebrews 4:12

I Make You an Overcomer

My dear children, you belong to God. So you have defeated them because God's Spirit, who is in you, is greater than the devil, who is in the world.
—1 John 4:4 ICB

I am training you to be an overcomer. This means you are learning to find Joy in the middle of a problem that would have defeated you in the past.

You can be an overcomer because of this one rock-solid fact: *I have overcome the world.* I have already won the biggest victory of all—the victory over sin and death! *You will still have trouble in this world.* So expect to face many hard times as you travel through this life. That's because you live on a planet that's always at war, and the devil—the enemy of your soul—never rests. But don't be afraid, because the One *who is in you is greater than the devil who is in the world.* This is a good reason to rejoice!

When you're in the middle of a tough problem, it's so very important to keep trusting Me. Whisper, "I trust You, Jesus" as often as you need to. I'm right beside you. Ask Me to help you learn from this trouble. Then look for the flowers of Joy that grow even in the soil of sadness and trouble. Feel My Presence with you; the sunlight of *My Face is shining upon you*, dear child.

READ ON YOUR OWN

John 16:33; Psalm 145:18; Numbers 6:25

August 11

My Ways and My Thoughts

"For as the heavens are higher than the earth, so are My ways higher than your ways, and My thoughts than your thoughts."
—Isaiah 55:9 NKJV

My Face is shining on you, loved one. Take time today to simply sit in My joyful Light. Try to get to know Me as I truly am. I'm always nearby, even closer than the air you're breathing. Staying aware of My Presence is a rich blessing. But the most important thing is to trust that I am with you no matter what's happening in your life, good or bad.

I am everywhere in the universe, all at the same time. And I'm bigger and more powerful than anything in the universe—I live beyond the limits of time or space. I am *the King that rules forever! I cannot be destroyed and cannot be seen. As the heavens are higher than the earth, so are My ways higher than your ways and My thoughts than your thoughts.* So don't expect to completely understand Me or My ways. When things don't go as you think they should, be willing to accept that *My wisdom and knowledge have no end! No one can understand My ways*, but they are always good!

Remember Job? He lost everything this world has to offer—his family, his riches, and his health. But he still *bowed down to the ground to worship Me.* I am greater than all your troubles!

READ ON YOUR OWN

1 Timothy 1:17; Romans 11:33 ICB; Job 1:20

Joyful Troubles

*You will have many kinds of troubles. But when these things
happen, you should be very happy. You know that these things
are testing your faith. And this will give you patience.*
—James 1:2–3 ICB

When you bump into huge boulders of trouble on your path through life, I don't want you to worry or give up. Instead, I want you to *be very happy*. That sounds impossible, but remember that My arms are wide open—ready to catch you, to calm you down, to help you do what seems impossible.

You *can* have Joy in the middle of the most puzzling problems because I am *God your Savior*, and I have already done the greatest miracle in your life, which is saving you from your sins. If you keep looking to Me, your risen Lord and King, your doubts and worries will be replaced by courage and strength. Even though you live on this earth, your soul already shares in My heavenly victory.

I have unlimited, endless Power, so "impossible things" are My specialty. I find Joy in them because they show My Glory so clearly. They also help you live the way I want you to: happily trusting in Me and depending on Me. So the next time you face something "impossible," turn to Me right away with hope in your heart, believing that I will help you. Admit that you can't handle it on your own, and hold tightly to Me. Trust Me and believe that *all things are possible with Me*!

READ ON YOUR OWN

Deuteronomy 33:27; Habakkuk 3:17–18; Matthew 19:26

You Are Free!

Those who are in Christ Jesus are not judged guilty.
—Romans 8:1 ICB

No matter how ashamed or guilty you're feeling because of a sin, remember that you are *not* being judged. Those who belong to Me, who know Me as their Savior, *are not judged guilty*. Just the opposite is true! In fact, you have already been judged "Not guilty!" in the courts of heaven.

I came to earth to set you free from sin. And I want to see you joyfully living in that freedom I bought for you on the cross. Learn to enjoy being guilt-free. Don't let yourself be dragged down by feelings of shame. This world is fallen—full of sin and evil—but *I have overcome the world*!

Thank Me for the grace I have poured out on you. And let your thankfulness encourage you to follow My will for you. The closer you live to Me, the easier it will be for you to understand how I want you to live—and the more your life will be filled with My Peace and Joy. Knowing Me personally will help you trust Me enough to feel My Peace even when you're surrounded by terrible troubles. And when your heart is *overflowing with thankfulness*, it has the wonderful "side effect" of giving you greater Joy. Beloved child, live free and be happy in My Presence!

READ ON YOUR OWN

John 8:36; John 16:33; Colossians 2:6–7

Wake Up Your Heart

Give me back the joy that comes when you save me.
Keep me strong by giving me a willing spirit.
—Psalm 51:12 ICB

When you admit your sins to Me with a humble heart, I gladly forgive you. But there's more: I *give you back the Joy* you had *when I first saved you. The salvation of your soul* is the source of *a Joy that cannot be explained*, and it is *full of Glory*! I want you to be forgiven and to live again in the wonderful excitement of being close to Me. I want to be first in your life—your *First Love*.

Keeping Me first in your heart takes work: All kinds of people and activities and things try to steal your attention each day. It's good that you have your favorite ways of spending time with Me, but there is also a danger in doing things the same way over and over again. It can become just another boring task that you feel you *have* to do. If this has happened, stop and try something new. Remember who I am: King of kings, Lord of lords, and Creator of this huge and awesome universe! Take extra time to worship and praise Me *before* you bring Me your other prayers and requests. This will wake up your heart to feel *My Glory* and the Joy of being with Me.

READ ON YOUR OWN

1 Peter 1:8–9; Revelation 2:4; John 17:24

True Peace

You, Lord, give true peace. You give peace to those who depend on you. You give peace to those who trust you.
—Isaiah 26:3 ICB

*Y*ou will seek Me and find Me when you search for Me with all *your heart.* What a wonderful mission! But it's also a challenging one. Spending time with Me and enjoying My Presence is a privilege given only to those who know I'm their Savior and Lord. To get the most out of being with Me, you need to seek Me with all your heart. But too often your heart is a tangled-up mess! Ask My Spirit to clear your heart and mind of all worries, lies, doubts, fears, and anything else that pulls you away from Me. He'll help untangle your thoughts, freeing you up *to search for Me with all your heart.*

I want you to look for Me not only in quiet times but when you're doing other things. Your amazing brain, which I created, is able to think about Me even when you're busy. Pray this simple prayer: "Jesus, help me remember You're with Me." Pray this over and over again, so that it plays like soft background music in your mind. And keep praying this as you think about other things. Because *when you depend on Me and trust Me, I give you Peace.*

READ ON YOUR OWN

Jeremiah 29:13; Psalm 112:7

A Child of the Light

In the past you were full of darkness, but now you are full of
light in the Lord. So live like children who belong to the light.
—Ephesians 5:8 ICB

I will bless My people with Peace. This promise from the Bible
is for everyone who trusts Me as their Savior. So when you're
feeling upset or worried, try praying, "Jesus, bless me with Your
Peace." This simple prayer will bring you into My Presence and
open up your heart to My help.

Peace and trust are wonderfully woven together in My
kingdom. The more you lean on Me in faith, the less afraid
you'll be. And if you are completely *trusting in Me*—without
doubting—you don't need to be *afraid of bad news*. Because I'm
both all-powerful *and* good, you can believe that this world isn't
spinning out of control. Yes, there's plenty of bad news, but I'm
not just sitting in heaven doing nothing. I'm always working,
even in the most terrible situations. I am always busy bringing
good out of evil.

My kingdom is about change: changing into good what the
devil meant for evil, and changing you to be more like Me. Join
Me in this important work. *Live as a child of the Light*. Together
we will bring others out of the darkness of their sins and into
the Light of My Presence.

READ ON YOUR OWN

Psalm 29:11; Psalm 112:7

I Chose You

Since God chose you to be the holy people he loves,
you must clothe yourselves with tenderhearted mercy,
kindness, humility, gentleness, and patience.
—Colossians 3:12 NLT

I chose you to be one of My *holy people* whom *I love.* I know you aren't perfect; I know you still sin and make mistakes. But you are *holy in My sight.* This is because I see you wearing the shining perfection of *My* righteousness from head to toe. As My follower, you are covered with My pure righteousness forever!

I love you very, very much. Let this life-changing truth soak deep into your heart, your mind, and your spirit. You are so much more than a son or daughter, a brother or sister, a student or friend. You are *beloved*—adored, My treasure! That is your true identity. When you look in the mirror, say to yourself, "I belong to Jesus. *I am my Beloved's.*" Repeat these words all through the day and just before you fall asleep.

Remembering that you are perfectly loved by Me, *the King of Glory*, will keep you standing on solid ground. Because you know who you are—My chosen child—you can love and serve the people around you. Have mercy on them. Be kind, humble, gentle, and patient with them. Yes, it will take work and practice, but My Spirit will help you. He lives inside you and loves to work through you, blessing you *and* those around you.

READ ON YOUR OWN

Ephesians 1:4; Songs of Songs 6:3; Psalm 24:10

I Will Lead You

He gives me new strength. For the good of
his name he leads me on paths that are right.
—Psalm 23:3 ICB

Are yesterday's failures dragging you down? Do you wish you could go back and do things differently? That happens to everyone, but the past is not something you can change. Yesterday's sins and mistakes cannot be undone. Even *I*—the eternal One who created time—respect the limits of time in your world. So don't waste energy worrying about the bad choices you've made. Instead, ask Me to forgive your sins and help you learn from your mistakes.

I hate to see My children weighed down by past failures. It's as if you're dragging heavy chains wrapped around your legs. When you're feeling this way, imagine Me cutting away those chains. After all, I came to set My children free from sin. When you look to Me for what you need, you are *truly free*!

Celebrate that I forgive you and give you a fresh start whenever you ask. Talk to Me about where you've messed up, and be ready to *learn from Me*. Let Me show you the changes I want you to make in how you live. If you'll trust Me, I'll *lead you on paths that are right*.

READ ON YOUR OWN

Matthew 11:28–29; John 8:36

A Joy-Filled Way to Live

"Everyone who hears these words of mine and puts them into practice is like a wise man who built his house on the rock."
—Matthew 7:24

Rejoice and be glad because you depend on Me. This will make you feel so safe!

Some people depend on themselves, on other people, or on the things in their life (like money or being popular) to help them feel safe. But they're building their lives on sand. When the storms of life come, they'll see how weak that foundation is—the "sand" they've been standing on will be washed right out from under them. On the other hand, when you depend on Me, you're building your life *on the Rock*. I am the foundation that's strong enough to keep you standing during any of life's storms.

But don't just depend on Me in stormy, troubled times. Depend on Me when the skies are clear and calm too. You'll need to practice every day, but relying on Me when everything is going great will prepare you for *whatever* lies ahead: blue skies or storms.

Relying on Me will also give you great Joy—because you'll need to keep talking to Me. This is an amazing honor and privilege that will give you strength. It will also encourage and guide you. When you pray, you will know you aren't alone. As you *walk in the Light of My Presence*, I will help you *rejoice in Me all day long*. Depending on Me is a Joy-filled way to live!

READ ON YOUR OWN

Psalm 89:15–16; 1 Thessalonians 5:16–17

You Are Safe in Me

*"On that day you will realize that I am in my Father,
and you are in me, and I am in you."*
—John 14:20

Find your safe place in Me. As this world you live in feels more and more scary, turn your attention to Me more and more often. Remember that I am with you at *all* times, and I have already won the most important victory of all—defeating sin and death. Because *I am in you and you are in Me*, you have an eternity of perfect, worry-free living waiting for you in heaven. There won't be even one moment of fear or stress in heaven. Instead, your worship of Me, *the King of Glory*, will fill you with Joy greater than you could ever imagine, forever and ever!

Let this *future hope*, this promise of heaven, give you strength and courage while you're living in this sinful, broken world. When something you've seen or heard or thought upsets you, bring those feelings to Me. Tell yourself that *I'm* the One who keeps you safe no matter what! If your mind starts whispering things like, "You're safe because of your money or your popularity or the stuff you own," stop and tell yourself: *"That's* not what makes me safe. Jesus makes me safe." Trust Me as you think about who I am—your Savior, your God, and your Friend forever. You are completely safe and secure in Me!

READ ON YOUR OWN

Psalm 24:7; Proverbs 23:18

My Love Never Changes

Jesus Christ is the same yesterday, today, and forever.
—Hebrews 13:8 NKJV

*P*ut your trust in Me, and you will find *My unfailing Love* shining on you, even in the middle of your hardest day. When you start to feel there's just no hope of things getting better, *decide* to trust Me. You'll probably have to make this decision over and over again. But remember who I am: the Creator of the universe, and your Savior, Lord, and Friend. You can count on Me because My Love for you never fails. It never runs out or fades away; it doesn't depend on how good or bad your behavior has been. Just as *I am the same yesterday, today, and forever*, so is My perfect Love for you—it never changes.

Lift up your prayers to Me and then wait in My Presence. Don't demand an answer, and don't pretend you have it all figured out and don't need Me. Worship Me while you wait for Me. As you do this, I'll change your heart and your thoughts, and I'll clear the road ahead of you. I won't let you see the whole future, but I will *show you the way* through this day—one step at a time. So trust Me with all your heart, My beloved child, because I'm taking wonderful care of you!

READ ON YOUR OWN

Psalm 143:8; Hebrews 1:1–2

I Am the Light

Here is the message we have heard from God and now tell to you: God is light, and in him there is no darkness at all.
—1 John 1:5 ICB

I am Light, and in Me there is no darkness at all. I am your God, and I'm perfect in every way. There's not one single speck of badness in Me. You live in a world where evil and ungodliness are everywhere. But don't forget: *I am the Light that shines in the darkness*! Nothing can put out, or even dim, the bursting brightness of My everlasting Light. Someday in heaven you will see My brilliance with your own eyes—and you will be filled to overflowing with incredible Joy. For now, though, you must *live by what you believe* about Me, *not by what you see* in this world.

When you are upset or afraid because of what's happening in the world or in your own life, grab hold of My hand and decide to trust Me. *Don't let evil defeat you. Defeat evil by doing good.* Remember that I am with you, and I've already beaten death and sin by dying on the cross and rising from the grave. *Nothing* can undo My awesome work! My actions have cut through the darkness so that My dazzling brightness could pour into your heart—and into the hearts of everyone who follows Me.

Spend time resting in My holy Light. My Face is shining on you. I'll chase away the darkness.

READ ON YOUR OWN

John 1:5; 2 Corinthians 5:7; Romans 12:21 ICB

August 23

Perfect and Complete

Let your patience show itself perfectly in what you do. Then you will be perfect and complete. You will have everything you need.
—James 1:4 ICB

When troubles *come at you from all sides*, think of them as a gift from Me. Don't waste your time and energy wishing things were different. Remind yourself that I am all-powerful and always loving—you are never without Me. Instead of drowning in all your problems, grab hold of My hand and trust Me to help you. Even though you can't handle your troubles by yourself, you and I *together* can handle anything! If you remember this when you have a problem, you can be joyful even in the middle of that problem!

You not only have My Presence with you, but you also have My Holy Spirit living inside you. He's ready to help at all times, so ask Him to—as often as you need to.

It's especially hard to wait for My answer when there's more than one problem to deal with. You need patience. This is why you need My Spirit: Patience is a gift He gives to everyone who believes in Me. *He* can help you be patient! Don't try to figure a way out of the struggle on your own, hoping it will be over quicker. Instead, keep waiting patiently for My perfect answer. This will make your faith *perfect and complete.*

READ ON YOUR OWN

James 1:2 MSG; Galatians 5:22–23; Romans 12:12

Rest with Me

And on the seventh day God ended His work which He had done, and He rested on the seventh day from all His work which He had done.
—Genesis 2:2 NKJV

Come to Me, My tired child, and *I will give you rest.* I know how very exhausted you are. Nothing in your life is hidden from Me. Yes, there is a time to push yourself to keep going, but there is also a time to rest. Even *I* rested on the seventh day after completing My work of creation—and I have endless energy!

Look for Me, and then just stay awhile in My loving Presence while I shine the warmth of My Love on you. Let favorite verses come to mind, bringing new life into your heart and spirit like fresh air flowing through an open window. If you suddenly remember something you don't want to forget—maybe something you need to do for school or for your parents—just scribble it down and then turn your attention back to Me. As you relax with Me, My Love will soak deep inside you. If you want to tell Me you love Me too, say so with whispers or out-loud words or songs.

I want you to know that I approve of you—and I approve of your rest. As you relax in My Presence, trust that you are loved and forgiven because of My work on the cross. Then both you *and* I will be renewed and refreshed.

READ ON YOUR OWN

Matthew 11:28; Numbers 6:25

I Live in You

*I do not live anymore—it is Christ living in me. I still
live in my body, but I live by faith in the Son of God.
He loved me and gave himself to save me.*
—Galatians 2:20 ICB

I live in you! These four words of truth change everything!
They make your life wonderfully better, both now and forever. Don't worry about whether or not you're a good home
for Me. I joyfully move into the heart of each and every one of
My followers—and then I patiently start working to "remodel"
what's inside. But I refuse to live in the hearts of those who
think they don't need Me or who believe they're already good
enough without Me. They are hypocrites and phonies. Such
people *are like tombs that are painted white. Outside, the tombs
look fine. But inside, they are full of the bones of dead people.*

As you think about the miraculous truth that *I am living in
you*, let your heart spill over with Joy! I'm not some short-term
visitor who stays only as long as you do what pleases Me. I have
come to live inside you forever. I warn you though: Sometimes
the changes I make can be painful. When My work in your heart
causes you to feel uncomfortable, hold even tighter to Me. *Live
by faith in Me*—the One who *loved you and gave Himself to save
you*. As you accept the changes I'm making, you'll become more
and more like the masterpiece I created you to be.

READ ON YOUR OWN

Matthew 23:27; Ephesians 2:10

Sing with Joy!

*Let them praise the L*ORD *for his great love and for the wonderful things he has done for them. Let them offer sacrifices of thanksgiving and sing joyfully about his glorious acts.*
—Psalm 107:21–22 NLT

No matter what's happening in your life, you can still *be joyful in Me* because I am *your Savior*. When the prophet Habakkuk wrote these words, his country was going to be invaded by the Babylonians—*a ruthless, feared, and dreaded people*. Yet even as he thought about this terrifying event, he was able to have Joy in His relationship with Me. This sort of Joy isn't natural—it's *super*natural. It's powered by the Holy Spirit, who lives inside all My followers.

Joy and thankfulness go together. *Praise Me for My great love and the wonderful things I have done. Sing joyfully* about My works. My Love for you will never let you down because I've already paid the whole price for your sins. Your salvation doesn't depend on you! The more you thank Me—for your salvation, for My Love, and for all My blessings—the more you'll see how blessed you really are. And a grateful heart will only make your Joy grow bigger. You can keep increasing your Joy by thanking Me in silent prayers, in written or spoken words, and with music. I love to hear you sing, so come to Me *with joyful songs!*

READ ON YOUR OWN

Habakkuk 3:18; Habakkuk 1:6–7; Psalm 100:2

Practice Waiting

*Why am I so sad? Why am I so upset? I should
put my hope in God. I should keep praising him.*
—Psalm 42:5 ICB

*I give strength to those who are tired; I give more power to those
who are weak.* So don't give up or be worried when you don't
feel strong. There are many different kinds of weakness, and
everyone is weak in some ways. In fact, I use weaknesses to
keep My loved ones humble, so that they'll remember they
need Me. I also use weaknesses to teach My children to wait on
Me in faith and hope. I have promised that those who wait on Me
and *trust Me will become strong again.*

This waiting isn't something to practice just every once in
a while. You need to practice it all the time. I created you to
depend on Me constantly, knowing that I am *the Living One who
sees you* always. Waiting on Me is closely connected to trusting Me. The more time you spend thinking about Me, the more
you will trust Me. And the more you trust Me, the more you'll
want to spend time with Me. Waiting on Me also makes your
hope in Me grow. This hope makes your life better in more ways
than you can count. It lifts you out of your troubles and lets you
praise Me for the help of My Presence.

READ ON YOUR OWN

Isaiah 40:29; Isaiah 40:30–31; Genesis 16:14

Wherever You Go

This God is our God for ever and ever;
he will be our guide even to the end.
—Psalm 48:14

I am with you and will watch over you wherever you go. A great and adventurous journey is just waiting for you, but you might be looking at it with both excitement and fear. In some ways you're eager to begin this new adventure. You're even expecting to find many good things along the way. But part of you is afraid of leaving your safe, comfortable life. When fearful thoughts try to take over, remind yourself that I will be watching over you all the time, wherever you are. I've promised you the comfort of My constant Presence—and I'll keep that promise forever!

The best thing you can do to get ready for the adventure ahead is to spend time with Me every day. Tell yourself over and over again, "Jesus is with me. He's taking good care of me." Imagine yourself holding My hand as we walk along together. Trust Me—Your Guide—to show you the way to go, one step at a time. I know the way perfectly, so don't worry about getting lost. Relax in My Presence, and enjoy the wonder of sharing your whole life with Me.

READ ON YOUR OWN

Genesis 28:15; Joshua 1:9

A Hidden Treasure

*"You will search for me. And when you search
for me with all your heart, you will find me!"*
—Jeremiah 29:13 ICB

The Light of My Presence shines on every moment of your life—past, present, and future. I knew you *before the creation of the world*, and *I have loved you with a Love that lasts forever.* You are never alone, so look for Me in everything that happens in your day. Search for Me as you would search for a hidden treasure. Try to "see" Me no matter what's going on. Don't let hard times, busy times, or even happy times keep you from finding Me.

Sometimes I let you know I'm with you in great and glorious ways that can't be missed. Other times, I show Myself in simple, quiet ways that only you can see. Ask Me to open your eyes and your heart to notice *all* the times and ways I speak to you.

As you go through this day, remind yourself to look for the Light of My Presence shining in your life. Don't think only about worldly worries or the things you need to do. Instead, think about *Me*; watch for the ways I'm with you in every moment. *Search for me. And when you search for me with all your heart, you will find me!*

READ ON YOUR OWN

Ephesians 1:4; Jeremiah 31:3 NLV; Psalm 89:15

Stand Strong!

That is why you need to get God's full armor. Then on the day of evil you will be able to stand strong. And when you have finished the whole fight, you will still be standing.
—Ephesians 6:13 ICB

I make you like a deer that does not stumble. I help you stand on the steep mountains.

I created deer with the ability to climb tall, steep mountains without stumbling—and to stand on those mountains without fear. And I created *you* to trust Me. That trust will give you strength to *walk on your high hills* of trouble.

It's so important to remember that you live in a world where your spiritual enemies never stop fighting against you. You have to stay alert and always be ready for battle. It's not a battle of swords but a battle of faith: Your enemies want to defeat and destroy your faith with lies and troubles and doubts.

Unlike the warriors of long ago who had servants to help them put on their armor, you must put on your own armor every day by praying and by studying My Word. No matter what happens, I want you to *be able to stand strong. And when you have finished the whole fight, you will still be standing.*

When you're in the middle of the battle, declare that you trust Me and that I'm there, helping you. You may sometimes feel as if you're losing the fight, but don't give up! To keep standing with Me in the middle of the battle—*this* is true victory!

READ ON YOUR OWN

2 Samuel 22:34; Habakkuk 3:19

Only One Thing

*"Don't store treasures for yourselves here on earth. Moths
and rust will destroy treasures here on earth. And thieves
can break into your house and steal the things you have."*
—Matthew 6:19 ICB

I am your Treasure. I am so much more valuable than anything you can see, hear, or touch. *Knowing Me* is the Prize that's greater than any other prize.

People pile up, insure, worry over, and hide the treasures of this earth to keep them safe. Yet the riches you have in Me can never be lost or stolen or ruined. In fact, the more you share Me with others, the more of My riches and blessings you'll get. And because I am unlimited, there will always be more of Me and My Treasure to discover—and to love.

Your world pulls you in so many different directions: School and sports, friends and family, church and hobbies all want your attention. And a lot of "stuff," even good stuff, gets in the way of enjoying time with Me. *You are worried and troubled about many things, but only one thing is needed*: Me! When you make Me that *one thing*, you choose a Treasure that *will never be taken away from you.*

Rejoice and be glad that I am always near. Knowing Me as your Savior, Lord, and Friend helps you see everything else in your life as it really is. I am the Treasure that will brighten every moment of your life!

READ ON YOUR OWN

Philippians 3:10; Luke 10:41–42

SEPTEMBER

You guide me with your advice.
And later you will receive me in honor.
I have no one in heaven but you.
I want nothing on earth besides you.

—Psalm 73:24–25 ICB

Feeling Weak? Don't Worry About It!

God, my strength, I will sing praises to you. God,
my defender, you are the God who loves me.
—Psalm 59:17 NCV

I am *your Strength*. I make you strong. This truth about Me is especially valuable on those days when you can't seem to do anything right—or almost can't keep going. Knowing that I'm your Strength is like always having a guide with you, showing you where to go, clearing away any dangers, and giving you the power to take the next step. *I hold your right hand*, and *I guide you with My advice*. Because I know absolutely everything there is to know, My advice is the best you could ever get. So don't worry about your weaknesses. They're teaching you to depend on Me. Trust that I am with you and that I will help you. This world isn't nearly as scary or dangerous when you realize you don't have to face it all by yourself.

I not only help in your weaknesses, I also use them to bring other people to Me. When you depend on Me to help you, My Light shines through you. Other people see *you* looking to Me, and they see *Me* making you strong. Let My Love and Light flow freely through you. And let them fill you with so much Joy that it spills over into the lives of those around you.

READ ON YOUR OWN

Psalm 73:23–24 ICB; 2 Corinthians 11:30; Romans 12:12

Listen and Love

"Do not come any closer," God said. "Take off your sandals,
for the place where you are standing is holy ground."
—Exodus 3:5

When people tell you their deepest secrets, worries, and fears, you are *on holy ground*. Be careful to listen to them in a loving way. Don't jump in with both feet and try to fix their problems for them. That dirties the holy ground. Some people will back away from you when you do this. Others are already so hurt and so wounded that they don't realize you've tried to take over. Either way, you have spoiled a wonderful chance to let Me work.

When you are on this sort of holy ground—holding someone's secrets in your hands—you need My Holy Spirit. Ask Him to guide your thoughts, to help you listen, and to help you love. As My Love shines through you, My healing Presence goes to work in the other person. And as you keep listening, the most important thing is to guide that person toward Me and My help.

If you treat others as I've taught you, both you and they will be blessed. They will feel *My unfailing Love* in their souls, and I will *show them the way they should go*. As you depend on Me to help you listen and love, My Spirit will flow through you like *streams of living water*. And I'll refresh your soul.

READ ON YOUR OWN

Psalm 143:8; John 7:38–39

Think About the Good Things

Think about the things that are good and worthy of praise.
Think about the things that are true and honorable
and right and pure and beautiful and respected.
—Philippians 4:8 ICB

*T*hink about the things that are good and worthy of praise. That may sound easy, but in this world it can actually be quite difficult. The people who report the news almost always aim their cameras at what is wrong. They rarely bother to report on all the many good things that are happening—*especially* the good things My people are doing.

Thinking positive thoughts is difficult because of this world's focus on the bad; also, it's the opposite of how you naturally think. Your mind is an amazing creation. But when Adam and Eve sinned against Me in the garden of Eden, everything on earth was hurt and damaged—even your mind. So trying to keep your thoughts on the best things doesn't come easily. You have to work at it all the time, choosing over and over again what your thoughts will be. Every second of every day, you must choose to look for what is good.

Yes, there are huge problems in this world, but there are also many, many things that are worthy of praise. And the One who is *most* worthy of praise is the One who's right beside you—Me! I'm even closer than your thoughts. Rejoice in *Me* and praise *Me*, My precious child!

READ ON YOUR OWN

Genesis 3:6; Proverbs 16:16; Psalm 73:23

A Way of Teaching You

*It is never fun to be corrected. In fact, at the time it
is always painful. But if we learn to obey by being
corrected, we will do right and live at peace.*
—Hebrews 12:11 CEV

I correct the people I love and discipline those I call My own. But My discipline isn't about punishment. It's a way of teaching you who you should be and how you should live. That's a goal that will take time to reach. Discipline isn't always pleasant. It can even be painful at times. So it's easy to feel that I've stopped loving you when I lead you down a rocky path. When hard times come, you have an important choice to make: Hold tightly to Me and trust that I'm doing what's best for you, or back away from Me and go your own way.

When you're able to see that My discipline is actually another way I show My Love for you, you can go through even the toughest times with Joy—just as some of My earliest disciples did. Peter was thrown into prison, and Paul was beaten, arrested, and shipwrecked. When you're struggling through a hard time, come to Me boldly—without fear. Ask Me to show you what I want you to learn and what I want you to change in your life. You can also ask Me to comfort you and cheer you up with My Love. Take time to rest in the Light of My loving Presence. As you look to Me, *the Light* of My Glory shines down on you!

READ ON YOUR OWN

Hebrews 12:6 CEV; Acts 5:41; 2 Corinthians 4:6

Sparkles of Joy

Let them give thanks to the Lᴏʀᴅ for his
unfailing love and his wonderful deeds for men.
—Psalm 107:8

Joy is a choice. There are a lot of things you can't control in your life, but you *can* control whether or not to be joyful. I made you *a little lower than the angels*, and I gave you an amazing mind. You can think things through and make choices and decisions. That ability gives you an important place in My kingdom. Your thoughts matter so much because it's *in* your thoughts that your feelings and actions begin. So make good choices about what you allow your mind to think.

Whenever you feel as if your Joy is gone, stop and remember these truths: *I am with you. I am watching over you* all the time. I love you with a perfect, *unfailing Love.* I have given you My Spirit, and this Holy Helper inside you has Power that is unlimited and unending. He can help you make sure that your thoughts agree with the truths of the Bible.

I'm always with you—that's a promise from My Word that you can count on. So look for *Me* and all the ways I'm working in your life. At first you may only see your problems. But keep looking until you see the Light of My Presence shining on those problems—and reflecting sparkles of Joy back to you.

READ ON YOUR OWN

Psalm 8:5; Genesis 28:15; Romans 8:9

I'm Taking Care of You

You give me a wide path on which to walk. My feet have not slipped.
—Psalm 18:36 ICB

I give you a wide path to walk on, so that your feet do not slip. I don't want you to think too much about what might happen in the future. And don't worry about whether or not you'll be able to handle it. Only *I* know what your future really holds. Only *I* totally understand what you are able to do. And finally, I am the One who can change your future—a little or a lot! In fact, I can widen the path you're walking on right now, pushing problems out of the way to make sure you don't stumble and fall.

I want you to understand how closely and lovingly I'm at work in your life. I love taking care of you, right down to all the details. I love "tweaking" and changing your situation, making it better for you and removing unneeded troubles. Remember that I am *a shield to all who trust Me*. Your job in this great life adventure is to trust Me. Walk with Me, talk with Me, and joyfully depend on Me. I won't remove every trouble, but I will widen the path you're on—to *bless you and keep you* from harm.

READ ON YOUR OWN

Psalm 18:30; Numbers 6:24

You Don't Have to Explain

*You know well everything I do. Lord, even before I say
a word, you already know what I am going to say.*
—Psalm 139:3–4 ICB

I have examined you, and I know all about you. I know well everything you do. Even before you say a word, I already know what
you are going to say. My dear child, you are *fully known*! I have
total knowledge of everything about you, even your most secret
thoughts and feelings. This truth could be terrifying—if you
were not My follower. But you *are* Mine, so you have nothing to
fear from Me. Because you have put your *faith in Me*, My perfect
righteousness is given to you, and it covers over all your sins.
You are a treasured member of My family!

My close relationship with you is a powerful cure for loneliness. Whenever you feel alone or afraid, talk to Me. Yes, I
hear your silent prayers, but whispering your prayers or saying them out loud can help you think more clearly. Because I
understand you perfectly, you don't have to explain things to
Me. You can just jump right in and ask Me to help you in this very
moment. Then spend a little while relaxing with Me, breathing
in *the Joy of My Presence*.

READ ON YOUR OWN

Psalm 139:1–2; 1 Corinthians 13:12;
Romans 3:22; Psalm 21:6

Helping You Destroy the Lies

We capture every thought and make it give up and obey Christ.
—2 Corinthians 10:5 ICB

While you wait with Me, spending time with me, I am giving you *a new way of thinking.* As the Light of My Presence shines into your mind, darkness runs away and lies are destroyed. However, there are many little places in your mind where those lies and old ways of thinking try to hide. My Spirit can search out and destroy those enemies, but you have to let Him.

Old ways of thinking don't die easily. When the Spirit's Light shines on a thought that could hurt you—like *you're not good enough for Me,* or *I don't really love you*—capture it by writing it down. Then show it to Me. Let's look at it together. I'll help you see the lies and replace them with My truth. I'll remind you: *You don't have to earn My Love. I'll always love you.*

The more you concentrate on Me and My Word, the more you can break free from hurtful, lying thoughts. Many of them were born in your mind when something really painful happened to you—or was said to you. You may have to capture the same lie many times before you can get rid of it completely. But all that work leads to a wonderful result: You'll be able to live free from that lie and find Joy in My truth.

READ ON YOUR OWN

Psalm 130:5; Romans 12:2; John 8:12

Let Me Show You Wonderful Things

"Call to Me, and I will answer you,
and show you great and mighty things."
—Jeremiah 33:3 NKJV

Your prayers are not useless cries in the dark. They rise up to My kingdom of Light, and I hear every one. *Call to Me, and I will answer you and show you great and mighty things.*

From the very beginning, mankind has struggled with eyes that don't see what's really important. So often, people don't even notice what's right in front of them. I can do the most amazing miracles right before their eyes, yet they treat My wonderful work as if they've seen it before. Or they call what I've done "a coincidence," "chance," or "luck." Only *the eyes of your heart* can see the reality of what I'm doing in this world.

When you come to Me, excited and ready to learn *great things* you've never heard before, then I rejoice! A good teacher enjoys seeing a student put extra work into discovering new things. In the same way, I love when you want to learn from Me. Being open to My teaching will help you understand *the hope* of heaven that *I have chosen to give you.* And you'll begin to see that *the blessings* I've promised to share with you *are rich and glorious.* You can look forward to living in heaven with Me. There is never any darkness in heaven because *the Glory of God is its Light.*

READ ON YOUR OWN

Ephesians 1:18; Psalm 143:10; Revelation 21:23

I Am the True Light

*The true Light was coming into the world.
The true Light gives light to all.*
—John 1:9 ICB

As the world becomes darker and filled with more evil, remember that *you are the light of the world.* Don't waste your time or energy being upset about things you can't control. Pray about those things, but don't let them drag you down. Instead, focus on doing what you can to brighten the place where I've put you. Use your time and your talents to push away the darkness. Shine *My* Light into the world!

I am *the true Light that shines on*—even in the most terrible conditions and situations. Your light starts with Me. It travels through you and then shines on to others. I created you to *reflect My Glory* and perfection. You do this best when you become more and more like the person I designed you to be.

Spend plenty of time with Me. Think about My Presence, which is always with you. And learn My Word, which will help you grow and understand how I want you to live. The time you spend with Me will feed your soul. It will comfort and encourage you. And through it, I'll not only give you strength, I'll also help you make others strong.

READ ON YOUR OWN

Matthew 5:14; John 1:5; 2 Corinthians 3:18

September 11

There Is No Unsafe Place

Control yourselves and be careful! The devil is your enemy. And he goes around like a roaring lion looking for someone to eat.
—1 Peter 5:8 ICB

You've probably heard the word *terrorist* on the news. Some people are saying—and feeling—that no place is really safe from terrorists. In one way, that's true. Evil people are cruel, and no one knows exactly what they're going to do, or where. But for you and for all My believers, the truth is this: There is really no place that is *unsafe*. Your true home is in heaven, and that's *an inheritance*—a lasting gift from Me—that no one can steal from you. It will never *be destroyed or be spoiled or lose its beauty*. Remember that I am Ruler over everything, including your life and the ones you love. Nothing can happen to you—or to them—except for what I let happen. Yes, there will be times when that's very hard for you to understand, but I promise to do only what's best for you.

The world you live in has been at war ever since Adam and Eve first sinned. The Fall in the garden of Eden made the earth a dangerous place where good and evil constantly battle each other. So you must *control yourself and be careful*. The devil is your worst enemy, but remember: I've already defeated him! *I have defeated the world!* And because you're My child, you're on the winning side—*My* side. With Me, *you can have Peace*. With Me, you are always safe.

READ ON YOUR OWN

1 Peter 1:3–4; Psalm 71:6; John 16:33 ICB

I'm in Control of Your Life

*This is the day the L*ORD *has made; we will rejoice and be glad in it.*
—Psalm 118:24 NKJV

*Y**our life is in My hands.* So *trust Me*, dear one. I'm training you to feel safe, even when everything around you is changing. It can actually be a relief to know you aren't in control of your life. When you accept that I'm the Ruler of all things and you choose to rest in My Power, then you're set free from worry and fear.

I'm not telling you to just accept whatever happens. And I'm not telling you to stop trying to make things better. I do want you to use the energy and abilities that I gave you, but do it with prayer. Pray about everything, and watch for Me in every moment. I am a God of surprises—look for Me in unexpected places.

I want you to *rejoice in this day that I have made.* Ask Me to take charge of every detail and event that will be part of it. Because I'm in control of your life, you don't have to worry about making things happen faster. Rushing and worry go hand in hand, and I've told you not to worry. If you let *Me* choose when things happen, I'll bless you *with a peace so great that you cannot understand it.*

READ ON YOUR OWN

Psalm 31:14–15; Philippians 4:6–7

September 13

I Am Watching Over You

"I am with you and will keep you wherever you go."
—Genesis 28:15 NKJV

Your life is a precious gift from Me. Open your hands and your heart to live in this day with Joy. I am your Savior and your Friend, but remember, I am also your Creator and God: *All things were created by Me.* As you go through this day that I'm giving you, look for signs of My Presence in it. *I am with you* and *watching over you* all the time.

On bright, joyful days, tell Me about all My wonderful gifts to you. As you thank Me for them, your Joy will grow. On dark and difficult days, hold tightly to My hand, trusting Me. *I will help you*, beloved child.

Your body and your physical life are amazing gifts. But your spiritual life is an even greater treasure that no amount of money can buy! People who don't know Me as their Savior will spend all of eternity separated from Me, and it will be terrible for them. But because you belong to Me, you'll live *with* Me forever. I'll give you a new body—one that will never get sick or tired.

I have saved you *by grace because you believe*. Let your thankfulness for this wonderful gift fill you with overflowing Joy!

READ ON YOUR OWN

Colossians 1:16; Isaiah 41:13; Ephesians 2:8

I Live to Help You

So be humble under God's powerful hand. Then he
will lift you up when the right time comes. Give all
your worries to him, because he cares for you.
—1 Peter 5:6–7 ICB

When a problem goes on and on and on, it can actually become an idol in your life. This happens when you start thinking about the problem more than Me. If you have a trouble that just won't go away, it's more important than ever to guard and protect your mind, being careful what you think about. If you don't, that problem can take up more and more of your thoughts—until it takes over and fills your mind with dark, ugly shadows! When you realize this has happened, tell Me. Pour out your feelings to Me as you try to get rid of those thoughts. Admit that you can't do this by yourself—that you need My help. *Humble yourself under My powerful hand.*

When a problem takes over your thoughts, it makes you worry. So please, *give all your worries to Me*, trusting that *I care for you*. You may have to do this over and over again—even thousands of times a day—but don't give up! Each time you give Me your worries, you're taking your thoughts off your problems and thinking about Me instead. And you'll think about Me even more as you thank Me for loving you so much. Remember that I not only died to save you from your sins, but *I live to help those who come to Me.*

READ ON YOUR OWN

1 John 5:21; Hebrews 7:25

The Tangled-Up Places

Be glad that you are his. Let those who ask the Lord for help be happy.
Depend on the Lord and his strength. Always go to him for help.
—1 Chronicles 16:10–11 ICB

When your life feels like it's all tangled up, I can smooth out those knotted places—even the ones in your heart and mind. So come to Me just as you are, with all your twisted-up problems and loose ends.

So many of your troubles are made worse by other people's problems! It's sometimes hard to sort out how much of the mess is yours and how much is theirs. Be willing to admit your own mistakes and sins, but also know this: The mistakes and sins of others are not your fault. I'm here to help you untangle all your troubles and find the best way through them.

Being a Christian is all about changing, and these changes happen throughout your entire life. Some of the knots from your past are hard to untie, especially when they've been made by people who keep on hurting you. Don't get stuck thinking about the past or trying to figure out how to fix things. Instead, keep turning to Me, asking for My help, and searching for My will. Wait with Me. Trust My timing. I will untangle those knots and smooth out your way. Be willing to live with problems that aren't fixed yet, but don't let them worry you. My Presence with you, right in this very moment, is My gift to you—an endless and wonderful blessing.

READ ON YOUR OWN

2 Corinthians 3:18; Lamentations 3:24

A Way of Life

Come into his city with songs of thanksgiving. Come into his courtyards with songs of praise. Thank him, and praise his name.
—Psalm 100:4 ICB

*C*ontinue praying and keep alert. And when you pray, always *thank Me*. I want you to make praying a way of life. Prayer is how you stay connected to Me. But it's not always easy. The devil hates your love for Me. His servants are hard at work trying to weaken your prayers or stop them altogether. So keep praying! Don't let the devil stop you from staying in touch with Me.

You can train yourself to call on Me in prayer, even while you're busy doing other things. Prayer invites Me into your world, helps you do your work better, and adds extra Joy to your life. Praying while you do other things is good, but it's also important to set aside time just to talk with Me. This isn't easy in your busy world! To really pray well, you need an alert mind that pays attention. You also need a thankful heart. Ask My Spirit, *the Helper*, to give power to your prayers, making you more alert and more thankful as you pray.

A mind that's wide-awake and a heart that's glad will not only help you pray better, they'll also help you live better. Always *give thanks to Me and praise My Name*.

READ ON YOUR OWN

Colossians 4:2 ICB; John 15:26

"Fear" of Me

The fear of the LORD is the beginning of knowledge,
but fools despise wisdom and instruction.
—Proverbs 1:7 NKJV

I am pleased with those who fear Me, who trust in My Love. "Fear" of Me can be a difficult thing to understand. It isn't being afraid that I'll harm you. Instead, it means to be in awe of Me, to respect My Power, to adore Me and follow My will for your life. *This* is where real wisdom begins.

The way you follow My will is to replace *your* thoughts and goals with *Mine*. This is the best way to live, because I created you and I know what's best for you. When your life shows that you "fear" Me, it pleases Me—you can feel My Joy shining on you.

Living by My will isn't easy. There will be lots of ups and downs on our journey together. But no matter what's happening, you can trust My unfailing Love. It will give you hope for the future. In your world today, many people are worried and afraid, and they feel there's no hope. They've trusted in the things of this world—and they've been let down. So they don't want to count on anyone or anything. But My Love will never let you down—it will never let go of you! Hold tight to My Hope, child. It's like a precious, golden rope that keeps you close to Me.

READ ON YOUR OWN

Psalm 147:11 ICB; Lamentations 3:22–23

Fill Your Day with Joy

*In the beginning was the Word, and the Word was with God,
and the Word was God. He was with God in the beginning.*
—John 1:1–2

If you want to fill your day with even more Joy, try to be more aware of the fact that I am always with you. An easy way to do this is to say: "Thank You, Jesus, for being with me." This is such a short, simple prayer that you can pray it as often as you want. These few, short words not only praise Me, but they also connect you to Me in a beautiful way. You don't have to *feel* Me near you in order to pray this way. But the more you thank Me for being with you, the more real I'll become to you. The truth is that *you live and move and exist* only because of Me. I want you to believe this in your heart, mind, and spirit.

You also grow more aware of Me when you look for signs of My Presence in your world. The wonders of nature and the blessings of loved ones all point to Me. I am also waiting for you in My Word, because I am the living Word. Ask My Spirit to show you what the words of the Bible mean. He will shine His Light in your heart and help you see the Glory of My Presence, which is always with you.

READ ON YOUR OWN

Acts 17:28; 2 Corinthians 4:6

Remember Me

I am very sad. So I remember you.
—Psalm 42:6 ICB

When you are feeling sad, the best cure is to *remember Me.* Think about who I am—*your Lord and your God*, your Savior and your Shepherd, the Friend who *will never leave you.* I know everything that's happening in your life, as well as all that you are thinking and feeling. You are so precious to Me that everything about you is important to Me. Remember all the ways I have taken care of you and helped you. Thank Me for each one that you can think of, and then relax in My loving Presence.

Tell Me about the things that are dragging you down. Yes, I already know all about them, but telling Me will take away some of that heavy load of sadness you've been carrying. In the Light of My Presence, you'll be able to see things more clearly. Together, you and I can figure out what's important and what's not. And as you spend time with Me, I'll shine down on you—blessing you, encouraging you, and comforting you. I promise you that this sadness will end, and soon you'll once *again be praising Me for the help of My Presence.*

READ ON YOUR OWN

John 20:28; Deuteronomy 31:8; Psalm 42:5

I Am Slow to Get Angry

The LORD is merciful and compassionate, slow to get angry and filled with unfailing love. The LORD is good to everyone. He showers compassion on all his creation.
—Psalm 145:8–9 NLT

I am merciful and compassionate, slow to get angry and filled with unfailing Love. Explore these wonders of My grace! My Love and blessings are poured out on you because of My finished work on the cross, where I died for your sins. Remember that *you have been saved by grace because you believe. You did not save yourself. It was a gift from Me.* And that's not all! *My* mercies—My compassions and care—*never stop. They are new every morning.* So begin your day expecting Me to give you fresh mercies and compassion. Every morning begins another day. Don't let yesterday's mistakes and failures keep you down. Learn from your mistakes and confess the sins you know about, but don't let them be *all* you think about. Instead, think about Me, My Love, and My blessings.

I am *slow to get angry.* So don't be too quick to judge yourself—or anyone else. Instead, be glad that I am *filled with unfailing Love.* In fact, Love is who and what I am. Your faith grows as you learn to give Me more and more of your attention and enjoy My loving Presence in your life. This will take work because the devil hates your being close to Me. Stay alert, and remember: Because you belong to Me, you *are not judged guilty*!

READ ON YOUR OWN

Ephesians 2:8; Lamentations 3:22–23; Romans 8:1

Thinking About You

*How precious it is, Lord, to realize
that you are thinking about me constantly!*
—Psalm 139:17 TLB

*C*ome to Me, and rest in My Presence. I'm *thinking about you constantly*, and I want you to think about *Me* more and more. Knowing that My Presence is with you can *give you rest* even when you're very busy. A sweet peace flows through you whenever you remember that *I am with you always*. Being sure of this also fills your heart, mind, and spirit with deep Joy.

Many of My children spend too much time thinking about the problems in their lives and in this world. When they hear about the terrible things that *might* happen, they lose their Joy—it gets buried under layer after layer of worry and fear. If you see that this has happened in your life, bring all those worries and fears to Me. Talk to Me about each one, so I can help you and guide you. Ask Me to take away those layers that have buried your Joy. As you trust Me to take care of all your worries and fears, your Joy will bloom again. Encourage that Joy to grow by speaking or singing praises to Me. Praise Me, *the King of Glory* who loves you all the time—forever.

READ ON YOUR OWN

Matthew 11:28; Matthew 28:20; Psalm 24:7

I Can Meet All Your Needs

*For since the world began, no ear has heard and no eye has
seen a God like you, who works for those who wait for him!*
—Isaiah 64:4 NLT

Don't worry about your weaknesses. Don't worry about
those things you can't do well. Instead, accept this truth:
You often need My help. In fact, it's those weaknesses that perfectly connect you to My endless Strength.

When you don't seem to have what you think you need,
you usually worry. That's how most humans react. But don't
do it! Stop your worrying by admitting, "I can't do it by myself,
Jesus"—and then thank Me for that weakness. Yes, thank Me! It
will free you from trying to be what you can never be: your own
Savior. Because you are weak and sinful, you need a Savior who
is strong and perfect—who can *meet all your needs*. You need Me!

Whether you are being quiet and still, or active and on the
go, you can be filled with My Strength. Being still with Me—
spending time alone with Me—makes our connection deeper
and stronger. *I work for those who wait for Me*, doing for you the
things you can't do for yourself. But there are many things you
can do. As you go through your day, doing what you can, depend
on *the strength I give you*. This glorifies Me and blesses you.

The next time you feel you just can't do something, turn to
Me right away. I'll be right there to meet you—with My Strength
and My Love.

READ ON YOUR OWN

Philippians 4:19; 1 Peter 4:11

Let Me Comfort You

"The mountains may disappear, and the hills may come to an end. But my love will never disappear. My promise of peace will not come to an end," says the Lord who shows mercy to you.
—Isaiah 54:10 ICB

I will not break a crushed blade of grass. I will not put out even a weak flame. I know that sometimes you feel as helpless as a crushed blade of grass and as weak as a flickering candle flame. And that's okay. Let your weakness help you open up to Me, dear child. Don't hold anything back—you can tell Me everything you're thinking and feeling because I understand you perfectly. As you tell Me your troubles, I will refresh you as if you jumped into a pool on a hot summer's day. I will also give you a *Peace so great you cannot understand it.* Instead of trying to figure everything out on your own, *lean on Me* and rest for a while. Just trust that I'm taking care of you—watching over you and working for you.

I *am* working to heal your hurts, and that happens best when you are resting in Me. *The mountains may disappear, and the hills may come to an end. But My love will never disappear. My promise of Peace will not come to an end. I will show mercy to you.* Whenever you're feeling weak, or hurt, or wounded, come to Me. Let Me comfort you and cover you with My endless Love and Peace.

READ ON YOUR OWN

Isaiah 42:3; Philippians 4:6–7; Proverbs 3:5

A Letter from Me

"I will send you the Helper from the Father. He is the Spirit of truth who comes from the Father. When he comes, he will tell about me."
—John 15:26 ICB

*Y*ou are a letter from Me. This letter is not written with ink, but with the Spirit of the living God. It is not written on stone tablets. It is written on your heart. Because you are one of My followers, the Holy Spirit lives in you. He gives you the ability and the power to do far more than you could ever do on your own. So don't be frightened by challenges or tough times. The Spirit—the third Person of the Trinity—lives *inside* you! Just think about what that means. You can do so much more than you think you can when you walk with Me and ask My *Helper* to give you strength for every step.

The Spirit writes on your heart, which makes it look more and more like *My* heart. This not only blesses you, but it also helps others want to know Me. When you're with people who don't know Me, My Spirit makes you a living letter to them—*from Me*. One of the shortest but best prayers is: "Help me, Holy Spirit." Use this prayer as often as you need to. Invite the Spirit to make the truths of My Word come alive through you.

READ ON YOUR OWN

2 Corinthians 3:3; Romans 8:9

Live in Peace

Always be willing to listen and slow to speak.
Do not become angry easily.
—James 1:19 ICB

*D*o your best to live in peace with everyone. At times there will be someone who stands against you or wants to pick a fight—for no good reason! If that's what happened, you aren't responsible for the problem. But often you really *did* add to the fight with something you said or did. When this is true, admit what you did and tell Me you're sorry for your part in the trouble. Then go to that person and try to make peace. Whether you did anything wrong or not, you need to forgive the person who hurt you. You may also need to forgive yourself for your part in the mess.

Dear child, *always be willing to listen and slow to speak. Do not become angry easily.* Take time—not only to think through what you should say, but to *listen* to the other person. If you listen carefully and wait a moment before you answer, you'll be much less likely to get angry in the first place.

When you haven't lived at peace with someone and it's partly your fault, don't give up hope. I paid the price for *all* your sins so that you can have Peace with Me—now and forever.

READ ON YOUR OWN

Romans 12:18; Romans 5:1

Loose Ends

Praise the Lord for the glory of his name.
Worship the Lord because he is holy.
—Psalm 29:2 ICB

Don't be surprised by the many loose ends in your life—those problems that never completely go away. Loose ends will always be part of living on this sinful, fallen planet. When I created Adam and Eve, I placed them in a perfect world: the garden of Eden. Because you came from them, it's only natural for you to wish for a world like they had. It's also *super*natural. That's because you're My follower, and your forever home is heaven—a more wonderful and amazing place than anything you could ever imagine! Your wishes for a perfect world will be answered there.

Whenever loose ends start to drag you down, look up to Me. Remember that I am the Perfect One, and I'm always with you. Tell Me your troubles so I can help you with them. Ask Me to guide you about what's important and what's not—I will show you what I want for your life. Just take time to rest with Me in My Presence and worship Me. Praising Me takes your thoughts off this troubled world and all its loose ends—and puts them on Me and My Glory. And while you're worshiping Me, you get a taste of My Glory.

READ ON YOUR OWN

Genesis 2:15; Psalm 73:23–24

The Gift of Me

"For God so loved the world that he gave his one and only Son, that whoever who believes in him will not perish but have eternal life."
—John 3:16

To all who accept Me and believe in Me I give the right to become children of God. Accepting Me and believing in Me are closely connected. To accept a gift, you must open your hands and your heart to the one giving it—and the gift I'm giving you is the best you could ever imagine: Me! When you accept Me as your Savior and God, you can believe that My gift of never-ending Life is real—and that it's for you.

Being a child of God is too wonderful to explain. I am both your Savior *and* your Friend who is always with you. As you travel through life in this dark world, I'm with you every step of the way. I not only give Light to your path, but I also fill your mind and heart with My Light. And I love to give you Joy, both now and forever. One day, even your brightest, happiest moment on earth will look dark when you compare it to the glorious Light of heaven! Because there you'll *see My Face* in all its shining Glory and you'll *be filled full* with My limitless Love.

READ ON YOUR OWN

John 1:10–12; Psalm 17:15 CEB

Wrestling with Fear

*There will never be night again. They will not need the light
of a lamp or the light of the sun. The Lord God will give them
light. And they will rule like kings forever and ever.*
—Revelation 22:5 ICB

When your world looks dark and dangerous, *pour out your
heart to Me*. Tell Me everything. I *will* listen, and I *do* care.
I am Ruler over all things—let that truth comfort you. Even
when the world looks terribly out of control, I am in control.
Yes, there are many things that are *not* as they should be and
not as I created them to be. It's good for you to dream of a perfect goodness—and someday, in heaven, those dreams will all
come true.

Think about the prophet Habakkuk. The Lord told him that
his land was about to be invaded by its enemies, the Babylonians.
He knew the attack would be horrible, and this knowledge upset
him deeply. Yet he wrote a song to Me, to say that he trusted Me
completely. His song ended with these words: *"But I will still be
glad in the Lord. I will rejoice in God my Savior."*

It's okay to wrestle with Me about your worries and fears.
But remember the point of that wrestling is for your trust in Me
to win out over everything that's upsetting you. Let Me fill you
with a Joy greater than your fears. You won't understand the
mysterious ways I work, but you can come to Me to find hope
and help. *I will give you Strength!*

READ ON YOUR OWN

Psalm 62:8; Habakkuk 3:17–19; Psalm 42:5

Your First Goal

We make it our goal to please him, whether
we are at home in the body or away from it.
—2 Corinthians 5:9–3

If your first goal in life is to please yourself, you'll be frustrated and upset most of the time. The belief that everything should go your way is based on a lie. What's the lie? That *you* are the center of your world and everything circles around you. The truth is that *I* am the Center, and everything circles around Me. So go ahead and make your plans, but be prepared to change them when you come and ask Me what I want for you. Then, if things go the way you planned, be happy and thank Me. But if things *don't* go the way you wanted, talk to Me about it and be ready to accept My will instead of yours.

Remember that you belong to Me, dear child. *You are not your own.* Knowing that you are Mine can be a great relief. It takes your thoughts off yourself and what you want. Instead of trying so hard to get your own way, your first goal should be to please Me. You might think this would be a burden, but actually, *the work that I ask you to accept is easy. The load I give you to carry is not heavy.* Just knowing that you belong to Me will give you deep and joyful *rest for your soul.*

READ ON YOUR OWN

Psalm 105:4; 1 Corinthians 6:19; Matthew 11:29–30

Knowing Me

God once said, "Let the light shine out of the darkness!" And this is the same God who made his light shine in our hearts. He gave us light by letting us know the glory of God that is in the face of Christ.
—2 Corinthians 4:6 ICB

The richest treasure I offer you is *the Light of the good news— the good news about Me*. This Light is what makes the gospel such amazingly wonderful news. Because it lights up the way to Me!

When you trust Me as your Savior, I set your feet on the path that leads to heaven. Being forgiven of your sins and given a future in heaven are fantastic blessings, but I have even more to send your way. I've *made My Light shine in your heart*. So *search for Me* with all your heart. When you find Me, you'll also find great Joy in knowing that you're in My Presence.

"Knowing" is a very important word. It means to be aware of something because of what you've gone through, what you've learned, what you've discovered, or what you've seen. So knowing Me means that you are *aware* of Me—that you've discovered Me and felt My Presence with you. It also means you've seen Me. Not My physical body, but the way I work in your life and in your world. *The devil who rules this world has blinded the minds of those who do not believe*, which keeps them from seeing or knowing Me. But *you* can know Me as you see My glorious Light shining in your life!

READ ON YOUR OWN

2 Corinthians 4:4; Psalm 27:8

OCTOBER

The LORD's unfailing love surrounds
the man who trusts in him.

—Psalm 32:10

Take Time to Rest

He makes me lie down in green pastures, he leads
me beside quiet waters, he restores my soul.
—Psalm 23:2–3

I want you to relax and enjoy this day. It's easy to focus so much on the things you want to get done that you push yourself too hard—and forget to rest. You judge yourself and decide how good a day you've had based on how much you've gotten done—schoolwork and practice, time with friends and family, chores. There's definitely a time and place for all those things. And I do want you to use the abilities and the hours I've given you. But I also want you to understand that it's okay to rest. In fact, it's important.

Rest in knowing that you're a child of God, *saved by grace because you believe* in Me. This is who you really are! You are a prince or princess in My heavenly kingdom.

Remembering you are Mine will help you balance your times of resting and busyness. Knowing that you're My child helps you understand that you're loved because of who you are, not what you do. And when you take time to rest, you'll do better work for My kingdom. I'll wake up your mind, and you'll be able to think more clearly—and more like Me. A rested soul is kinder and more loving to others. So spend time with Me, and let Me *lead you beside quiet waters* of rest.

READ ON YOUR OWN

Genesis 2:2–3; Ephesians 2:8 ICB

My Truth

Come, let's sing for joy to the Lord. Let's
shout praises to the Rock who saves us.
—Psalm 95:1 ICB

I will judge the world with fairness and the nations with truth. This promise is full of blessing and encouragement for you. It means that someday all evil will be judged. My perfect justice will finally—and forever—win!

You have nothing to fear from My judgment because you're My follower and you are clothed in My perfect righteousness. But those who won't trust Me as their Savior have *everything* to fear. Someday time will run out, and they won't have another chance to put their faith in Me. On that day, My anger and justice will be terrifying for everyone who doesn't believe. They will be so scared that they'll even *call to the mountains and rocks, "Fall on us. Hide us from the face of the One who sits on the throne. Hide us from the anger of the Lamb!"*

I will judge everyone by My truth. Many people in this world refuse to believe that there is one truth—*My* truth—but it's a rock-solid fact. One day everyone will be judged by My truth, whether they believe in it or not. For you and for all believers, My truth is like a rock that you can build your life on—working, playing, and praising Me. And that's a very good reason to *sing for Joy*!

READ ON YOUR OWN

Psalm 96:13 ICB; Isaiah 61:10; Revelation 6:16 ICB

I Am God with You

"The virgin will be with child and will give birth to a son, and they will call him Immanuel"—which means, "God with us."
—Matthew 1:23

*N*o one can explain the things I decide. No one can understand *My ways.* That's why trusting Me is always your best answer when you don't understand what I'm doing in your life. My *wisdom and knowledge* are too great, too deep, for Me to explain to you. This shouldn't surprise you. After all, I have no limits of any kind—no beginning and no end. *I have always been, and I will always be.*

I am also *the Word who became a man and lived among you.* I became completely human: I had a human body and died a terrible death to save those sinners who believe in Me. I served people with My life *and* My death. Both prove that you can trust Me, even when you don't understand My ways.

You can have great Joy because your loving Savior and ruling Lord is wiser than wise! And you can come close to Me at any time by tenderly whispering My Name. I stay so close by your side that I can always hear you: now and tomorrow and forever. I am *Immanuel—God with you*—and I will never leave you.

READ ON YOUR OWN

Romans 11:33 ICB; Psalm 90:2 ICB; John 1:14 ICB

No Fear

Where God's love is, there is no fear, because God's perfect love takes away fear. It is punishment that makes a person fear. So love is not made perfect in the person who has fear.
—1 John 4:18 ICB

Do not let your fear of mistakes keep you from trying things or make you worry about what might happen. In this life you *will* make mistakes sometimes. You're human, after all; you only know and understand so much. When you have a big decision to make, find out all you can about it. Also, come to Me for help. I'll *guide you with my advice* as you think things through with Me. When the time is right, go ahead and make the best choice you can, even though you don't know how everything will turn out. Pray that what I want will be done. Then leave the rest to Me.

It is punishment that makes a person fear. If you've ever been punished for something you didn't do, or punished too hard for a little mistake, it's natural for you to be afraid of making more mistakes. When you're faced with a choice, worry can cloud your thinking, even causing you to freeze up. The cure is to remember that *I am with you* and completely on your side. You don't have to worry about doing things well enough for Me to keep loving you. Absolutely nothing—not even your very worst mistake—*can separate you from My Love*!

READ ON YOUR OWN

Psalm 27:8; Psalm 73:23–24 ICB; Romans 8:38–39

Don't Be Afraid of Bad News

*The Lord God is coming with power. He will
use his power to rule all the people.*
—Isaiah 40:10 ICB

I don't want you to *be afraid of bad news*. The only way to keep out the fear is to *trust Me*. There is so much bad news in this world, but instead of being scared, boldly trust Me. *Believe* in Me! Be encouraged by how My death on the cross saved you; be amazed at how I rose up from the dead. It's a miracle! I am your living Savior! I am the Almighty God! I am Ruler over everything, including all the events of this world. No matter what happens, I am still in control.

When the things around you or the things in this world seem to be spinning out of control, come to Me and *pour out your heart*. Tell Me everything you're feeling. Instead of worrying and fretting, put your energy into praying. I'll not only comfort you, but I'll also be your Guide. I'll help you find the way to go. *And* I'll remember your prayers as I decide what will happen in your world. I answer your prayers in ways that are far, far beyond what you can understand.

Don't be afraid of bad news or let it spook you. Instead, calm your heart and mind by trusting Me. I won't let you down.

READ ON YOUR OWN

Psalm 112:7 ICB; Psalm 62:8; Isaiah 9:6

Ask Me for Wisdom

If any of you needs wisdom, you should ask God for it. God is generous. He enjoys giving to all people, so God will give you wisdom.
—James 1:5 ICB

Ask Me for wisdom, child. I know how much you need it! Everyone needs it. Even King Solomon *asked that I give him wisdom*, and I gave him as much wisdom and understanding as there is *sand on the seashore*. This precious gift is also important for you, especially when you're making plans and choices. So turn to Me for the wisdom you need, and *trust Me* to give you all that you need.

One part of wisdom is seeing that you must have My help in everything you do. It's easy to forget about Me and just dive into those things you have to do. But sooner or later you'll bump into a problem. Then you have an important choice to make: Keep going, or stop and ask for My understanding and guidance. The closer you live to Me, the more easily and the more often you'll seek My help.

The fear of the Lord is where wisdom begins. "Fear of the Lord" isn't being afraid of Me; it's respecting Me and being completely amazed at Me because of who I am. Yes, I'm your Friend. But remember, I am the great and mighty and all-powerful God! Knowing who I am—and worshiping Me for who I am—is the very best beginning place for wisdom.

READ ON YOUR OWN

James 1:6; 1 Kings 3:9; 4:29 ICB;
Proverbs 1:7 ICB; Mark 13:26

Remember Who I Am

"I am the Alpha and the Omega, the Beginning and the End," says the Lord, "who is and who was and who is to come, the Almighty."
—Revelation 1:8 NKJV

Train your mind to think great thoughts about Me! So many Christians are defeated because they let their thoughts be taken over by less important things like homework worries, practices, friends' problems, their own struggles, and so on. Yes, *in this world you will have trouble*, but don't let your troubles become the main thing you think about. Remember that I'm with you, and *I have defeated the world*. I am closer to you than the air you breathe—and yet I am the all-powerful God, *the King of kings and Lord of lords*. I am also the Savior who loves you and the Friend who never leaves you.

One of the best ways to understand how great I am is to praise Me. Praise connects you to Me—and to the Father and the Holy Spirit—in an amazing and glorious way. True praise brings My kingdom of Light into your world and chases away the darkness. One beautiful way to praise Me is to sing or read the Psalms. Filling your mind with the truth of My Word will help keep sadness away. So when troubles attack, take time to think about who I am: your Savior and Friend who is the Almighty God!

READ ON YOUR OWN

John 16:33 ICB; Revelation 19:16

My Greatest Commandment

"'Love the Lord your God with all your heart and with all your soul and with all your mind.' This is the first and greatest commandment. And the second is like it: 'Love your neighbor as yourself.'"
—Matthew 22:37–39

I want you to think about Me more and more. Most people think mostly about themselves. My followers can fall into that trap too. But thinking mostly about yourself keeps you from growing into who I created you to be.

When you love someone, you think about him or her very often, which helps you love that person even more. So the way to think about Me more is to love Me more—*with all your heart and soul and mind*. This is *the greatest commandment*, and it's the most important goal for you. Of course, you won't be able to do it perfectly in this life. But the more you understand and delight in My wonderful, *unfailing Love* for you, the more deeply you can love Me. Ask My Spirit to help you in this great adventure!

There are two parts to this adventure. The first is learning how deep, wide, and never-ending My Love for you is—and letting that amazing Love into your heart. The second is to love Me more and more. That's the way you break free from thinking mostly about yourself. And I just love helping you break free!

READ ON YOUR OWN

Psalm 52:8; 1 John 4:19; John 8:36

Accept My Forgiveness

*If we confess our sins, he will forgive our sins,
because we can trust God to do what is right. He will
cleanse us from all the wrongs we have done.*
—1 John 1:9 NCV

Be careful not to decide how valuable you are based on what you do or how well you do it. When you're unhappy with something you've said or done, talk to Me about it. Ask Me to help you sort out what's a sin and what is not. Tell Me about—confess—anything you know you've done wrong, and then accept My forgiveness with a thankful heart. That way, you can live in the wonderful freedom of knowing you are My beloved and forgiven child.

Don't ever let your mistakes and sins make you feel less loved. Remember that *those who are in Christ Jesus are not judged guilty*. Because you are Mine, I declared you "Not Guilty" forever! You are precious to Me, and *I take delight in you*. So don't get down on yourself.

You aren't perfect—that's part of being human. But knowing that you're not perfect humbles you and helps you remember that you need Me. Pride is such a deadly sin—it's the sin that got Satan tossed out of heaven. So being humble is a blessing. Thank Me for the things that shrink your pride—and come closer to Me. Let *My priceless, unfailing Love* fill you up!

READ ON YOUR OWN

Romans 8:1 ICB; Zephaniah 3:17; Psalm 36:7

Delight in Me

*Delight yourself in the LORD; and He
will give you the desires of your heart.*
—Psalm 37:4 NASB

A difficult problem can actually become an idol in your mind. That's because if you think about anything—good or bad— more than you think about Me, that thing can be an idol for you. In a way, you are worshiping it with your mind. So it's smart to check up on your thoughts.

Most people believe that only the fun things in this world can become idols. But a problem, especially one that lasts a long time, can also be an idol if it takes over your thoughts. Realizing this has happened is the first step in breaking free. Next, you need to bring the problem to Me and confess that it is on your mind way too much. Ask for My forgiveness, which I will freely give to you. Then ask for My help as you work to *capture every thought and make it give up and obey Me.*

I'm teaching you to *think about Me* more and more. But to do this, you have to *want* to, and you have to *practice* at it. It's important that you enjoy thinking about Me—and that you're happy in My loving Presence. *Delight yourself in Me,* dear child. Make *Me* the One your heart wants.

READ ON YOUR OWN

Acts 10:43; 2 Corinthians 10:5 NCV; Hebrews 3:1 ICB

Praise Me in Times of Trouble

The Lord is my strength and shield. I trust him, and he helps me. I am very happy. And I praise him with my song.
—Psalm 28:7 ICB

I am your *Strength and Shield.* I'm constantly working in your life to give you energy and strength and to protect you—sometimes in wonderful and amazing ways. The more completely you trust Me, the happier your heart will be!

I want you to trust Me with your whole heart. Rest in knowing that I am Ruler of all things—I control the *entire* universe. When the world seems to be spinning out of control, grab on to Me, confident that I know what I'm doing. I'll weave all the events of your life together to create beautiful blessings for you, both in this world and in heaven.

While you're in the middle of a problem, your greatest challenge is to keep on trusting that I am good *and* I am in control. Don't expect to understand what I'm doing. *Just as the heavens are higher than the earth, so are my ways higher than your ways. And my thoughts are higher than your thoughts.*

You know those times when trouble seems to be staring you in the face? I am pleased that you praise Me even then. It shows Me that you know I'll make something good out of the worst events. Your praise is an act of faith. It encourages you and honors Me. I am happy when My children *give thanks to Me in song*—especially when they're right in the middle of a problem!

READ ON YOUR OWN

Psalm 18:1–2 ICB; Isaiah 55:9 ICB

A Beautiful Puzzle

*"For I am the LORD, your God, who takes hold of your right
hand and says to you, Do not fear; I will help you."*
—Isaiah 41:13

Learn to lean on Me more and more. I know just how weak you really are. That's where My powerful Presence comes to meet you: right in the middle of those places of weakness! My strength and your weakness fit together perfectly, like the pieces of a beautiful puzzle created long before you were born. In fact, *when you are weak, then My Power is made perfect in yo*u. This mystery makes no sense to the world, but it's true.

It's important to lean on Me anytime you're feeling that you aren't "good enough" or that you just can't do everything you need to do. Remember that you and I together are *more* than enough. To feel My nearness, try closing your hand just as if you're grabbing hold of Mine. Listen to My promise: *I take hold of your right hand and say to you, "Do not fear; I will help you."*

I also want you to lean on Me even when you *do* feel you can handle things on your own. This will remind you that I'm always near and that you always need Me. I'm much, much smarter and wiser than you could ever imagine! So let Me guide your thoughts as you make plans and choices. Leaning on Me helps you not only make good choices but also grows your friendship with Me—the One who *will not leave you or forget you.*

READ ON YOUR OWN

2 Corinthians 12:9 ICB; Philippians 4:13;
Deuteronomy 31:6 ICB

Shut Out the Noise

Pray in the Spirit on all occasions with all kinds of
prayers and requests. With this in mind, be alert
and always keep on praying for all the saints.
—Ephesians 6:18

*B*e alert and always keep on praying. With My Spirit's help, you can learn to be more and more wide-awake to Me—aware of My Presence. This isn't an easy assignment though. That's because the world is constantly trying to pull your attention away from Me. Too much noise and too many electronic screens make it hard for you to find Me sometimes. But I'm always close by—as close as a whispered prayer.

People who are the best of friends love to spend time together so they can enjoy their friendship. I am your very best Friend—and I want to spend time with you. Just you. When you shut out the noise of the world to be alone with Me, I'll fill your soul with *the Joy of My Presence*! This makes your love for Me grow stronger and helps your own spirit stay wide-awake and alert. Praying becomes easier when you know in your heart that I am close by—My Presence is *with* you!

Praying not only blesses you, but it also gives you a way to serve Me. Rejoice and be glad that you and I can work together, through prayer, as I build My kingdom on earth.

READ ON YOUR OWN

Acts 17:27–28; Psalm 21:6; Matthew 6:10

Follow *Me*

Guide me in your truth. Teach me, my God,
my Savior. I trust you all day long.
—Psalm 25:5 ICB

I will guide you from now on. Rejoice and be happy that the One who leads you through each day will never leave you. I am the God you can always count on—the One who goes before you into the future and who also stays right beside you in this moment. I never let go of your hand. *I guide you with My advice, and later I will receive you in honor* in heaven.

Many people depend too much on their human leaders. They want someone else to make their decisions for them. Evil leaders can use this weakness against their followers, pushing them to do things they wouldn't usually do—even terrible things. But everyone who trusts Me as their Savior has a Leader they can completely trust and depend on.

I guide you with My truth and teach you My ways so you can make good choices. I've given you a wonderful map, the Bible. You can count on it. My Word will never lead you the wrong way. *My Word is a lamp to guide your feet and a light for your path.* Follow this Light. Follow *Me*. I am the One who knows the very best way for you to go.

READ ON YOUR OWN

Psalm 48:14 ICB; Psalm 73:23–24 ICB; Psalm 119:105 NLT

I Hold You Close

He will feed his flock like a shepherd. He will carry the lambs in his arms, holding them close to his heart. He will gently lead the mother sheep with their young.
—Isaiah 40:11 NLT

I protect you with My saving shield. I hold you up with My right hand.

I won the greatest victory of all time with My death on the cross and the miracle of rising from the dead. I won the battle against sin and death. And I did it for you and for all who choose to trust Me as their Savior and God. I did everything I planned to do! Your part in this victory is simply to believe—believe that you need a Savior to pay the price for your sins and that I am the only Way you can be saved.

Your belief and faith in Me sets you on the path to heaven. At the same time, My shield of victory protects you as you journey through this world. Use My shield to stop the fiery arrows of the devil. When you're under attack, call out to Me: "Help me, Lord! I trust in You."

In each moment of your life, depend on Me to take care of you. My right hand will hold you and help you keep going when times are tough. I have great Power—greater than anything you could ever dream up on your own! I use My mighty right hand not only to protect you but to gently lead you. Sometimes I even carry you in My arms, holding you close to My heart.

READ ON YOUR OWN

Psalm 18:35 ICB; John 14:6; Ephesians 6:16

Just Whisper My Name

But I am always with you. You have held my hand.
—Psalm 73:23 ICB

Problems come and go, but I am always with you. I'm writing the story of your life—through the good times *and* the hard times. I can see the big picture: from before you were born to the day you will join Me in heaven. I know exactly what you'll be like when heaven becomes your home forever. And I'm constantly working to change you into that perfect creation. You are royalty in My kingdom!

My Presence with you—all the time—is a precious treasure. But it's a treasure that most of My followers don't value. They've been taught the truth that *I am always with them*, but they often think and act as if they're all alone. This makes Me sad.

When you whisper My Name with love, it brings you closer to Me, even in your toughest times. And that closeness blesses both you and Me. This simple prayer—*"Jesus"*—tells Me that you believe I'm really with you and that I'm taking care of you. The fact of My Presence is greater than any problem you're facing, no matter how big that problem may seem. So *come to Me* when you're feeling *tired and have a heavy load* to carry. *I will give you rest.*

READ ON YOUR OWN

2 Thessalonians 2:13; Matthew 11:28 ICB

The Champion

Let us run with endurance the race God has set before us. We do this by keeping our eyes on Jesus, the champion who initiates and perfects our faith.
—Hebrews 12:1–2 NLT

I am the *Champion who makes your faith perfect*. The more problems you have, the more important it is to *keep your eyes on Me*. If you look only at your problems or the troubles in this world, you'll lose hope. So whenever you're feeling dragged down by worry, or fear, or sadness, break free of those feelings by turning to Me. I'm always with you, so you can talk to Me anytime. Instead of just letting your thoughts run wild, think about *Me*. This gives your thoughts a purpose and brings you closer to Me.

Rest with Me for a little while. Enjoy the loving protection of My Presence. As you look out over this broken and sinful world, rejoice and be glad because *nothing can separate you from My Love*! I'll keep this promise to you in any situation you face. No matter how terrible or hopeless things may look, I'm still in control. I am the Champion who fights for you, and I laugh at those who think they can beat Me. Remember: *My never-failing Love surrounds you*!

READ ON YOUR OWN

Romans 8:38–39; Psalm 2:4 ICB; Psalm 32:10 ICB

Trust and Thank Me

Yes, God's riches are very great! God's wisdom and knowledge have no end! No one can explain the things God decides. No one can understand God's ways.
—Romans 11:33 ICB

Trust in *My unfailing Love*. I will never stop loving you. Thank Me for all the good in your life, even the good you don't see. When evil seems to be winning in the world around you, it can look as if things are spinning out of control. But believe in this truth: I am not sitting up in heaven just twisting My hands helplessly, wondering what to do next. I am still in control, and I am doing so much good behind the scenes. So thank Me for *all* your blessings—the ones you see and the ones you don't.

My wisdom and knowledge are much, much greater than any words could say. *No one can explain the things I decide. No one can understand My ways.* That's why trusting Me *at all times* is so important. Don't let the confusing events that are happening around you shake your faith in Me. When your world feels unsteady, thanking Me and trusting Me—as often as you can—will help you stay steady. Remember: *I am always with you. I guide you with My advice. And later I will receive you in honor* in heaven. Let this hidden treasure—My gift of a future in heaven—make your heart sing with Joy!

READ ON YOUR OWN

Isaiah 54:10; Psalm 62:8; Psalm 73:23–24 ICB

October 19

I'll Help You Believe More

I do believe! Help me to believe more!
—Mark 9:24 ICB

I want you to live close to Me, knowing that I'm here with you. Listen to Me, trust Me, and thank Me. I'm always near. Open yourself to Me completely—heart, mind, and spirit. Ask the Holy Spirit to help you find Joy in My living Presence.

Try to stay aware of Me all through this day. There's never one moment when I don't know everything that's happening to you. I'm always alert, listening carefully and watching closely—and I want you to be the same way with Me. Pay close attention to Me, but also pay attention to the people I bring into your life. Listening to others while you pray for My guidance is a gift to them and a blessing for you.

The Bible is full of instructions to trust Me and thank Me. It's always right to believe Me and My promises. Remember: I am completely worthy of your trust—I deserve it because I'll never let you down! But I understand that you are weak, and sometimes you have doubts. Tell Me about them, and I'll *help you believe more.*

Thank Me often as you go through each day. Some of the best times to thank Me are when you first wake up and just before you fall asleep. This thankfulness will fill you with My Joy—until you overflow with it!

READ ON YOUR OWN

Revelation 1:18; James 1:19; Psalm 28:7

Ask the Helper

"I will ask the Father, and he will give you another Helper.
He will give you this Helper to be with you forever."
—John 14:16 ICB

When the task you need to do looks difficult or even impossible, refuse to be afraid or overwhelmed. Train yourself to think of your tough assignments in a more positive way. Don't tell yourself, "I *have* to do this task," but say instead, "I *get* to do it!" This will make all the difference in the way you see things. This kind of thinking has the power to change hard chores into something you can enjoy. It's not a magic trick though. You'll still have to do the work. But changing the way you think about that work can help you do it with confidence and a happy heart.

As you go about your work, it's important that you stick with it. If you grow tired or discouraged, or if you feel like giving up, remind yourself: "I *get* to do this!" Thank Me for giving you the ability and the strength to do what needs to be done. Being thankful clears your mind of "I can't do it" thoughts and brings you closer to Me. Remember that My Spirit lives inside you and He is *your Helper*. Ask Him to help you when you're not sure what to do. As you think through problems and look for answers, He will guide your mind. And *whatever you do, work at it with all your heart*—as if you were *working for Me*.

READ ON YOUR OWN

Colossians 4:2; Colossians 3:23

First Place

My mind and my body may become weak.
But God is my strength. He is mine forever.
—Psalm 73:26 ICB

Hold on to *things* with loose hands, but hold on to *Me* tightly. This means don't be so attached to your stuff that you put it first in your life. All those things are blessings from Me, so accept them and enjoy them *with thankfulness*. But don't forget that, in the end, *I* am the Owner of everything, and I want to have first place in your heart.

It's also important to hold on to *people* with open hands. Love and value your family and friends, but don't let them become idols in your life. Don't put them before Me. If your life revolves around anyone other than Me, you need to tell Me you're sorry and change your ways. Return to Me, dear child. Make Me *your First Love*, and try to please Me above all else.

Another thing to hold on to loosely is your desire to be in charge. When your life is going smoothly, it's easy to feel as if you're in control. Enjoy these peaceful times, but don't expect them to go on forever. Instead, hold tightly to My hand—in good times, in hard times, at all times. Good times are even better, and hard times are easier to bear, when you're depending on Me. *I am your Strength*, and *I am yours forever*.

READ ON YOUR OWN

Colossians 2:6; Revelation 2:4; Psalm 73:23–26 ICB

Tell Me Your Troubles

*People, trust God all the time. Tell him all
your problems. God is our protection.*
—Psalm 62:8 ICB

Don't be afraid to tell Me how weak and tired you feel sometimes. I know exactly how big your troubles are. Nothing
about you is hidden from Me.

Even though I know everything about you, I wait for you to
talk to Me about your troubles. *Tell Me all your problems. I am
your protection*—your refuge. When you share your struggles
with Me, I'll hold you close and fill you with My sweet Peace.
You don't have to pretend that everything is okay. You can be
real with Me—and with yourself. Then you can rest in the safety
of My Presence, trusting that I understand you perfectly and
that I *love you with an everlasting Love.*

Relax with Me, My child. Stop trying so hard to be perfect. *Be still* while My Presence refreshes and renews you.
Then, when you're ready, ask Me to show you what to do next.
Remember that I never, ever leave your side. I am right beside
you, *holding you by your right hand.* Let this give you the courage and confidence you need to keep going. And as you walk
through your day, hear Me whispering to your heart, *"Do not
fear; I will help you."*

READ ON YOUR OWN

Jeremiah 31:3; Psalm 46:10; Isaiah 41:13

Comfort Others

We have small troubles for a while now, but they are helping us gain an eternal glory. That glory is much greater than the troubles.
—2 Corinthians 4:17 ICB

Don't think of sadness and suffering as your enemies. Let them remind you that you're on a journey to heaven—a far better place than this world. Yes, I will give you some joys and comforts along the way, but they aren't the kind that last forever. When you reach your home in heaven, that's when I'll shower you with *pleasure forever*. In that wonderful place, *there will be no more death, sadness, crying, or pain*. The Joy that will fill you there is a Joy that will never end.

Because you have put your trust in Me, I can promise that your sadness and suffering will come to an end one day. So try to see your troubles as *small and only here for a little while—but helping you gain an eternal glory. And that glory is much greater than the troubles*!

While you're living in this world, be thankful for the joys and comfort I bless you with. Then reach out to those who are hurting. After all, *I comfort you every time you have trouble so that you can comfort others when they have trouble.* When you offer help to hurting people, your own sadness becomes something useful and helpful. And you bring Glory to Me!

READ ON YOUR OWN

Psalm 16:11 ICB; Revelation 21:4 ICB; 2 Corinthians 1:4 ICB

I Am the Way and the Truth

*Jesus answered, "I am the way and the truth and the life.
No one comes to the Father except through me."*
—John 14:6

Joy that lasts forever can only be found in Me. There are lots of things in this world that will give you happiness, and sometimes they can even turn into a deeper Joy—especially when you share your delight with Me. I pour blessings into your life, and I'm thrilled when you thank Me for them. So come to Me often with thanksgiving, and the Joy of being in My Presence will increase your happiness even more.

But on those days when you're so upset that you can barely remember what Joy feels like, that's when you need to search for Me the most. Don't let your feelings or the things you see happening around you drag you down. Instead, tell yourself these truths about Me: *I am always with you. I hold your hand. I guide you with My advice. And later I will receive you in honor* into heaven.

As you walk through this sinful, broken world, hold on to My truths with all your might. Remember that I am *the Truth*, and hold tightly to Me. Follow Me, because I am also *the Way*. The Light of My Presence is shining in your life. Look for it, and it will light up the path in front of you, showing you the way to go.

READ ON YOUR OWN

Psalm 105:4; Psalm 73:23–24 ICB

The Answer to Any Trouble

Let your constant love comfort me,
as you have promised me, your servant.
—Psalm 119:76 GNT

*L*et My constant Love comfort you. Comfort eases sadness and troubles. It also gives strength and hope. The best source of these blessings is found in My nonstop Love that will never, ever fail you. No matter what's happening in your life, My Love can calm you down and cheer you up. But, in order to receive My comfort, you must come to Me for help. It's okay. I'm always here for you, and I love to give you everything you need.

I have a complete and perfect understanding of you and everything in your life. My understanding of what's happening is far greater than yours. So be careful of thinking too much about your troubles. Don't try to figure things out all on your own, and don't leave Me out of the answer. When you realize you've forgotten Me, turn to Me with this simple prayer: "Help me, Jesus." These three words remind you that I'm the most important answer to any trouble you'll ever face. Relax with Me awhile. Let My loving Presence comfort you. Yes, *in this world you will have trouble. But be brave! I have defeated the world!*

READ ON YOUR OWN

Psalm 29:11; Psalm 42:5; John 16:33 ICB

Learn to Be Joyful

You will teach me God's way to live.
Being with you will fill me with joy.
—Acts 2:28 ICB

Learn to be joyful, even when things don't happen the way you want. Don't wake up in the morning saying, "Today, I'll make everything go my way." Every day you'll bump into at least one person or thing that refuses to follow your wishes. It could be something as small as a bad hair day or as huge as an illness or a fight with a friend. My plan for you is *not* to make your every wish come true, or to make your life easy. My plan is for you to learn to trust Me in good times, in bad times, and in all the times in between.

If you think you *must* have your own way in everything, you'll end up frustrated and upset most of the time. Yet I don't want you wasting energy or tears over what has already happened. The past cannot be changed, but you have My help here and now. And you have My Hope for the future. So try to relax. Trust in My control over your life. Remember: I'm always close to you, and there are overflowing treasures of *Joy in My Presence*. In fact, My Face *smiles on you*, and My Joy shines upon you!

READ ON YOUR OWN

Psalm 62:8; Proverbs 23:18; Numbers 6:25 NLT

When People Expect Too Much

Lift up your hands in the sanctuary and praise the LORD.
—Psalm 134:2

Come to Me, My tired and weary child. Find rest in My Presence. Let Me refresh you. I am always right by your side, ready to help you—but sometimes you forget about Me.

Your attention is easily pulled away by the demands of other people. They expect you to do certain things and to act a certain way, and they say so in different ways. Their words may be gentle and kind, or they may say things that make you feel guilty. If their demands grow too big, or become too many, they can pile up and crush you.

When you find yourself sinking under a *heavy load* of things other people expect you to do, come to Me for help. Ask Me to lift that load off of you. Talk to Me about all the things that worry you. Let the Light of My Presence shine on those things, showing you what's important and what isn't. My Light will also comfort you and give you strength as it soaks deep into your spirit.

Open up your heart to My healing Presence. *Lift up your hands* to Me in joyful praise as My blessings pour down on you, and take time to rest with Me. Relax, dear child, while I *bless you with Peace.*

READ ON YOUR OWN

Matthew 11:28 ICB; Psalm 29:11

Bring Me Everything

I was in trouble. So I called to the Lord.
The Lord answered me and set me free.
—Psalm 118:5 ICB

Many people only bring part of themselves to Me in prayer. They don't bring Me the things they are ashamed of or embarrassed by. Other people are so used to living with painful feelings—like feeling lonely, afraid, or guilty—that they never think to ask for My help with these troubles. And still other people get so tied up in their problems that they forget I'm right there with them. That's not the way I want you to live, dear child.

I want to heal each and every part of you that hurts. I know some of those hurts have been with you for so long that you think they're actually part of *you*. You take them with you wherever you go, barely seeing how they drag you down. I want to set you free and show you a new way to live—without those hurts. But because you're so used to carrying them around, it will take time and work to let them go.

Bring those hurts to Me, over and over again. I *will* heal you. Each time you come to Me, you'll be healed a little bit more. And each time, I'll give you more of My Joy!

READ ON YOUR OWN

Romans 8:1; Psalm 126:3

Do Something Good

How terrible it will be for people who call good things bad and bad things good. They think darkness is light and light is darkness. They think sour is sweet and sweet is sour.
—Isaiah 5:20 ICB

*D*o not let evil defeat you. Defeat evil by doing good. Sometimes it feels as if you're being blasted by all the bad things happening in the world. News reports are frightening, and people are calling good things bad and bad things good. If you don't keep talking to Me, all this bad stuff can really upset you. The many horrors that you see make Me sad, but they don't surprise Me. I know how wicked human hearts can be; I know how much people lie. Unless someone is changed by a saving faith in Me, that person's ability to do wrong has no limits.

Instead of losing hope because of the terrible things in this world, be a light shining in the darkness. When evil seems to be winning, I want you—more than ever—to do something good. Sometimes this will mean working against the evil that's right in front of you, like standing up to a bully or helping someone who's been hurt. Other times, fighting evil will mean doing whatever you can to share My goodness—with whatever ability or opportunity I give you. Either way, you'll spend less time talking about how bad this world is and more time doing something good.

READ ON YOUR OWN

Romans 12:21 ICB; Jeremiah 17:9

You Need Me

Now we hope for the blessings God has for his children.
These blessings are kept for you in heaven. They cannot
be destroyed or be spoiled or lose their beauty.
—1 Peter 1:4 ICB

Walk close to Me. Trust My Love for you, and depend on Me with Joy. The friendship I offer you sparkles like jewels because of My precious promises in the Bible. Promises like these: I love you with a perfect, *everlasting Love*. I am always with you—every nanosecond of your life. I know everything about you, and I've already taken the punishment for your sins. Your future *blessings—which are kept in heaven for you—cannot be destroyed or be spoiled or lose their beauty*. I will guide you through your life, and *afterward I will take you into heaven's Glory*—to live forever with Me!

Because you are human, you must depend on something or someone, so depend on Me. Many people hate the fact that they can't do everything on their own. They work hard to pretend that they can. But I created you to need Me all the time, and I want you to be joyful about this. When you understand and accept how much you need Me, your eyes will open to My loving Presence more and more. And this awareness will draw you closer to Me, where you can enjoy My company and My friendship.

READ ON YOUR OWN

Jeremiah 31:3; 1 Peter 1:3 ICB; Psalm 73:24

Let Me Be Your Shield

God's way is perfect. All the Lord's promises prove true.
He is a shield for all who look to him for protection.
—2 Samuel 22:31 NLT

I am a Shield for you. *I am your protection and your Strength. I always help in times of trouble.* When your world is feeling unsafe and you feel afraid, think about these precious promises. I will personally shield and protect you, just as I protect all My children who come to Me. I will be your safe place in the middle of every problem.

Letting Me be your Shield means *trusting in Me* and *pouring out your heart to Me*—holding nothing back. No matter what's going on with you, it's always the right time to tell Me that you trust Me. Sometimes you'll have to deal with whatever "thing" is happening before you have time to really talk to Me. I understand that. Just whisper the quickest of prayers—"Jesus, I trust You." Then, as soon as you can, tell Me everything you're feeling. This time with Me will give you real comfort. It will also make our relationship stronger and help you see what to do next.

My Presence is a shield that's always there for you. Whenever you're feeling afraid, turn to Me and say: "Jesus, be my Shield"—and I will be.

READ ON YOUR OWN

Psalm 46:1 ICB; Psalm 62:8

NOVEMBER

Trust God all the time.
Tell him all your problems.
God is our protection.

—Psalm 62:8 ICB

A Safe Path

He is the God who makes me strong, who makes my pathway safe.
—Psalm 18:32 GNT

I am the God who makes you strong. *I make your path safe.* Come to Me just as you are—with all your sins, mistakes, and weaknesses. Admit what you've done wrong, and ask Me to forgive you. I'll take your sins as far away from you *as the east is from the west*—and I'll never remember them again. Then stay with Me in My Presence.

It's okay to let Me see all your weaknesses; I know them anyway. Your weaknesses are like empty "jars" just waiting to be filled with My Power. Let Me pour My strength into you, dear child.

I want you to thank Me for your weaknesses because they teach you to depend on Me. And My Power is always enough for what you need. So rejoice—be filled with Joy!

As you go through your life, I'm the One who makes your path safe. I protect you from worry and from too much planning. Instead of looking ahead to the future, which you can't know, look to Me as you travel the path of *this* day. Keep talking to Me, and let Me guide you. I'll walk beside you. I'll also walk ahead of you to clear away dangers. Trust Me to make your path the very best it can be for you.

READ ON YOUR OWN

Psalm 103:12; 2 Corinthians 12:9; 2 Corinthians 4:7

My Comfort Brings Joy

I was very worried. But you comforted me and made me happy.
—Psalm 94:19 ICB

*W*hen you are very worried, turn to Me for comfort. Other words for "comfort" are *compassion*, *understanding*, *help*, *encouragement*, and *relief*. I'll happily give you all these things—and much more—because you're My child. I know that when you're worried, you're tempted to think only about yourself and your problems. But the more you think about yourself, the more you forget about Me and all the help I can give you. When your thoughts are focused on your problems, this only makes you worry more! Let the uncomfortable feeling of worrying be like an alarm, waking you up to the fact that you've forgotten Me. To fix this, all you have to do is whisper My Name. Invite Me into your thoughts and troubles, and I will be right there with you.

Worship Me, and seek My Face. In Me, you'll find comfort and understanding. I'll encourage and help you. I already know all about your problems, and I also know the best way to fix them. As you relax in My loving Presence, I'll give you strength and help you stop worrying. I promise that *nothing in all creation can separate you from My Love*. My comfort is full of blessings, dear child, and *it brings Joy to your soul*.

READ ON YOUR OWN

Psalm 27:8 ICB; Romans 8:38–39

The Master of Your Life

"This is eternal life: that people know you, the only true God, and that they know Jesus Christ, the One you sent."
—John 17:3 NCV

It's time to stop pretending that you're in control of your life. When everything is going smoothly, you like to feel as if you're in charge. But the more you see yourself as being the master—the one in charge—the harder you will fall when tough times come.

I *want* you to enjoy the easy times and be thankful for them. But don't start thinking that's the way life will always be. Just as on some days the weather must include rain and storms, there *will* be storms of trouble in your life sometimes—you won't always be sure of what to do. If you try to be in control and demand that everything in your life go your way, you'll be crushed when real troubles come.

I'm training you to *trust Me at all times*, because *I am your Refuge*—your place of safety. I use troubles to set you free from the false idea that you're in control of your life. Find your safety in *knowing Me*. I'm the Master who rules over all the storms of your life—and over the sunny days too.

READ ON YOUR OWN

James 4:13–14; Psalm 62:8 ICB

Whatever You Do

I keep the Lord before me always. Because
he is close by my side I will not be hurt.
—Psalm 16:8 ICB

Living your life close to Me gives you a taste of how wonderful heaven will be. Yet living close to Me is very challenging. It takes work to keep your thoughts, your heart, and your spirit focused on Me.

In the Psalms, David wrote about living in My Presence. He said that *he kept Me before him always*. David was a shepherd, so he had plenty of time to think about Me and enjoy being with Me while he watched over his sheep. David discovered that living each day with Me beside him was a beautiful thing. I'm teaching *you* to live this way too. But you'll have to work at it. It will take a lot of effort and willpower. You may worry that all this work will take you away from the other things you do, but being close to Me actually fills *every* activity with My energy and Life.

Whatever you do, do it *for* Me. Also, do your work *with* Me, and I will help you. Even boring chores can glow with the Joy of My Presence when you do them for Me. Remember that *nothing in all creation will ever be able to separate you from Me*. That means you and I can keep going on this amazing adventure *together* for all eternity!

READ ON YOUR OWN

Colossians 3:23–24; Romans 8:39

I Guard and Guide You

Even when walking through the dark valley of death I will not be afraid, for you are close beside me, guarding, guiding all the way.
—Psalm 23:4 TLB

*D*o not be afraid. I am close beside you, guarding and guiding you all the way.* So many times you don't even realize that My Presence is with you, even though I'm always there.

Fear can be like an alarm clock for your heart. It wakes you up to the fact that you need to reach out to Me. When you feel your worries and fears growing, take time to relax and let the Light of My Presence shine on your life and into your heart. As you rest in the warm Light of My Love, those icy-cold fears will start to melt away. While My Love is warming you, tell Me how much you love and trust Me.

Remember that I am a God who will both guard you and guide you. If you knew how much bad stuff I protect you from, you would amazed! But the most important protection I give you is guarding your soul—the part of you that lives forever. Because you are My follower, your soul is safe and secure with Me. *No one can snatch you out of My hand.* I will lead you all through your life, and *I will be your Guide* all the way to heaven.

READ ON YOUR OWN

John 10:28; Psalm 48:14

Love with Patience

*Be joyful because you have hope. Be patient
when trouble comes. Pray at all times.*
—Romans 12:12 ICB

*L*ove is patient. In 1 Corinthians 13, the apostle Paul gave a long list of words to describe what Christian love should be like. The very first one is "patient." Being patient is being able to face troubles calmly. It's not getting upset when you have to wait or deal with rude people or hard problems.

Paul knew patience was very important, but this world doesn't agree. Even My followers forget to be patient sometimes. And when it comes to love, patience is almost never the first thing people think about. There is one exception to this: a loving mother or father. The demands of children help good parents learn to be patient. How many times has your mom or dad put aside what they wanted or needed to take care of you?

I want My followers to include plenty of patience in their love for one another. Patience is also part of the fruit of the Spirit in Galatians 5. So when you're having trouble being patient, My Spirit can help you be more calm and more understanding with others.

Remember that I love you with a perfect and *unfailing Love*: I am endlessly patient with you and all your mistakes. Ask the Holy Spirit to help you love others with My beautiful, patient Love.

READ ON YOUR OWN

1 Corinthians 13:4; Galatians 5:22–23; Psalm 147:11

Enough Trouble

"So don't worry about tomorrow. Each day has enough trouble of its own. Tomorrow will have its own worries."
—Matthew 6:34 ICB

*E*ach day has enough trouble of its own. That means you can expect to face *some* kind of trouble every day, big or small. I want to help you handle those troubles calmly and with confidence. The things that surprise you do *not* surprise Me, because I know everything. I am *the Beginning and the End*. And I am completely with you, right by your side. I'm ready to guide and comfort you through the toughest times.

Having *enough* trouble in each day can help you live better *right now*. Your mind likes to have something challenging to think about. And if you didn't have enough to think about today, your mind would probably start worrying about the future. I'm teaching you to keep your thoughts focused on My Presence in this present moment.

Troubles shouldn't keep you from enjoying My Presence. Just the opposite! Troubles bring you closer to Me when you and I work as partners to handle them. Your trust and confidence in Me will grow as long as we're dealing with your problems together. And the pleasure of being with Me will increase your Joy too!

READ ON YOUR OWN

Revelation 21:6; Romans 12:12

What Other People Think

And besides, the leaders liked praise from
others more than they liked praise from God.
—John 12:43 CEV

*B*e careful of loving praise from men more than praise from *Me.* One of the results of Adam and Eve's fall into sin is that people are too worried about what others think of them—who their friends are, how good they are at sports or school, or how they look. And all those commercials for things that promise to make you look better or be more popular only encourage this dangerous focus on your outside image.

I don't want you to be worried about how other people see you, so I have shielded and protected you from being able to read other people's minds. What they think about you is really "none of your business." People's thoughts are *not* something you can trust, because their minds can get twisted by their own sins, weaknesses, and fears. Even if people praise you to your face, some of their thoughts about you may be very different.

I am the only One who sees you as you really are. No, you aren't perfect. But when I look at you, I see you brightly clothed in My perfect righteousness! Instead of trying to get *praise from others*, think about how *I* look at you. My Face is shining with Joy because I love you so much!

READ ON YOUR OWN

Isaiah 61:10 CEB; Numbers 6:25–26

I Want You to Know My Love

*Christ's love is greater than any person can ever
know. But I pray that you will be able to know that love.
Then you can be filled with the fullness of God.*
—Ephesians 3:19 ICB

Trust Me to lead you step by step through this day. I will only give you enough Light for one day at a time. If you try to look ahead into the future, even if it's only as far ahead as tomorrow, you won't be able to see what's there. Only I know the future! *My Face shines upon you* in this present moment. *Right now* is where you'll find My unfailing, never-ending Love for you.

My Love is even stronger than the love a mother has for her baby. *Even if a mother could forget her baby, I will not forget you!* You are so precious to Me that *I have written your name on My hand*. Forgetting about you is something I will *never* do.

I want you to *be able to know My great, great Love* and to feel it working in your life. When you decide to follow Me, the Holy Spirit comes to live inside you, and He will help you. Ask Him to pour in so much of My Presence that your whole body and soul are *filled* with Me! Then you can experience how great My Love for you really is.

READ ON YOUR OWN

Numbers 6:25; Song of Songs 8:7; Isaiah 49:15–16 ICB

Finding Peace in Hard Times

He is the God of all comfort. He comforts us every time we have trouble, so that we can comfort others when they have trouble. We can comfort them with the same comfort that God gives us.
—2 Corinthians 1:3–4 ICB

I want you to comfort others *with the same comfort I have given you*. No matter what you are going through, My Presence and comfort are enough—they're exactly what you need and *all* you need. As a Christian, every hard time you face has an important reason and a useful purpose. Suffering can make you stronger, and it can prepare you to help others who are struggling. So talk to Me about your hard times. Ask Me to use them for My purposes. Of course, you can try to solve your problems, but be careful not to miss the blessings that are hidden inside them.

When tough times bring you closer to Me—causing you to look for My help—you grow wiser and stronger in your faith. This prepares you to help others as they face hard times of their own. Your understanding of people who feel hurt will touch their lives. And because you've been through hard times yourself, you'll know better how to help and comfort others.

I'm training you to face troubles with Me by your side. As you learn to do this, your own peacefulness will grow. And even though troubles are still painful at the time, they will bless you later on with *a peaceful harvest of right living*.

READ ON YOUR OWN

Philippians 4:19; Hebrews 12:11 NLT

Saved by Grace

Since we are receiving a Kingdom that is unshakable, let us be thankful and please God by worshiping him with holy fear and awe.
—Hebrews 12:28 NLT

There's a poisonous attitude that's flooding this world. It's called *entitlement*, and it's the belief that you deserve to be given something without having to work for it. You've probably seen it in your school, when kids haven't done all their assignments but expect to get a good grade, or they feel they should make the team without practicing. But this is the opposite of what the Bible teaches. The apostle Paul commanded Christians to *stay away from any believer who refuses to work.* Paul himself *worked and worked, night and day.* He even said: "If anyone will not work, he will not eat."

One way to explain *entitlement* is the feeling that you should be given things just because you want them. But thankfulness is the opposite—it's being grateful for what you've *already* been given. Think about this: If I gave you what you really deserved, you'd never be allowed into heaven because of your sins! So be thankful that I *don't* give you what you deserve. Be thankful that *My mercy is great* and *you have been saved by My grace.*

Thinking you ought to be given more than what you have just makes you unhappy. But being thankful will fill you with Joy. And when you're thankful, you *worship Me with holy fear and awe*—which makes your Joy even greater!

READ ON YOUR OWN

2 Thessalonians 3:6–10 ICB;
Ephesians 2:4–5 ICB; Psalm 107:1

Full of Grace and Truth

"Let your light shine before men, that they may see your good deeds and praise your Father in heaven."
—Matthew 5:16

I am *full of grace and truth*. Because of your sins, you don't *deserve* My Love and My Presence in your life, but I give it to you anyway. That's "grace." To be given something you don't deserve is humbling—and that's a good thing. It protects you from the sin of pride. My priceless gift of grace opens up the gates of heaven to you. And because you know Me as your Savior, I look on you with loving approval. You don't deserve My Love and you can't earn it, but it's yours anyway—to keep forever. You can't lose it! So *trust in My Love*, and *be happy because I saved you*.

I'm not only full of truth, but *I am the Truth*. This world throws all kinds of news and stories at you, and many of them are twisted with lies. It's hard to know what to believe and who to trust. But you can find the perfect Truth that never, ever changes—in Me and My Word, the Bible. I won't ever lie to you.

Knowing Me is like being lifted out of quicksand: I put your feet on a rock and give you a firm place to stand. This safe foundation for your life makes you shine like a star in this dark world. Trust My Truth. *Let your light shine* so that *many will see your good deeds* and put their trust in Me.

READ ON YOUR OWN

John 1:14; John 14:6; Psalm 13:5–6 ICB

True Strength

"If you come back to me and trust me, you will be saved.
If you will be calm and trust me, you will be strong."
—Isaiah 30:15 ICB

I am your living God, and I want you to trust Me with quiet confidence. The prophet Isaiah wrote that *in quietness and confidence is your strength*. This means that quietly trusting Me is the way to be strong. People often think that strength has to be loud. They try to control others by yelling, showing their muscles, or making crazy promises they'll never keep. These people are like playground bullies—they seem strong, but they're really weak. They can only feel strong when they're putting others down and controlling them.

True strength comes from quietly trusting in *Me* and *My* promises. Rejoice that I am the *living* God, not just a lifeless statue or idol. *I am the One who lives. I was dead, but look: I am alive forever and ever!* My Power is greater than all the power in the universe, but I come to you gently and with Love. Spend time with Me, dear child, telling Me you trust Me. As you relax with Me, I'll give you My Strength, and I'll make sure you're ready for any troubles that are coming your way. While you're thinking about Me, use Bible verses to help you pray. You can always come closer to Me by simply whispering: *"I love You, Lord. You are my Strength."*

READ ON YOUR OWN

Revelation 1:18 ICB; Psalm 18:1 ICB

Taste and See My Goodness

*Taste and see that the L*ORD* is good. Oh,*
the joys of those who take refuge in him!
—Psalm 34:8 NLT

I am always with you, My child, whether you feel My Presence or not. Sometimes you may feel abandoned—as if I have left you alone in a desert. But I have not. You can call out to Me and *know* that I'm right by your side, ready to help you. *I am close to everyone who prays to Me.* Throw all your doubts into the wind and whisper My Name with sweet trust. Tell Me your troubles and ask Me to guide you—then change the subject. Praise Me for My greatness and My majesty. Praise Me for My Power and Glory! Thank Me for all the good things I have done and am doing in your life. You will find Me there with you in your praises and thanksgiving.

Taste and see that I am good! The more you think about Me and My blessings, the better you can taste My goodness. Enjoy the sweetness of *My unfailing Love.* Take in the hearty flavor of My strength. Satisfy the hunger of your heart with the Joy and Peace of My Presence. Believe that *I am with you and will watch over you wherever you go.*

READ ON YOUR OWN

Psalm 145:18 ICB; Isaiah 54:10; Genesis 28:15

The Prince of Peace

*Then Jesus came to them and said, "All
power in heaven and on earth is given to me."*
—Matthew 28:18 ICB

C *ome to Me*, and rest in My Presence. I am the *Prince of Peace*.
You need My Peace all the time, just as you need *Me* all the
time. So often, when things are going just the way you want in
your life, you forget how much you need Me. Later, when you
hit bumps in the road, you get worried and upset. After a time,
you'll remember to come back to Me and ask for My Peace. And
I'll gladly give it to you—though it will be hard for you to accept
it until you calm down. How much better it would be if you just
stayed close to Me *all* the time!

Remember that I am the Prince of Peace, and I am royalty!
All power in heaven and on earth is given to Me. When you're going
through a hard time, come to Me and tell Me your troubles. Yet
don't forget who I Am! Don't get angry and shake your fist at
Me. Don't tell Me that I have to do things your way. Instead, pray
these words from David in the Psalms: *"Lord, I trust You. I have
said, 'You are my God.' My life is in Your hands."*

READ ON YOUR OWN

Matthew 11:28; Isaiah 9:6; Psalm 31:14–15 ICB

Safe and Secure

How great is your goodness! You have stored it
up for those who fear you. You do good things for
those who trust you. You do this for all to see.
—Psalm 31:19 ICB

You are safe, secure, whole, and complete in Me. So stop worrying and trying to fix everything on your own. Come to Me with the things that upset you. Trust Me enough to be honest and tell Me everything. *Give all your worries to Me, because I care for you* and I am taking care of you! Then rest for a while *in the shelter of My Presence.*

If you wander away from Me and leave Me out of your life, you will no longer feel whole and complete. That restless, broken feeling you have at those times is a gift from Me—it reminds you to come back to Me, your *First Love.* I want to be the center of your thoughts and feelings, as well as your plans and actions. When you live as I want you to live, I give your life meaning and purpose.

You are on the path that leads to heaven, and I am the Friend who is always with you—walking right beside you. Yes, you *will* have troubles along the way, but *be brave! I have defeated the world!* In Me you are always safe, secure, whole, and complete.

READ ON YOUR OWN

1 Peter 5:7 ICB, Psalm 31:20;
Revelation 2:4; John 16:33 ICB

My Words Are True

Your words are true from the start.
And all your laws will be fair forever.
—Psalm 119:160 ICB

My words are true—perfect, never-changing, and forever true! More and more people in this world believe that truth can change, or that it's not even real. But those are lies! Because these people have been hurt or lied to by others, they don't notice what is *true, honorable, right, pure, beautiful, and respected* in this world. Instead, they focus on all the things that are false, wrong, dirty, and ugly. They lose hope and act in ways that hurt themselves. *The devil who rules this world has blinded the minds of those who do not believe. They cannot see the Light of the good news*—the good news of the gospel truth about Me.

The gospel is a pure Light that shines with the Glory of who I am and all that I have done! This good news has unlimited Power to change sadness to Joy. My Spirit lives inside everyone who chooses to be My child. Not only do My children carry My Light inside them, but they can shine that Light into the lives of others. Join Me in this wonderful adventure. Use the gifts and opportunities I give you to share the good news about Me. I know you often feel weak, but your weakness works perfectly with My Strength. In fact, *when you are weak, My Power is made perfect in you*.

READ ON YOUR OWN

Philippians 4:8 ICB; 2 Corinthians 4:4 ICB;
2 Corinthians 12:9 ICB

I Won't Let Go

*But when Peter saw the wind and the waves, he became
afraid and began to sink. He shouted, "Lord, save me!"*
—Matthew 14:30 ICB

I am the Lord, and I am *your Strength*. On those days when
you're feeling strong yourself, this truth may not mean as
much to you. But My Strength is always there for you, especially when you need hope and encouragement. Whenever
you're feeling weak or tired, your lack of strength can help you
remember to look to Me and hold tightly to Me. Call out to Me at
any time, *"Lord, save me!"*—and I'll be there.

Let *Me comfort you with My Love* that never ends and never
lets you down. When you feel as if you're drowning in troubles,
you need to hold on to something strong, something that won't
fail, something you can trust no matter what. My powerful
Presence protects you and gives you strength. I hold you close,
dear child—I have a tight hold on you, and I won't let go.

Because I'm always close by, you don't have to be afraid
of feeling weak. In fact, when you're weak, that's when *My
Power is made perfect in you*. Your weakness and My Power fit
together perfectly like two pieces of a puzzle. So, thank Me for
your weaknesses, and trust in My Strength—it's always there
for you.

READ ON YOUR OWN

Psalm 59:17; Psalm 119:76 ICB; 2 Corinthians 12:9 ICB

Face Your Sins

If we say that we have no sin, we are
fooling ourselves, and the truth is not in us.
—1 John 1:8 ICB

There has never been a person who did not sin—except Me. So don't be afraid to face your sins. *If you say that you have no sin, you are fooling yourself, and the truth is not in you.* When you *confess your sins*, it actually sets you free. That's because you know that *I will forgive your sins and make you clean from all the wrongs you have done.*

The good news is that I have already paid for all your sins by dying on the cross. When you confess and tell Me what you've done wrong, you're admitting that these *wrongs* are actually *sins*. And since *I am the Truth*, confessing your sins brings you even closer to Me. It also *sets you free* from feelings of guilt or shame.

When you realize you've sinned—in your thoughts, your words, or your actions—tell Me right away. You don't need a long or fancy prayer; it can be as simple as: "Forgive me, Lord, and make me clean." I've already done the hard part: I've already been punished for your sins. Your part is to live in the Light of My Truth. I am your Savior, and I *am the Light of the World.*

READ ON YOUR OWN

1 John 1:9; John 14:6; John 8:32; John 8:12

Live in This Moment

Since no man knows the future, who can tell him what is to come?
—Ecclesiastes 8:7

Let Me teach you how to spend more of your time in this day. Tomorrow doesn't really exist—at least not in the way most people think about it. When you start planning how your future will be, you're really just using your imagination. I am the *only* One who knows what will happen in your tomorrows. That's because I am eternal—I have always been alive, and I will never die. Time has no hold on Me. I can be in the past, present, and future all at the same time.

As you go through each day, I open up the future to you step by step. However, even as you're stepping forward in time, you can never step farther than the present moment. When you understand that looking ahead too much is a waste of time, you can live more fully now. But your mind is used to wandering into the future. So it will take time to train your thoughts to stay in the present, and it won't be easy. When you find yourself thinking a lot about the future, remember that you are wandering in a fantasyland. This reminder will help you return to "right now"—where I am waiting for you, ready to wrap you up in *My unfailing Love*.

READ ON YOUR OWN

Revelation 1:8; Psalm 32:10

The Joy of Thanksgiving

Come into his city with songs of thanksgiving. Come into his
courtyards with songs of praise. Thank him, and praise his name.
—Psalm 100:4 ICB

Thanksgiving isn't just a holiday you celebrate every year. It's an attitude of the heart, and it creates Joy. Thanksgiving is something the Bible commands you to do. When you're thankful, you *worship Me with respect and awe.* You cannot worship Me in the right way if your heart isn't thankful. Your worship may look good on the outside, but your ungrateful attitude will block you from truly praising Me.

Whenever you're struggling in your heart or your spirit, stop and check your "thankfulness tank." If your tank is almost empty, ask Me to fill you with gratefulness. Search for things to thank Me for, even writing them down if you want to. Slowly, over time, you'll stop seeing all the things that are wrong in your life, and you'll start seeing all the things that are right.

No matter what's happening around you, you can always *be joyful in God your Savior.* Because I died on the cross and rose from the dead, you have an amazing future waiting for you in heaven. And I promise it will be yours forever! Celebrate this gift of salvation. I give this gift to you—and to *everyone* who trusts Me as the One who saves them from their sins. Let your heart overflow with thanksgiving, and I will fill you with My Joy.

READ ON YOUR OWN

Hebrews 12:28 ICB; 1 Corinthians 13:6;
Habakkuk 3:17–18

Be Grateful for My Grace

I mean that you have been saved by grace because you believe.
You did not save yourselves. It was a gift from God.
—Ephesians 2:8 ICB

Thank Me for the amazing gift of My grace. *You have been saved by grace because you believe. You did not save yourself. It was a gift from Me. You cannot brag that you are saved by the work you have done.* Because I died on the cross and you have trusted in Me as your Savior, you have been given the greatest gift of all: eternal Life. Even the faith you need to be saved is a gift. And the best thing you can do is to thank Me with a grateful heart. You can never thank Me too much or too often for My grace.

During this Thanksgiving holiday, think about what it means to have all your sins forgiven. It means you are on the path that leads to heaven—not to hell. You are headed toward *a new heaven and a new earth*. It also means that every day of your life is a treasure. As you go through *this* day, remember to thank Me often for My incredible gift of grace. Being grateful for grace will fill your heart with Joy—and make you even more thankful for all the *other* blessings I give you.

READ ON YOUR OWN

Ephesians 2:9; John 3:16;
Matthew 10:28; Revelation 21:1

I Am Good!

Thank the Lord because he is good. His love continues forever.
—Psalm 107:1 ICB

*T*hank Me because I am good. *My Love continues forever.* I want you to take time to think about the many blessings I've given you. Thank Me for the gift of life—your life and the lives of those you love. Be grateful for the everyday things I give you too: food and water, a home, clothing, and so on. Then remember the greatest gift of all: eternal life for everyone who knows Me as their Savior.

As you think about all that I have done for you, also think about who *I Am*—and delight in Me. I am one hundred percent Good! There has never been a single speck of darkness or evil in Me, and there never will be. *I am the Light of the World.* And My Love for you will go on and on and on, for all eternity.

Even now I wrap you in My loving Presence. No matter what's happening around you, I am always close by. Don't worry about whether or not you can feel My Presence. Just *trust* that I am with you, and let *My unfailing Love* be like a soft blanket that comforts you.

READ ON YOUR OWN

John 8:58; John 8:12; Psalm 107:8

Find Joy in Today

"Martha, Martha, you are getting worried and upset about too many things. Only one thing is important. Mary has chosen the right thing, and it will never be taken away from her."
—Luke 10:41–42 ICB

Every day I shower blessings on you. Accept them with the Joy of a thankful heart—but don't hold on to those blessings too tightly. Be ready to give them back to Me. Yes, I want you to enjoy every good thing I give you. The best way to do this is to live in this present moment. Don't worry about tomorrow. *Today* is the best time to find Joy in the gifts I've given you. Since you don't know what tomorrow will be like, make the most of the blessings you have today, such as family, friends, talents, and your things. And look for ways that you can be a blessing to someone else.

When I take away something or someone that you treasure, it's okay to be sad and upset. It's also important to come closer to Me during this time. Hold tightly to *Me*, dear child, and remember that *nothing* can take Me away from you. *I am your Rock. You can run to Me for safety.* Many times, I'll surprise you with *new* blessings to comfort you and help you keep going. So be on the lookout for all the good things I have stored up for you!

READ ON YOUR OWN

Matthew 6:34 ICB; Psalm 18:2 ICB; Isaiah 43:19

Give Glory to Me

Your word is a lamp to guide me and a light for my path.
—Psalm 119:105 GNT

I created you to give glory to Me. Make this idea the center of your thoughts as you go through this day. You can give Me glory by thanking Me, praising Me, and worshiping Me. Thank Me often. Search for My blessings as if you were searching for hidden treasure—and when you find one, thank Me!

Praise Me not only in your prayers and songs, but also with your words to other people. Tell them about the amazing things I've done. Announce that I am great and mighty! Join with others at church to worship Me. When you are gathered together in My Name, you can feel how awesome My Presence is.

Whenever you need to make a decision, think about what would please Me and show others My glory. This will help you choose wisely and stay more aware of Me. Instead of getting stuck in your thoughts and not knowing what to do, ask Me to guide your mind as you think things out. I know everything about you and everything about what's happening. The better you know Me, the better I can guide your choices. So learn more about Me by spending time in the Bible—because *My Word is a lamp to guide you and a light for your path.*

READ ON YOUR OWN

1 Thessalonians 5:18 TLB; Psalm 96:3;
2 Corinthians 4:17–18 ICB

War by Worship

Control yourselves and be careful! The devil is your enemy. And he goes around like a roaring lion looking for someone to eat.
—1 Peter 5:8 ICB

Thanking Me wakes up your heart and helps you think more clearly, so that you can enjoy being in My Presence. When your thoughts are all fuzzy or you feel far away from Me, take a moment to thank Me for *something*. There are always plenty of things to choose from. Thank Me for My eternal gifts of salvation, grace, and faith. Or thank Me for one of the zillion ordinary, everyday blessings I pour into your life. Think back over the past day, and make a list of all the good things I've given you in just that one day. Not only will this make you feel better, it will also wake up your mind so you can think more clearly.

Remember that *the devil is your enemy. And he goes around like a roaring lion looking for someone to eat*. That's why it's so important to *control yourself and be careful*! When you let your mind wander away from Me, it's easier for the devil to attack. But there's a simple answer to that problem. As soon as you realize that your mind has wandered, you can drive the devil away by thanking and praising Me. This is war by worship—and it works!

READ ON YOUR OWN

Ephesians 2:8–9; 2 Corinthians 9:15

Live by What You Believe

We live by what we believe, not by what we can see.
—2 Corinthians 5:7 ICB

Thankfulness and trust are like close friends who are always ready to help you. When you've had a rotten day and the world seems scary, it's time to turn to these faithful friends. Stop for a moment and take some deep breaths. Look around. Search for beauty and blessings, and when you find them, thank Me. Thankfulness links you to Me in a wonderful way. Talk to Me with words of praise about the many good gifts I've given you. Try to thank Me with gladness and excitement, no matter how you're feeling. As you come up with more things to be thankful for, you'll find yourself becoming more joyful.

It's also helpful to say that you trust Me—out loud or in a whisper. Do this often! It reminds you that I'm with you and that you can always count on Me. There will be times in your life when it's harder to trust Me. But when those times come, look at them as new chances to learn to trust Me more. *Live by faith—by what you believe* about Me. Don't waste the opportunities that hard times give you. Use them to come closer to Me. I welcome you with open arms!

READ ON YOUR OWN

Psalm 92:1–2; Psalm 118:28; James 4:8

A Brighter and Stronger Love

I pray that Christ will live in your hearts because of your faith. I pray that your life will be strong in love and be built on love.
—Ephesians 3:17 ICB

*Y*ou love Me because I first loved you. The truth is that *you were spiritually dead because of your sins and the things you did wrong against God.* You weren't even able to love Me until My Spirit brought your soul to life. Because of the work of My Spirit, you were able to turn away from your sins. You were also given eternal Life and never-ending Love. As you think about this miracle of being saved from sin, let your heart be filled with thankfulness and Joy.

In order to grow in your faith, you must learn to be thankful. Thankfulness opens your heart and mind to My Word, the Bible. And My Word is what helps you grow in wisdom and understanding. A thankful attitude will help you discover the countless blessings I pour out to you, even in the middle of hard times. A thankful heart also protects you from losing hope and feeling sorry for yourself. It makes you more aware of My Presence—which is always with you. And it helps you understand how great and amazing My Love for you really is! So practice being thankful, My loved one. Your thankfulness will feed your love for Me, making it grow brighter and stronger!

READ ON YOUR OWN

1 John 4:19; Ephesians 2:1 ICB; Ephesians 3:16–18 ICB

Live Life to the Fullest

"A thief comes to steal and kill and destroy.
But I came to give life—life in all its fullness."
—John 10:10 ICB

A *good person can look forward to happiness.* This means that My followers can expect good things to happen. That's because I have taken away your sins and covered you in *My* perfect goodness and righteousness. I have Joy waiting for you in every day, so wake up each morning excited to find it.

Some of My followers never find the joys I've prepared for them. This is because they think too much about the problems in their lives or the troubles in the world. Instead of living life to the fullest and enjoying everything it has to offer, they live afraid—trying to avoid all pain and risk. But by doing this, they also miss out on Joy, and they aren't as good at sharing My kingdom with others. That's *not* how I want you to live.

As you wake up each morning, turn to Me and expect wonderful things. Invite Me to prepare you for any troubles that might be in the day ahead. Also ask Me to open your eyes to the good things I've planted all through your day—things to make you happy. Then take My hand and let Me share in everything you face along the way—not just the troubles, but also the joys!

READ ON YOUR OWN

Proverbs 10:28 ICB; Isaiah 61:10

Choose Joy

I will still be glad in the Lord. I will rejoice in God my Savior.
—Habakkuk 3:18 ICB

Joy is a choice—and it's a choice you're asked to make many times each day, for as long as you live in this world. When you reach heaven, the most wonderful Joy will be yours without even trying! You won't have to *choose* to be joyful; it will just happen naturally. And it will never go away.

While you walk through this sinful world, I want to help you make wise choices. You must be aware of—and stay aware of—this truth: Joy is a choice in every moment. So make it your goal to find Joy in every part of your day. If you notice you're feeling discouraged or upset or frustrated, let those prickly feelings "poke" you to remember Me. Turn to Me and talk to Me. You can pray something like, "Jesus, I choose to be joyful because You are *God my Savior*. Nothing can take me away from Your loving Presence."

Live like a winner, dear child, by looking for more and more of *Me* in each day.

READ ON YOUR OWN

Psalm 27:8; Romans 8:38–39

DECEMBER

With joy you will drink deeply from the fountain of salvation!

—Isaiah 12:3 NLT

December 1

You're Working for Me

The Lord God took the man and put him in the
Garden of Eden to work it and take care of it.
—Genesis 2:15

*I*n all the work you are doing, work the best you can. Work as if you were working for the Lord, not for men. Rushing through your school assignments or doing just enough to get by on your chores is not pleasing to Me—and it's not good for you. I know it's tempting to hurry through the things you don't want to do, being sloppy and careless just to get them done. But sooner or later this attitude will get you into trouble, and you'll end up feeling bad about yourself. Instead, try doing your tasks with a thankful heart—thankful you have a room to clean and homework that gives you a chance to learn. You'll do a much better job, and you just might start to enjoy what you're doing.

Every moment of your life is a gift from Me. Instead of feeling that someone owes you something "easier" or "better," do all you can with what I give you—including the work I give you. When I put Adam and Eve in the garden, I told them *to work it and take care of it*. Even that perfect garden was not a place to be lazy or to goof off.

No matter what your job is, remember that you are really *working for Me*. Give Me your very best efforts, and I'll give you Joy in return.

READ ON YOUR OWN

Colossians 3:23 ICB; 2 Thessalonians 3:11–12

The Water of Life

*God, you are my God. I search for you. I thirst for you like
someone in a dry, empty land where there is no water.*
—Psalm 63:1 NCV

When you are "thirsty" for Me, I will let you drink for free *from the spring of the water of Life.* This spring never runs dry, so take a deep, long drink of its water—a deep, long drink of Me. You can "drink" of Me by following Me, spending time talking and listening to Me, and reading My Word. Then, I can live in you more and more. Let the water of Life soak deep inside you, making you feel like new. Because this water is free, you can have as much of it as you want—as much of *Me* as you want. I am *Christ in you. I am your only hope for the Glory* of heaven!

I want you to *thirst for Me* more and more. Thirst is a powerful thing—to keep on living, you need water even more than food. Pure water is a much healthier choice for your body than bottled drinks full of sugar or chemicals. In the same way, thirsting for Me more than for things is important for your spiritual health. The things of this world may satisfy you for a little while, but only *I* will perfectly satisfy the thirst of your soul.

Be glad that what you need most—the water of Life—is free of charge. *Draw water from the springs of salvation with Joy!*

READ ON YOUR OWN

Revelation 21:6 ICB; Colossians 1:27; Isaiah 12:3 CEB

December 3

The Blessings of Believing

You have not seen Christ, but still you love him. You cannot see him now, but you believe in him. You are filled with a joy that cannot be explained. And that joy is full of glory.
—1 Peter 1:8 ICB

*E*ven though you do not see Me, you believe in Me. I am far more real than the things you *can* see—more complete, never changing, and without end. When you believe in Me, you are trusting in rock-solid Truth. I am the unbreakable *Rock*. You can keep standing firm and strong on *Me*, no matter how much the waves of life are crashing around you. And because you belong to Me, I am loyal and devoted to you. You are My much-loved child, and I want you to *run to Me for safety*—I am your safe place.

Believing in Me has countless blessings. The most precious one is *the saving of your soul*, forever and ever. Your belief in Me also makes your life here in this world so much better. It helps you know who you are (My beloved child) and Whose you are (Mine!). As you talk to Me and spend time with Me, I'll help you find your way through this sinful world. I will fill your heart with hope and give you more Joy. The better you know Me, the more I can *fill you with a Joy so great that it can't be explained*.

READ ON YOUR OWN

1 Peter 1:9 ICB; Psalm 18:2 ICB; Romans 8:25

With All Your Heart

*Trust the Lord with all your heart. Don't
depend on your own understanding.*
—Proverbs 3:5 ICB

I want you to trust Me enough to relax and enjoy being in My Presence. I didn't create you to live with constant fear and worry, as if you're always in the middle of an emergency. Your body is wonderfully designed to "power up" when you need to act quickly—and then "power down" when the emergency is over. But because you live in such a messed-up world, it's hard to let your guard down and relax. It's hard to "power down." I want you to remember that I'm with you all the time. And I am completely worthy of your trust. *Pour out your heart to Me.* Give Me all those things that are worrying you, and let Me take care of them. Then you can "power down" and relax.

The more you *lean on Me*, the more you can enjoy being with Me. As you relax and rest in My Light, I will shine My Peace into your mind and heart. You'll feel My Presence with you more and more, and *My unfailing Love* will soak deep inside you. *Trust in Me*, dear one, *with all your heart*. I won't let you down.

READ ON YOUR OWN

Psalm 62:8; Psalm 52:8

December 5

When Your Mind Wanders

God created human beings in his image. In the image of
God he created them. He created them male and female.
—Genesis 1:27 ICB

I created you in My image, which means I've made you a lot like Me. Because you're made in My image, you have the amazing ability to talk to Me. You can also choose what you think about. Many of your thoughts come and go, just wandering in and out of your mind. But you can control them more than you might think. The Holy Spirit told the apostle Paul to write: *"Think about the things that are good and worthy of praise. Think about the things that are true and honorable and right and pure and beautiful and respected."* The Bible wouldn't teach you to think this way if it wasn't possible to do it.

Because both good and evil are in this world, you can choose whether to think about things that are *good and worthy of praise* or about terrible, unhappy things. Yes, sometimes you have to face the evil and sin around you. But each day also gives you plenty of chances to think about *pure and beautiful* things. When your mind is just wandering, it often wanders toward things that upset you—like past mistakes you wish you hadn't made or worries about your future. But I am here *with you* in this present moment, waiting for you to remember My Presence. Train yourself to turn your thoughts to Me often. This will brighten even your darkest days and bring you Joy.

READ ON YOUR OWN

Philippians 4:8 ICB; Matthew 1:23; Acts 2:28

Trust and Love

*Lord, I trust you. I have said, "You
are my God." My life is in your hands.*
—Psalm 31:14–15 ICB

Trust Me, dear child. Every time you have a worried or fearful thought, you need to look to Me—over and over again. Say My Name out loud to remind yourself that I'm with you, ready to help. Repeat these words of the Bible back to Me: *"Lord, I trust you. You are my God. My life is in your hands."* Say this Bible verse to Me, *"I love you, Lord. You are my strength."* Remember that I am your Savior and King. I *take great delight in you*. You're a part of My royal family forever!

When you connect with Me in prayer, it stops the scary thoughts that like to wander through your mind. So the more often you talk to Me, the more free you'll become—free from those pesky worries and fears. Because *I am the Truth*, living close to Me will help you understand what is true and what is just a lie. This protects you from being tricked by lies.

Trusting Me and loving Me are beautiful ways of living close to Me. Your trust and love help you think more about *Me*, which protects you from thinking too much about yourself and your fears. Come to Me over and over again—I'll keep you safe and secure in the shelter of My Presence.

READ ON YOUR OWN

Psalm 18:1 ICB; Zephaniah 3:17; John 14:6

Through the Lens of Thankfulness

The mountains may disappear, and the hills may come to an end. But my love will never disappear.
—Isaiah 54:10 ICB

I want you to learn to *be joyful always* by finding your Joy in Me *first*. One way to do this is by remembering that I love you all the time—no matter what's happening. *The mountains may disappear, and the hills may come to an end. But my love will never disappear.*

When things don't go the way you want, or when you've failed in some way, you may be tempted to doubt My Love for you—but don't! My loving Presence is like a solid rock that you can stand on in any storm that tries to knock you over. In *Me* you are safe and secure for all eternity. I am *the Lord who has compassion on you*; I am always loving, caring, and kind.

Another way to multiply your Joy is to *give thanks* no matter what happens. Ask My Spirit to help you view your life through the lens of thankfulness. Just as looking through a piece of colored glass will change the way you see things, looking through the lens of thankfulness will change the way you see your life. Search for the blessings I've scattered throughout your day—and thank Me for each one you find. I encourage you to keep looking through your lens of thankfulness by *thinking about the things that are good and worthy of praise.*

READ ON YOUR OWN

1 Thessalonians 5:16–18 ICB; Philippians 4:8 ICB

I Give You Peace

May the Lord of peace himself give you peace at all
times and in every way. The Lord be with all of you.
—2 Thessalonians 3:16

I am *the Lord of Peace.* In fact, I am the *only* source of true Peace. Peace isn't something that's separate from Me—it's a part of who I am. So I'm giving you Myself when I give you this gift. Yet you can't just grab this gift on the run. Instead, you need to spend time with Me, thinking about Me and enjoying being with Me.

You live in the middle of a fierce spiritual war, and My Peace is an important part of your armor. To stay on your feet in this battle, you must wear tough and strong combat boots. But these aren't boots that can be bought in a store. These boots are the *Good News of Peace.* This good news promises that I love you and I am *for you.*

Many of My followers lose My Peace because they think I'm always watching them, just waiting for them to mess up. I *do* watch over you, but I always see you through eyes of perfect Love. Instead of punishing yourself when you've failed, remember that My death on the cross was enough to take away *all* your sins. I love you *with unfailing Love*—just because you're Mine! Rejoice in My Peace. It is yours to enjoy *at all times and in every way.*

READ ON YOUR OWN

Ephesians 6:15 ICB; Romans 8:31; Psalm 90:14

Shine with My Light

*You are chosen people. You are the King's priests. You are a
holy nation. You are a nation that belongs to God alone. God
chose you to tell about the wonderful things he has done.
He called you out of darkness into his wonderful light.*
—1 Peter 2:9 ICB

As you walk through this life with Me, look for the hope and promise of heaven shining on your path. It will light up your life and the way you see this world. Remember that you are one of My *chosen people. You belong to Me alone. I called you out of darkness into My wonderful light.* Just think about how amazing this is! *I chose you before the creation of the world*—so nothing can separate you from Me. You belong to Me forever! I brought you out of the darkness *of sin and death* and into the beautiful Light of an eternal Life with Me.

The brightness of My Presence helps you in so many ways. The closer you live to Me, the more clearly My Light will help you see the way ahead. As you soak in the Light of My Love, *I give you strength and bless you with Peace*. My Light also blesses those around you as it shines through you. The time you spend thinking about Me helps you become more like Me—and it helps you shine My Light into the lives of others. I'm constantly calling My loved ones out of darkness and into My wonderful, dazzling Light. And when you shine with My Light, both you and others are blessed!

READ ON YOUR OWN

Ephesians 1:4 ICB; Romans 8:2; Psalm 29:11

Evil Will Not Win

*Be still in the presence of the Lᴏʀᴅ, and wait patiently
for him to act. Don't worry about evil people who
prosper or fret about their wicked schemes.*
—Psalm 37:7 ɴʟᴛ

*B*e still in My Presence, and wait patiently for Me to act.
Spending quality time with Me is so good for you, dear
child. I'm delighted when you say no to all the other things
demanding your attention and choose to spend time alone with
Me instead. I know how hard it is to sit quietly with Me—I don't
expect you to do it perfectly. Still, I treasure each time you try. I
look at you with Love and approval when you *search for Me with
all your heart*. This close and precious connection between us
helps you trust Me as you wait for Me to act.

*Don't worry about evil people who prosper or fret about
their wicked schemes.* Sometimes it seems that the ones who
are doing wrong are the ones who are winning. Don't give up
though. Trust that I'm still in control and that My justice will
win in the end. *I will judge the world with fairness and the nations
with truth.* Until that happens, look for ways to share My truth
with this world. Keep your eyes and your thoughts on Me as you
go through this day. Be willing to follow wherever I lead you.
Do not let evil defeat you or upset you. *Defeat evil by doing good*!

READ ON YOUR OWN

Jeremiah 29:13 ɪᴄʙ; Psalm 96:12–13 ɪᴄʙ; Romans 12:21 ɪᴄʙ

Good News of Great Joy

The angel said to them, "Do not be afraid. I bring you good news of great joy that will be for all the people. Today in the town of David a Savior has been born to you; he is Christ the Lord."
—Luke 2:10–11

I am *the Rock that is higher than you*—higher than anything you face. This means I will lift you up above your troubles so that you'll be safe. I am your Rock and your Refuge. You can find shelter in Me at any time and in any place.

Come to Me, dear child. Rest in the Peace of My Presence. Take a break from trying to figure everything out. Admit that there are many, many things you'll never understand and never be able to control. *Just as the heavens are higher than the earth, so are my ways higher than your ways. And my thoughts are higher than your thoughts.*

When the world around you looks confusing and evil seems to be winning, remember this truth: I am the Light that keeps on shining—no matter what. And My Light *always* chases away the darkness.

Because you are My follower, I want you to shine brightly in this dark and troubled world. Whisper My Name and sing songs of praise to Me. Tell others the *good news of great Joy*—that I am the *Savior, who is Christ the Lord*! I'm also the One who is always with you. Keep looking to Me, and My Presence will light up your path—showing you the way I want you to go.

READ ON YOUR OWN

Psalm 61:2; Psalm 18:2; Isaiah 55:9 ICB

You Are Precious to Me!

You do not own yourselves. You were bought by God for a price.
—1 Corinthians 6:19–20 ICB

When I came into your world, I came as both God and man. I came to *a world that was My own*. Everything belonged to Me then—and it still does! Most people think their things belong to them, but the truth is that everything you have belongs to Me. And so do *you*.

There may be times when you feel all alone, but this is just not true. I'm *always* with you. I paid an incredible price for you—by suffering terrible pain and dying on the cross for your sins. The huge price I paid shows how precious you are to Me! Think about this powerful truth whenever you start to doubt what you're worth or wonder if you're important. You are Mine—My treasured child! You have been *saved by grace because you believe* in Me, your Savior.

Because you are worth so much to Me, I want you to take good care of your whole self: your body, mind, and spirit. Take time to think about the words of the Bible, letting them sink into your mind and heart. Since *your body is a temple for the Holy Spirit*, protect your body and your feelings from people who would hurt you. Also, I want you to help others learn the good news about Me—the free gift of *eternal life for whoever believes in Me*. Always be ready to share My Joy.

READ ON YOUR OWN

John 1:11 ICB; Ephesians 2:8–9 ICB; John 3:16 ICB

December 13

Joy and Truth

"When the Spirit of truth comes he will lead you into all truth. He will not speak his own words. He will speak only what he hears and will tell you what is to come."
—John 16:13 ICB

*E*veryone who belongs to the truth listens to Me. That's because I *am* the living Truth. I was born and came into your world for this reason: *to tell people about the truth.*

Many people believe there is no real truth—there's no right or wrong. They believe what is wrong for one person may be right for another. Evil people use this way of thinking to twist the facts and to get others to do what they want. They say evil things are good, and good things are evil. I hate this! There is a place for those who tell lie after lie without ever being sorry, and it is in *the fiery lake of burning sulfur.* These people will not be in heaven.

Remember that *the devil is a liar and the father of lies.* The more you listen to Me, especially by reading the Bible, the more you will know and treasure My Truth. The Holy Spirit living inside you is *the Spirit of Truth.* Ask Him to show you what is real and what is a lie. He'll help you make your way through this world where so many people lie and twist the facts. It will be a struggle, but keep fighting to stay on *My* side—the side of truth. Live close to Me, the living Truth, and you'll find Joy in My Presence.

READ ON YOUR OWN

John 18:37 ICB; Revelation 21:8 ICB; John 8:44

Don't Stop Trying

*We all show the Lord's glory, and we are being changed
to be like him. This change in us brings more and more
glory. And it comes from the Lord, who is the Spirit.*
—2 Corinthians 3:18 ICB

*D*on't get tired and stop trying. When you're facing troubles
that just go on and on, it's easy to get so tired that you want
to give up. Problems that won't go away can wear you out and
wear you down. But if you think too much about the problems,
you might start sliding into a black hole of gloom and feeling
sorry for yourself.

There are different kinds of "tired." When your body doesn't
get enough rest, your heart and mind can end up exhausted
too—so that you don't even feel like trying anymore. But I've
made it possible for you to rise above your troubles if you will
look only to Me. I paid greatly for this help that I offer you—by
suffering death on the cross. Thinking about how I was willing to
suffer so much for you can give you the strength to get through
your own troubles.

Worshiping Me is a wonderful way to find new strength.
When you praise Me in the tough times, it shows your faith in
Me—and My wonderful Light shines on you, making you feel
stronger and better. As you keep thinking about Me even in your
troubles, you *show My Glory* to others. And you *are changed to be
like Me, with more and more Glory*.

READ ON YOUR OWN

Hebrews 12:2–3 ICB; 2 Corinthians 5:7

The Father and Me

"Anyone who has seen me has seen the Father."
—John 14:9

When the prophet Isaiah told about the coming of My birth, he called Me the *Eternal Father*. You may wonder how I, the Son, can be called "Eternal Father." It's possible because of the Trinity. The Trinity is God the Father, God the Son, and God the Holy Spirit. Even though we are three Persons, we are also one. This is a wonderful mystery. When the Jews were questioning Me in the temple, I said, *"I and the Father are one."* Later, when My disciple Philip asked Me to show the Father to the disciples, I said, *"Anyone who has seen Me has seen the Father."* So never think of Me as just a great teacher. I am God, and the Father and I live in perfect oneness and unity.

As you get to know Me better, you are also growing closer to the Father. Don't let the mystery of the Trinity confuse you. Simply come to Me, and know that I am everything you could ever need. I am your only Savior, and I am enough.

During this busy Christmas season, keep turning your thoughts back to Me and My holy Presence. Remember that I am *Immanuel—God with you*—and rejoice! Be happy because I have come into the world and into your life.

READ ON YOUR OWN

Isaiah 9:6; John 10:30; Matthew 1:23

Do Not Be Afraid

Be full of joy in the Lord always. I will say again, be full of joy.
—Philippians 4:4 ICB

W hen an angel appeared *to shepherds living out in the fields* near the city of Bethlehem and told them about My birth, he said: *Do not be afraid. I bring you good news of great Joy.* That instruction of "Do not be afraid" is repeated in the Bible more than any other command. It is a loving and tender command—and it is for you! I know how easy it is for you to feel afraid, and I don't judge you for it, but I *do* want to help you break free from your fears.

Joy is a powerful cure for fear! And the greater your Joy, the stronger the cure is. The angel's words to the shepherds were full of *great* Joy. Don't ever forget what amazingly good news the gospel is! You admit your sins and turn away from them. You trust Me as your Savior. I forgive *all* your sins and bless you with eternal life in heaven. And I give *Myself* to you—pouring out My Love on you and promising that I will be with you forever. Take time today to think about the angel's wonderful words to the shepherds. *Be full of Joy in Me*, because I am your Savior.

READ ON YOUR OWN

Luke 2:8–10; 1 John 3:1 ICB

Sing to Me!

Let all who take refuge in you rejoice;
let them sing joyful praises forever.
—Psalm 5:11 NLT

*S*ing for Joy to Me, because I am *your Strength*. Christmas music is one of the best blessings of the holiday season, and it doesn't have to cost anything. You can sing carols at church or at home, or in the car, on the bus, or just walking outside. As you are making a "joyful noise" to Me, pay close attention to the words. They are about Me and the miracle of My birth in this world. Singing from your heart fills you with Joy and energy. Your songs of Joy also bless Me.

I created you to praise Me and to enjoy being with Me forever. So it's no surprise that you feel more alive when you praise Me through song. I want you to learn to enjoy me in more and more areas of your life, not just in church or when you're praying. Before you get out of bed each morning, remind yourself that My Presence is right there with you. Say: *"Surely the Lord is in this place."* This will wake you up to how wonderful it is to be close to Me all the time! And *I will fill you with Joy in My Presence.*

READ ON YOUR OWN

Psalm 81:1 ICB; Genesis 28:16; Acts 2:28

I Am Mighty God!

For to us a child is born, to us a son is given, and the government will be on his shoulders. And he will be called Wonderful Counselor, Mighty God, Everlasting Father, Prince of Peace.
—Isaiah 9:6

I am your Savior, and I am *Mighty God*! Much of the Christmas season is centered around Me as the Baby in the manger. Yes, I did begin My life on earth in this humble way. I put aside My heavenly Glory and became completely human. Yet I never stopped being God—that's how I was able to live a perfect life on earth, without any sin, and to perform such amazing miracles.

I am with you, My child. I am *your God—the mighty One who will save you*! Let this combination of My tender nearness and My incredible Power bless you.

When I came into this world, I came to a world that was My own—it already belonged to Me because everything was made by Me. My own people did not accept Me. But some people did accept Me. They believed in Me, and I gave them the right to become children of God. This gift of salvation is priceless. It gives meaning to your life and a direction for you to walk in—and it makes heaven your forever-home.

During this season of giving and receiving presents, remember that the very best present of all is eternal Life. Thank Me for this wonderful gift by rejoicing and celebrating. *Be full of Joy in Me always*!

READ ON YOUR OWN

Zephaniah 3:17 ICB; John 1:11–12 ICB; Philippians 4:4 ICB

Finding True Joy

You will teach me God's way to live. Being with you will fill me with joy. At your right hand I will find pleasure forever.
—Psalm 16:11 ICB

I am *Immanuel, God with you*—every moment of every day. My Promise to always be with you means that nothing can take away your Joy. Many people try to find their pleasure in things that don't last, but My Presence with you is eternal. Rejoice and be glad, dear child, because you know that your Savior *will never leave you or forget you*.

The way that time keeps passing can steal some of your Joy if you let it. But don't let it! It's true that your best days on earth don't last forever. Vacations end, birthdays end, and the Christmas season ends—no matter how much you might want to "stop the clock" and keep enjoying things just as they are. Even though the pleasures of this world don't last, I *do* want you to enjoy them. Just be sure you understand that they won't satisfy your soul's thirst for true Joy. Your search for lasting Joy will fail—and leave your soul "thirsty"—unless what you're searching for most of all is *Me*! *I will teach you My way to live. Being with Me will fill you with Joy.*

READ ON YOUR OWN

Matthew 1:23; Deuteronomy 31:8 ICB

Your Hope Will Overflow

I pray that the God who gives hope will fill you with much joy and peace while you trust in him. Then your hope will overflow by the power of the Holy Spirit.
—Romans 15:13 ICB

No matter how lonely you may feel, you are never alone. Christmas can be a hard time for a lot of people because they're not with the ones they love. This might be because someone has moved away, or there has been a divorce, or because a loved one has gone on to heaven. The happiness that is all around at Christmas can make lonely people feel even more alone. But I give all My children the most wonderful help—My Presence is always with them.

Remember this prophecy that was said about Me: *"The virgin . . . will give birth to a Son, and they will call Him Immanuel"—which means "God with us."* Long before I was born, I was announced as the God who is *with you*. This is an amazing truth that nobody and nothing can ever take away from you.

Whenever you're feeling lonely, take some time to enjoy being with Me. Thank Me for *wrapping you with a robe of righteousness* that covers all your sins and makes you holy. Ask Me—*the God who gives hope*—to *fill you with much Joy and Peace*. Then, with the help of My Spirit, *your hope will overflow* into the lives of people around you.

READ ON YOUR OWN

Matthew 1:23; Isaiah 61:10; 2 Corinthians 5:21

December 21

I Became Poor for You

*You know the grace of our Lord Jesus Christ. You know
that Christ was rich, but for you he became poor. Christ did
this so that by his being poor you might become rich.*
—2 Corinthians 8:9 ICB

I was rich, but for you I became poor. The heart of Christmas is
My birth on the earth. This was a priceless gift of great, great
value. But it made Me incredibly poor! I gave up all the dazzling
beauty and riches of heaven to become a helpless baby. My
parents were poor, young, and far away from their own home
when I was born in that stable in Bethlehem.

I did many miracles during My life on earth, but they were
all to help others—not Myself. After forty days and nights without food, fasting in the wilderness, Satan came and temped Me
to *turn stones into bread.* But I refused to do this miracle even
though I could have, and even though I was so hungry! I lived
as a homeless man for years. I could have given Myself a life of
comfort and wealth, but I didn't—for your sake.

Because I was willing to live as a poor man, you are incredibly rich! My life, death, and resurrection from the grave opened
up the way for My followers to become *children of God.* Because
of Me, you will one day receive all the riches and blessings of
heaven. My Presence—which is always with you—is also a precious gift. Celebrate these amazing gifts today and every day
with thanksgiving and Joy!

READ ON YOUR OWN

Matthew 4:1–4; John 1:12; Luke 2:10

The Light That Gives Life

"I am the light of the world. The person who follows me will never live in darkness. He will have the light that gives life."
—John 8:12 ICB

I am the Light of the world! Many people celebrate the Christmas season by lighting up their homes with candles and decorated trees. This is a way of remembering that I came into the world—that My eternal Light broke through the darkness of sin and opened the gates of heaven. Nothing can change this amazing plan to save you. Everyone who trusts in Me and follows Me is adopted into My royal family forever.

My Light shines in the darkness. And the darkness has not overpowered the Light. This means that no matter how much evil you see in this world, and no matter how many people refuse to believe in Me, I keep shining just as bright. My Light is a beacon of hope for anyone who really wants to see it. So it's important to look toward My Light as much as possible. *Keep your eyes on Me*, dear child. And be careful to make good choices about your thoughts. When you turn your thoughts to Me, you can find Me as you walk through this life. Ask My Spirit to help you keep looking toward Me and following Me. Because *the person who follows Me will never live in darkness. He will have the Light that gives Life.*

READ ON YOUR OWN

Ephesians 1:5; John 1:5 ICB; Hebrews 12:2 CEV

December 23

New Strength

His power at work in us can do far more than we dare ask or imagine.
—Ephesians 3:20 CEV

*T*hose who trust Me will find new strength. Spending time alone with Me shows that you trust Me. Waiting with Me is so good for you, but it's very different from what the world says you should be doing. The world encourages you to stay busy and try to do several things at once—like studying while you watch television and hang out with friends. During the Christmas season, there are even *more* things to get done and more places to go. So I encourage you to take a break from all the busyness. Turn to Me and rest in My Presence for a while. Christmas is really all about *Me* anyway.

Spending time with Me is an act of faith—it's believing that your prayers really do make a difference. *Come to Me when you're tired and carrying a heavy load.* Be real with Me about everything you're thinking and feeling, and bring Me all your worries. Then rest in My Presence. Let Me take your heavy load and carry it for you. Trust that *My Power can do far more than you could dare ask or imagine.*

As you leave the quietness and head back into all the busyness, keep listening to Me: I'll be whispering "I am with you" all throughout your day. And be thankful that you have *new strength* because you've spent time with Me.

READ ON YOUR OWN

Isaiah 40:31 CEV; Psalm 27:8; Matthew 11:28 ICB

Get Your Heart Ready

*Then a very large group of angels from heaven joined
the first angel. All the angels were praising God,
saying: "Give glory to God in heaven, and on earth let
there be peace to the people who please God."*
—Luke 2:13–14 ICB

It's time to get your heart ready to celebrate My birth. Listen to what John the Baptist said: *"Prepare the way for the Lord. Make the road straight for him."* This is another way of saying: Clear away anything that would keep you from spending time with Me.

Christmas is the time to rejoice because it's when I came to this earth *to live among you.* I actually *became a Man* and lived in your world. You hear about My birth so often but don't let it become just another story. Understand that I am the greatest Gift—better than all the gifts you will ever receive!

Clear out the clutter in your heart so you can think about the miracle of My birth. Imagine the shepherds out in the fields that night, watching over their sheep. First they saw one angel, and then a very large group of angels came and lit up the sky, calling out: *"Give glory to God in heaven, and on earth let there be peace to the people who please God."* Be amazed and celebrate the Glory of My birth, just as the shepherds did so long ago. Praise Me with Joy; your Lord has come!

READ ON YOUR OWN

Mark 1:3 ICB; John 1:14 ICB; Philippians 4:4

My Gift to You

*The Word became a man and lived among us. We
saw his glory—the glory that belongs to the only Son
of the Father. The Word was full of grace and truth.*
—John 1:14 ICB

I am *the living Word that became a man*. I have always been, and
I will always be. *Before the world began, there was the Word*
(God's Son). *The Word was with God, and the Word was God.* As
you think about Me as a tiny baby, born in Bethlehem, don't forget that I am God. This baby who grew up and became both a
man and a Savior is also the Almighty God! That's the only way
salvation could have happened. Giving My life for you on the
cross would not have been enough to save you if I were only a
man. So rejoice and celebrate because *the Word*, who came into
this world as a helpless baby, is really God. I am your Savior *and*
your God.

    *I was rich, but for you I became poor. I did this so that you might
become rich.* No Christmas present could ever be as wonderful
as the treasure you have in Me. I take away your sins so that
they are as far away from you *as the east is from the west*. As My
child, you are not judged guilty for what you do wrong. I forgive
you—and I give you the gift of wonderful Life that will never
end! As you think about this amazing gift and thank Me for it, I
fill your heart with Joy.

READ ON YOUR OWN

John 1:1 ICB; Hebrews 1:1–2;
2 Corinthians 8:9 ICB; Psalm 103:12

Adding Up Joy

*I will give an offering to show thanks
to you. And I will worship the Lord.*
—Psalm 116:17 ICB

I am the greatest Gift you could ever think of! When you have *Me*, you have everything you need—for this life and your life in heaven. I have promised to use *My wonderful riches to give you everything you need.* But sometimes My children don't enjoy the treasures I give them because they aren't thankful. Instead of celebrating all that they have, they are constantly wishing for what they don't have. This makes them feel unhappy and unsatisfied.

I'm training you to *give thanks to Me whatever happens.* First, thank Me for the blessings you can see in your life. Then stop and think about the awesome gift of knowing Me. I am your living God, your loving Savior, your Friend who never leaves you. No matter how much or how little you have in this world, your relationship with Me makes you incredibly rich! So when you're counting your blessings, be sure to include the unlimited, endless treasure you have in Me. When you add Me into the equation of your life, your thankfulness grows by leaps and bounds. Whatever you have + Me = a fortune too great and too big to be counted!

READ ON YOUR OWN

Philippians 4:19 ICB; 1 Thessalonians 5:18 ICB

A Fountain of Joy

Happy are the people who know how to praise you.
Lord, let them live in the light of your presence.
—Psalm 89:15 ICB

I give you a Joy that doesn't depend on what's happening in your life. That's because I give you Myself! *All the treasures of wisdom and knowledge are hidden in Me.* Because I am endlessly wise and I know all things, you'll never run out of treasures to search for.

I am a fountain of Joy—ready and eager to flow into your life. Open your heart, mind, and spirit wide to receive the gift of Myself. My Joy isn't like the joy of this world—you can have My Joy even in the middle of your toughest times. No matter how things are going, *the Light of My Presence* still shines on you. Look up to Me with a trusting heart. If you keep searching for Me, My joyful Light will shine through even the darkest storm clouds. Let this heavenly Light soak deep inside you. Let it brighten the way you look at the world and fill you with delight.

Remember that you have blessings kept for you in heaven. They cannot be destroyed or be spoiled or lose their beauty. Because you believe in Me, I will fill you with a Joy that cannot be explained. That Joy is full of Glory—and it is yours to keep, both now and forever!

READ ON YOUR OWN

Colossians 2:3; Psalm 89:16 ICB; 1 Peter 1:3–4, 8 ICB

A Heavenly Gift

We have this treasure from God. But we are
only like clay jars that hold the treasure. This shows
that this great power is from God, not from us.
—2 Corinthians 4:7 ICB

*H*ow priceless is My unfailing Love! It is truly a heavenly gift. Remember what I did to get this gift for you? I was tortured, shamed, and killed on a cross. My willingness to suffer so much for you shows how very, very much I love you!

I want you to understand how amazingly rich you are in Me. I have given you the priceless treasure of My eternal Love! This gift makes you much richer than any billionaire on earth, because it's worth more than all the money in the world. You may own very little of this world's things, but you can stand up tall as you walk through your life—knowing that this wonderful treasure inside you is yours to keep forever. Because you're My beloved child, you are truly rich!

Rejoice and be glad that My Love is worth more than anything money can buy, and it will never fail you. You can always count on My Love—it's even more dependable than the rising of the sun. So let this unfailing Love fill you with sparkling Joy as you walk along *the path of Life* with Me.

READ ON YOUR OWN

Psalm 36:7; Psalm 16:11

December 29

Let Peace Rule Your Heart

*Let the peace of Christ rule in your hearts, since as members
of one body you were called to peace. And be thankful.*
—Colossians 3:15

*L*et My Peace rule in your heart, and be thankful. To let My
Peace control your heart is a difficult assignment, so ask
My Spirit help you. Because the Spirit lives inside you, His *Love,
Joy, and Peace* are always available to you. A simple way to
invite His help is to pray: "Holy Spirit, fill me with your Peace."
Try sitting in a quiet place until you feel calm. When you're very
relaxed, it's easier for you to receive My Peace and enjoy being
in My Presence.

While you rest in My Presence, take time to thank Me for all
the good things I give you. As you think about Me and My many
blessings, let your heart be filled with thankfulness and even
leap for Joy. One of the greatest gifts you could ever imagine is
My *robe of righteousness*—it covers all your sins with My perfect goodness. This wonderful *coat of salvation* is a priceless
blessing for all who trust Me as their Savior. This gift of righteousness—of being covered by My perfection forever—was
paid for with My blood when I died on the cross. Wrap yourself
in this precious robe, and be warmed by My Peace and Joy.

READ ON YOUR OWN

Galatians 5:22–23; Psalm 28:7; Isaiah 61:10 ICB

The Most Joyful Way to Live

You guide me with your counsel, and
afterward you will take me into glory.
—Psalm 73:24

I am the Alpha and the Omega, the Beginning and the End. What I see is not limited by time because *I* am not limited by time. I have always been, and I will always be. I am able to see and understand everything all at once—the past, the present, and the future. This makes Me the perfect Person to be in charge of your life. I know the day you will join Me in heaven just as well as I know the day you were born. I also know everything in between. Unlike Me, you are *finite*—limited by time—and sinful. There are many things you cannot understand. So trust Me rather than depending *on your own understanding*. That's the best way to live—and it's the most joyful way too.

The end of this life is not something to be afraid of. It's simply a first step into heaven for everyone who believes in Me. I can see that "someday" just as clearly as I see today. And because I am the Omega—the End—I am already there in that day. I'll be waiting when it's time for each of My sons and daughters to step into heaven. So when this journey through life gets hard, think about that wonderful day when you'll see Me face to Face in heaven—and rejoice!

READ ON YOUR OWN

Revelation 21:6 ICB; Proverbs 3:5; Hebrews 12:2

December 31

The Light of Heaven
Shines on You

God is our God forever and ever. He will guide us from now on.
—Psalm 48:14 ICB

As you come to the end of this year, take some time to look back—and also to look ahead. Ask Me to help you think over all the things that have happened this year: the hard times as well as the good times. Try to see *Me* in each of those memories, because I was right there with you—watching over you and helping you every step of the way.

When you were holding tight to Me in tough times and asking for My help, I comforted you with My loving Presence. I was also there when your heart was full of Joy. I was with you on the mountaintops of happiness, in the valleys of sadness—and *everywhere* you were!

Your future stretches out before you—all the way to heaven. I am the Friend who will never leave you and the Guide who knows every step of the way ahead. I'll show you the best way to go as you walk through this life. The Joy that waits for you in heaven is so great and so *full of Glory* that it *cannot be explained*! As you get ready to step into a new year, let the Light of heaven shine on you and light up the path before you.

READ ON YOUR OWN

Isaiah 41:13; Psalm 16:11; 1 Peter 1:8–9 ICB

About the Author

Sarah Young's devotional writings are personal reflections from her daily quiet time of Bible reading, praying, and writing in prayer journals. With sales of more than 20 million books worldwide, *Jesus Calling*® has appeared on all major bestseller lists. Sarah's writings include *Jesus Calling*®, *Jesus Today*®, *Jesus Lives*™, *Dear Jesus*, *Jesus Calling*® *for Little Ones*, *Jesus Calling*® *Bible Storybook*, *Jesus Calling*®: *365 Devotions for Kids*, and *Peace in His Presence*—each encouraging readers in their journey toward intimacy with Christ. Sarah and her husband were missionaries in Japan and Australia for many years. They currently live in the United States.

Jesus Calling® was written to help people connect not only with Jesus, the living Word, but also with the Bible—the only infallible, inerrant Word of God. Sarah endeavors to keep her devotional writing consistent with that unchanging standard. Many readers have shared that Sarah's books have helped them grow to love God's Word. As Sarah states in the introduction to *Jesus Calling*®, "The devotions . . . are meant to be read slowly, preferably in a quiet place—with your Bible open."

Sarah is biblically conservative in her faith and reformed in her doctrine. She earned a master's degree in biblical studies and counseling from Covenant Theological Seminary in St. Louis. She is a member of the Presbyterian Church in America (PCA), where her husband, Stephen, is an ordained minister. Stephen and Sarah continue to be missionaries with Mission to the World, the PCA mission board. Sarah spends a great deal of time in prayer, reading the Bible, and memorizing Scripture. She especially enjoys praying daily for readers of all her books.

**IF YOU ENJOYED THIS DEVOTIONAL,
YOU MAY ENJOY THESE OTHER
DEVOTIONALS FOR KIDS BY**

Sarah Young

Jesus Calling®:
365 Devotions for Kids

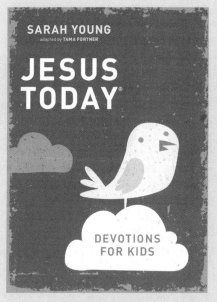

Jesus Today®
Devotions for Kids

OTHER BOOKS FOR KIDS BY

Sarah Young

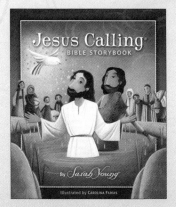

Jesus Calling® Bible Storybook
Hardcover

Jesus Calling®
for Little Ones
Board Book

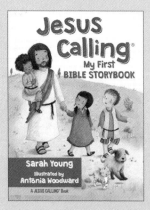

Jesus Calling®
My First Bible Storybook
Board Book

Sarah Young's

First 365-Day Devotional
Since *Jesus Calling*®

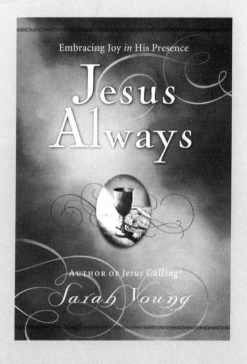

Embrace Joy in the Presence of the Savior who is always with you.

Visit www.jesuscalling.com/jesus-always